Lotus Race Cars
1961-1994
Photo Album

Edited with introduction by
Norman Hayes

Iconografix
Photo Album Series

Iconografix seeks collections of archival photographs for reproduction in future books. We require a minimum of 120 photographs per subject in our Photo Archive Series and Photo Album Series, and a minimum of 500 photographs per subject in our Photo Gallery Series. We prefer subjects narrow in focus, i.e., a specific model, or manufacturer, railroad, racing venue, etc. Photographs must be of high-quality, suited to reproduction in an 8x10-inch format. We willingly pay for the use of photographs.

If you own or know of such a collection, please contact: The Publisher, Iconografix, PO Box 446, Hudson, Wisconsin 54016 USA.

Iconografix
PO Box 446
Hudson, Wisconsin 54016 USA

Iconografix books are offered at a discount when sold in quantity for promotional use. Businesses or organizations seeking details should write to the Marketing Department, Iconografix, at the above address.

Library of Congress Card Number 97-075279

ISBN 1-882256-84-0

98 99 00 01 02 03 04 5 4 3 2 1

Printed in the United States of America

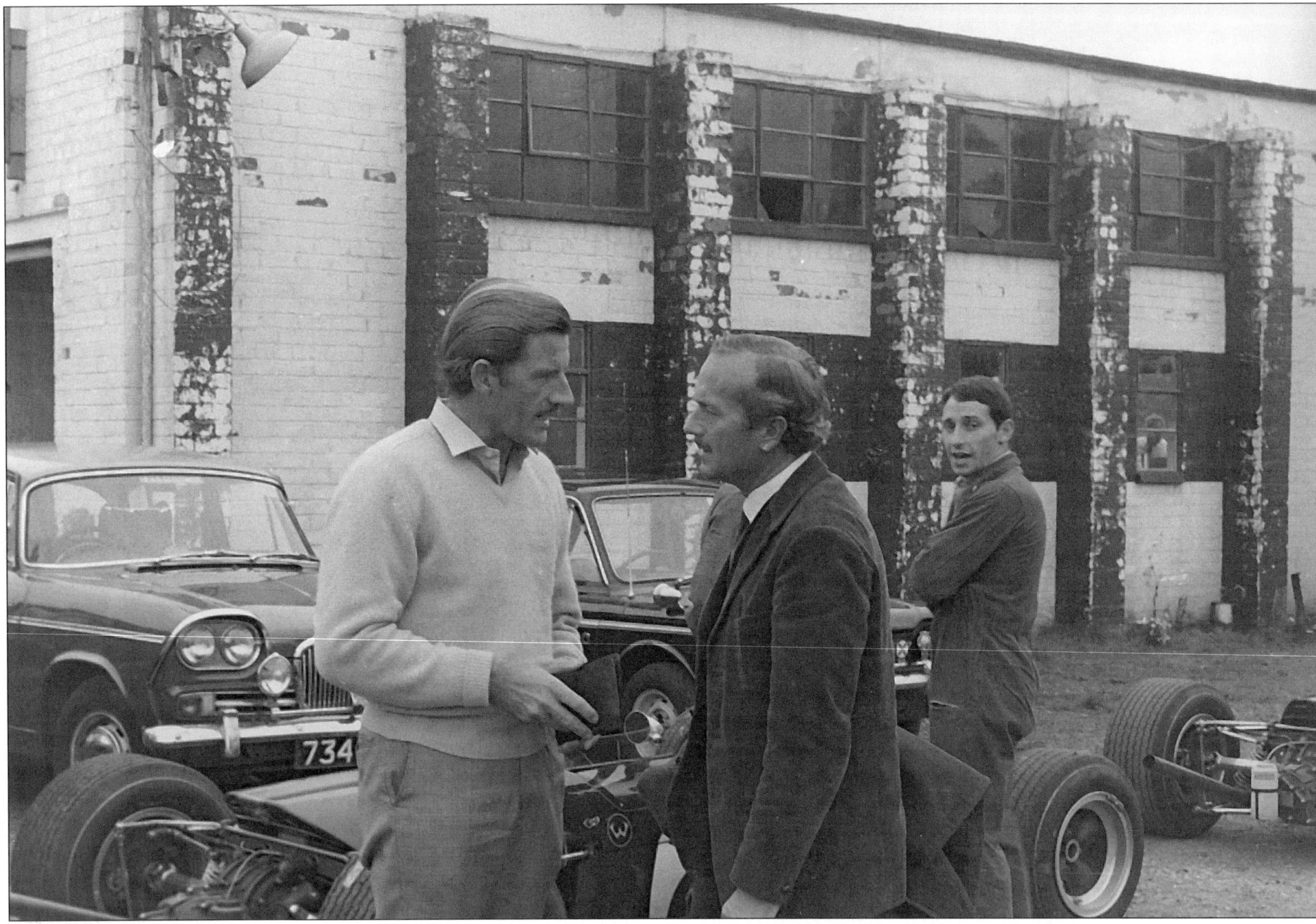

Colin Chapman (center), the founder of the Lotus Company, talking with Graham Hill (left) in the Oulton Park paddock during the 1967 International Gold Cup Race.

INTRODUCTION

From before WWII, England had been an also ran on the world's Grand Prix stage. That changed in the 1960s when, under the direction and management of Colin Chapman, Lotus transformed Grand Prix racing. While becoming one of the dominant constructors, Lotus also became the team to be beat. Chapman's designs were synonymous with radical extremes in race car design and dominated racing for many years. Indeed, Chapman's ideas were copied by almost every other racing manufacturer.

Lotus was born in 1948 when Anthony Colin Bruce Chapman modified an Austin Seven, designated the Mk. 1. Building the car for his own use in reliability trials, the Mk. 1 brought Chapman instant success in the trials world, winning two class awards in the first trials that he entered. Next was the Mk. 2, again an Austin Seven but with a Ford 10 engine in place of the Austin engine. The Mk. 2 was first entered in a 16 lap scratch race at Silverstone in 1950, winning with ease. It met with equal success in many other races and sprints. Eventually the car was sold to renowned trials specialist Mike Lawson, who won many trials and championships in the car.

The Mk. 3 Lotus was designed for the 750 circuit racing formula that existed at the time. Again Chapman started with an Austin Seven, modifying the engine within the rules of the 750 formula. The Mk. 3 was so successful in this formula, because of the engine modifications, that the 750 Motor Club changed the rules. Chapman had gained too great of an edge over his rivals. This was one of Chapman's strong points--he would look at the governing rules trying to find ways around them, often with great success.

In 1957 Lotus produced the Mk. 12, Chapman's first serious single seater racing car. The earlier Mk. 6 to Mk. 11 were two seater sports cars that won many races between 1954 and 1957--including index of performance and class wins at Le Mans. Team Lotus's first Grand Prix entries of the Mk. 12, with 1960cc Coventry Climax FPF engines, were at Monaco in 1958, where Graham Hill retired after 70 laps with transmission problems while Cliff Allison finished the race sixth. The last of the Lotus front engine racing cars were the Mk. 16 single seaters, produced for 1958 and 1959. Dubbed the 'mini-Vanwall', the Mk. 16 was designed by Chapman with the assistance of Frank Costin, an aerodynamicist who had designed the bodywork for the Vanwall cars. Hill and various other drivers had little success with the car due to problems with failing brakes, chassis breakages and wheels falling off.

Lotus's first rear-engine single seater, the Mk. 18, was used in all forms of racing cars produced by Team Lotus--from Formula 1 to Formula Junior. More successful than its predecessor, it took GP wins in 1960 for Stirling Moss in the Monaco Grand Prix, United States Grand Prix at Riverside, California and Fl Gold Cup at Oulton Park. Innes Ireland took wins in minor Fl races at Goodwood, Silverstone and Snetterton. In 1961 Innes Ireland won the United States Grand Prix at Watkins Glen in the new Coventry Climax engine Mk. 21, while Stirling Moss won the Monaco and German GPs. The Mk. 19, dubbed the 'Monte Carlo', was a rear engine sports car with a fiberglass body, and was run by the UTD-Laystall team with great success the same year.

Another highlight of Chapman's early racing cars was the lightweight Mk. 23 sports car with a Ford-Classic based 1500cc engine. Jim Clark, in the Mk. 23, made a great impression on its first outing at the Nurburgring 1000 km. race. From the start he led the all conquering Ferraris of the time, but the exhaust pipe began to leak in the eleventh lap, gassing Clark, who crashed as a result.

For 1962 Lotus had the Mk. 24 and the Mk. 25–the trend setter for all future Grand Prix and other formula cars. The Mk. 24 did not win any GPs but did win minor F1 races in the hands of Clark and Jack Brabham. However, the Mk. 25 created a sensation by introducing a monocoque chassis. With a V8 Coventry Climax engine, it was first entered for Jim Clark at the 1962 Dutch Grand Prix. Leading the race until he encountered problems, he finished ninth overall. Clark took his first Grand Prix win driving the new Mk. 25 at the 1962 Belgian Grand Prix, later winning both the British and the United States GPs. Clark took the 1963 World Championship in the Lotus Mk. 25 by winning seven of ten GPs run that year.

Lotus and Clark began 1964 with the Mk. 25--its third season. Though now outdated, he still managed to win three GPs with the car before Lotus introduced the Mk. 33. Though Clark had little success during the rest of 1964, he won the 1965 Drivers' World Championship with six outright victories.

Lotus entered the 1963 Indianapolis 500 with a Lotus Mk. 29, with a 4260cc Ford Fairline-derived engine. Two cars were produced--one for Jim Clark, the other for Dan Gurney. Clark led for most of the first half of the race, but with a mixture of yellow flags during the second half of the race Clark dropped back and finished second, while Gurney finished seventh. In 1964 Team Lotus returned with Mk. 34s, running four cam Ford V8 engines. Again Clark and Gurney drove the two cars. Jimmy qualified on pole, while Gurney took his place in the second row of the grid. Clark led until his left-rear Dunlop tire stripped its tread. The resultant vibration destroyed the suspension, causing Clark to crash into the retaining wall without injury. Gurney was called in immediately as a safety measure.

At Indianapolis in 1965 Clark drove the new Mk. 38 with a full monocoque chassis to victory. He was backed by his teammate Bobby Johns, a veteran stock car racer who finished in seventh place.

The year 1966 saw the 'Return of Power' or so it was termed because of the increase in size of the racing engines from 1500cc to 3000cc. Some of the teams, including Lotus, did not have engines ready for the start of the season. Lotus relied on the old 1500cc Coventry Climax in its original form, later enlarging it to 2000cc. In the second half of the season they brought out the new Mk. 43 using a 3000cc B.R.M. H16 engine. However, the car wasn't a success because of the unreliable engine. In spite of this, Clark scored an unexpected win in the United States Grand Prix at Watkins Glen.

Ford, a world wide motor manufacturer, became involved in Grand Prix racing during the 1967 season when they provided the engine designers and builders Cosworth Engineering Ltd. with the money to build a new Ford badged engine for the sole use of Colin Chapman's Lotus Cars. Designated the Ford Cosworth DFV V8, Chapman and his team designed a car around the engine. The resulting Mk. 49 won the Dutch Grand Prix on its debut with Clark at the wheel. From 1967 to 1969 the Lotus 49 scored twelve World Championship Grand Prix victories, with Graham Hill winning the World Championship in 1968.

Another interesting and radical design from Lotus was the Mk. 56, with a Pratt & Whitney gas turbine engine and Ferguson 4wd, built for the 1968 Indianapolis 500 race. After securing second place on the starting grid, Graham Hill was running in the top five until the 111th lap when his suspension broke and put him into the turn two wall without any injury.

The gas turbine car was again used in 1971 for Grand Prix racing. Having been modified for circuit racing and numbered Mk. 56B, it only ran in two GPs, the Dutch and British driven respectively by Dave Walker and Reine Wisell, with both cars retiring during the race.

The Mk. 72 made it's Grand Prix debut in 1970 at Jarama for the Spanish Fl race. It didn't win, but for the next six years it dominated the Grand Prix scene with twenty wins, three Constructors' titles, a posthumous Drivers' World Championship for Jochen Rindt in 1970--who was killed during practice for the Italian Grand Prix at Monza, and a Drivers' World Champion for Emerson Fittipaldi in 1972. The Mk. 72 was probably one of the most successful Grand Prix cars of all time.

In 1976, with Mario Andretti and Ronnie Peterson driving, the cars were no longer called Lotus, having been renamed John Player Specials after their main sponsor. Although the Mk. 77 was full of innovations in the braking and suspension area, it was a very difficult season. The cars were unreliable and the JPS cars could only muster a first for Andretti and three third position finishes during the year.

Chapman's genius showed again for the 1977 season when he and his design team revealed their latest creation in the form of the Mk. 78 'wing car', which harnessed ground-effect aerodynamics. The underwings, beneath the car, created a low pressure area generating download on the car. Mario Andretti was heard to remark that the Mk. 78 'felt as though it was painted to the road'. Andretti took four wins and Nilsson took one during the season with Mario finishing third in the Drivers' World Championship.

The following year the Mk. 79 appeared at the Belgian Grand Prix and won on its debut. This car, a much refined Mk. 78, was now considered to be a true ground-effects vehicle. It had side skirts along the length of the car to prevent air from escaping from underneath the car, thus enclosing the low pressure beneath the car and sucking the chassis to the ground. Andretti won five GPs with the car in 1978, securing the Drivers' World Championship. Ronnie Peterson, who tragically died after an accident in the Italian Grand Prix, also won one race in the new car and finished second in the Drivers' World Championship.

Lotus had miserable years in 1979 and 1980, when the new Mk. 80 and Mk. 81 didn't live up to the previous year's success. Elio de Angelis had joined Andretti as the second driver. In 1981, Nigel Mansell was hired by Chapman, who expected great things from him and de Angelis. They raced the Mk. 81s for half of the season with the best place going to Mansell--a third place in the Belgian Grand Prix. When the Mk. 87 was introduced for the second half of the season, de Angelis put in good performances, placing in the points five times.

Lotus entered the field of Rallying in 1979. In cooperation with Talbot Sunbeam, a Lotus engine was dropped into the chassis. Tony Ponds debuted the car in the Manx Rally. The car proved the fastest car in the event and led the rally from the first stage only to be sidelined later with engine troubles. Later in the year the car, in Pond's hands, gave a very impressive display of speed on the Lombard RAC Rally of Great Britain. He was quickest over a number of stages but while challenging for the lead he crashed on ice in the forests of Wales.

The following year--1980, Henri Toivonen and his navigator Paul White in their Talbot Sunbeam Lotus hardly put a wheel wrong when they won the Lombard RAC Rally of Great Britain. In the same rally the Lotus engined car of Guy Frequelin and Jean Todt (present Ferrari team manager) finished third. The Talbot Sunbeam Lotus cars were still dominant in 1981, winning the World Makes Rally Championship.

The Mk. 91, introduced in 1982, was quite good looking with the driver seated near the front. The most productive of the two drivers that year, de Angelis finished in eight races, including a win in the Austrian Grand Prix. Mansell missed two GPs with minor injuries, finishing in six of the races he entered. Worse was to come for Team Lotus, when Colin Chapman succumbed to a massive heart attack just before Christmas at the age of 54 years.

Peter Warr took over the running of Team Lotus, but just before his death Chapman had signed a deal with Renault Sports to use their turbocharged V6 engines for the new formula in 1983. The Lotus cars with the turbo engines were known as Mk. 93T and later that year 94T, after technical input from Gerard Ducarouge, which had improved the car. Mansell had the most success during the season by finishing nine times compared to two for de Angelis.

Team Lotus and Ducarouge made improvements to the new 95T in 1984, making it one of the best handling cars during the season. The cars were remarkably reliable with de Angelis finishing in the points on eleven occasions out of the 16 races that were run. Mansell finished only five races but scored points each time.

From 1985-1988 the Renault V6 turbo engined 97T and 98T took six wins with Senna driving, and one with de Angelis. Senna finished Fourth in the Drivers' World Championship in 1985 and 1986.

Lotus changed engine manufacturers in 1987 for the 99T, moving from a Renault V6 turbo to the Honda V6 turbo. Senna took a couple of wins during the season and third place in the Drivers' World Championship.

Lotus 100T, for 1988, was the last of the turbo cars, since rule changes banned turbo cars for the following year. It wasn't an impressive car--Piquet retired from seven races and finished sixth in the Drivers' World Championship.

The Lotus Team began a downhill slide in 1989, and was almost bankrupt by 1991, when their main sponsors, Camel cigarettes, announced that they would be taking their money elsewhere. Lotus was saved at the last minute by a consortium of business people, who carried on building cars using a variety of engines. The 1989 Mk. 101 used a Judd engine, the 1990 Mk. 102 a Lamborghini with Warwick and Donnely driving. For 1991 they had switched back to a Judd engine with Hakkinen and Herbert driving. The following year another engine change, for the Mk. 107, to a custom Ford V8 with the same drivers. Herbert was retained for his third season in 1993, driving a modified car--the Mk. 107B. He was accompanied by the second driver Alessandro Zanardi (later to become the 1997 CART champion of United States). They finally went bankrupt in 1994 after completing the season with a pair of Lotus 109s using Mugen Honda engines, and again using Herbert and Zanardi as their drivers.

Senna was the last driver to win a Grand Prix for the Lotus team, and that was in 1987 when he took the chequered flag in the U.S. Grand Prix at Detroit. It was this lack of success that led to the downfall of a household name in Formula 1.

Team Lotus had entered 490 GPs since its first appearance at Monaco in 1958, with 79 victories, 71 fastest laps and 107 pole positions, seven World Constructors' titles and six World Drivers' Championships. For the period, apart from Ferrari, they were one of the best teams in Grand Prix racing.

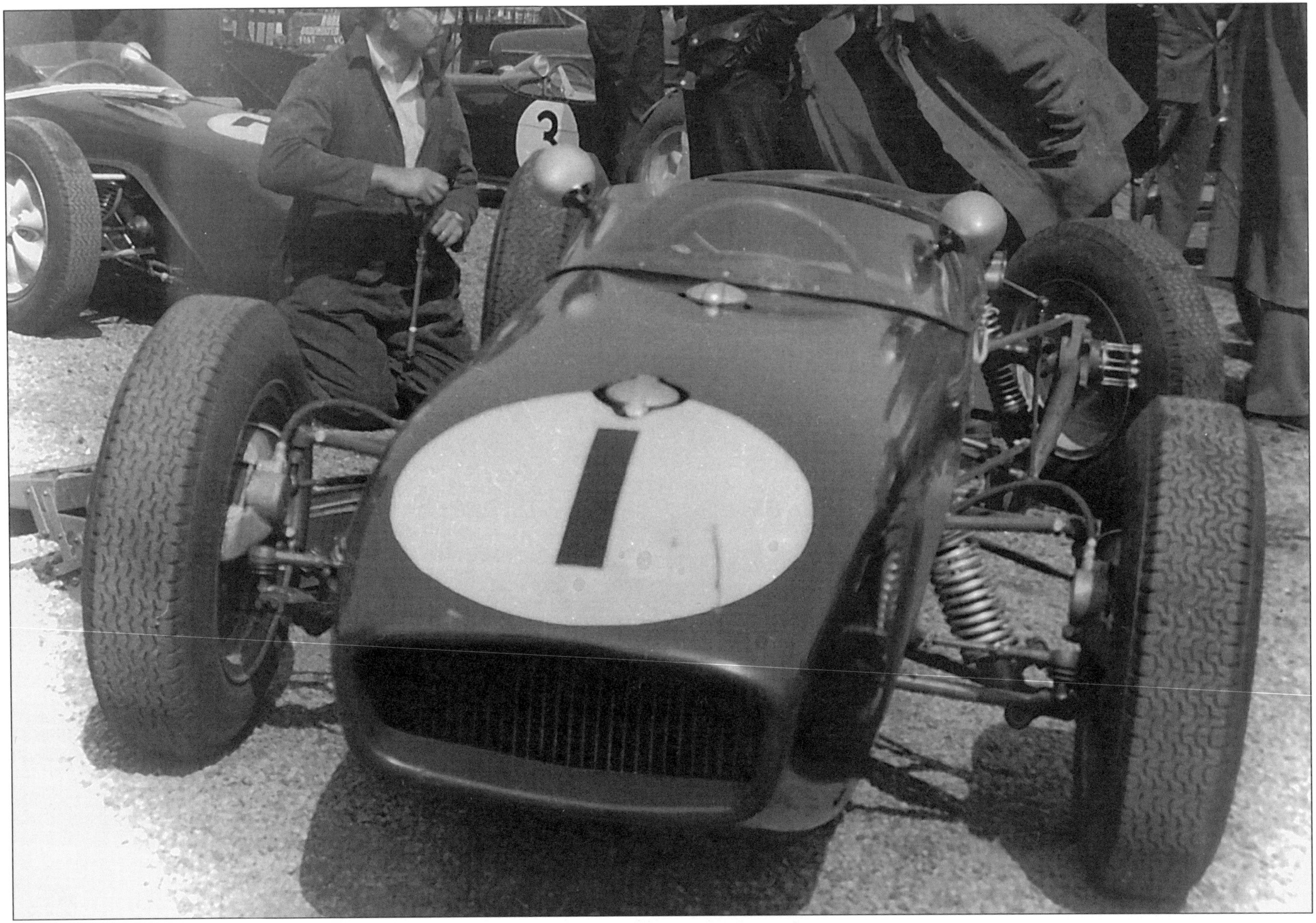

Innes Ireland's Lotus 18 at the 1960 Aintree International 200 Meet.

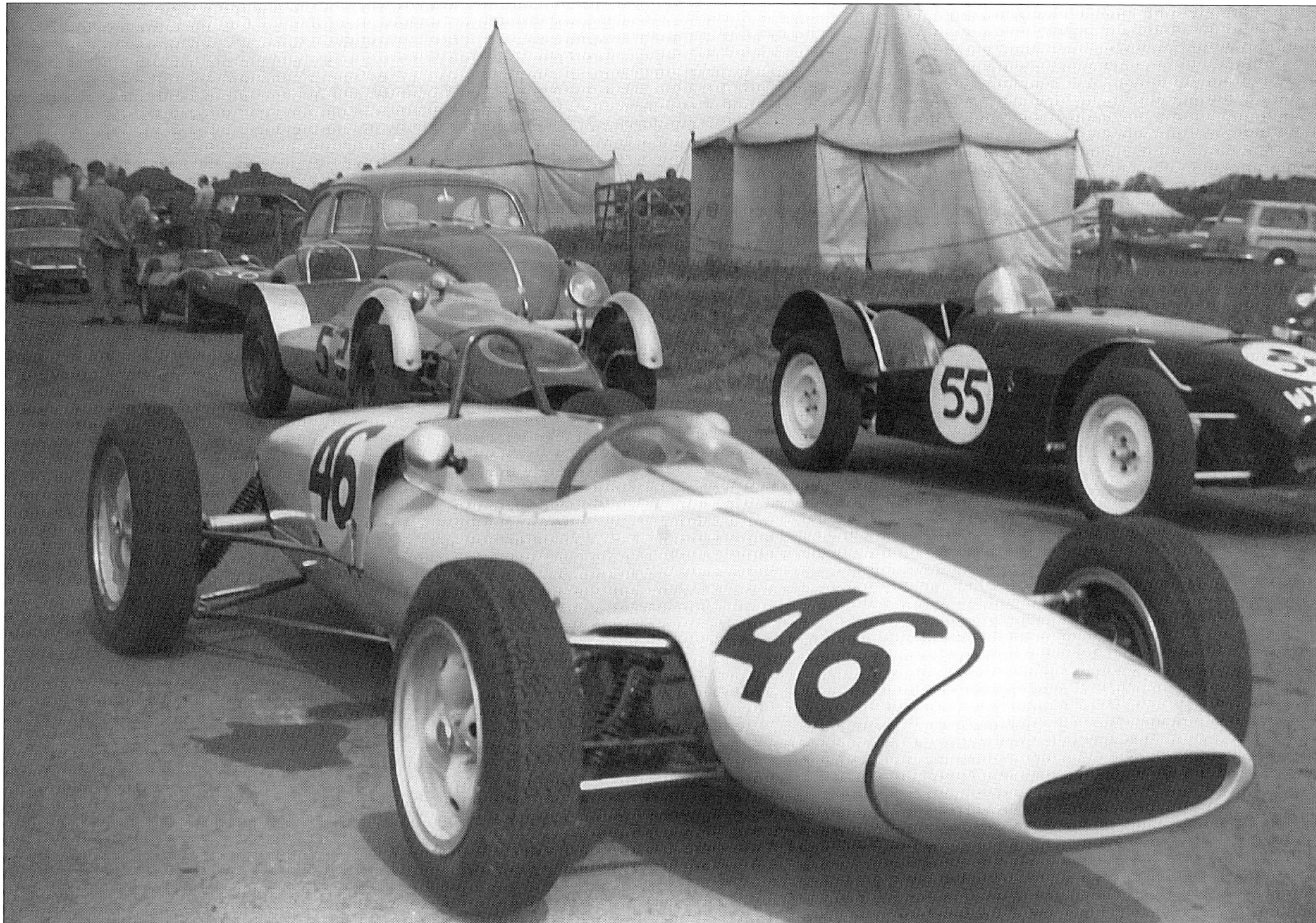

M. Cleaver's Lotus 20 at the 1961 Aintree Spring Meet.

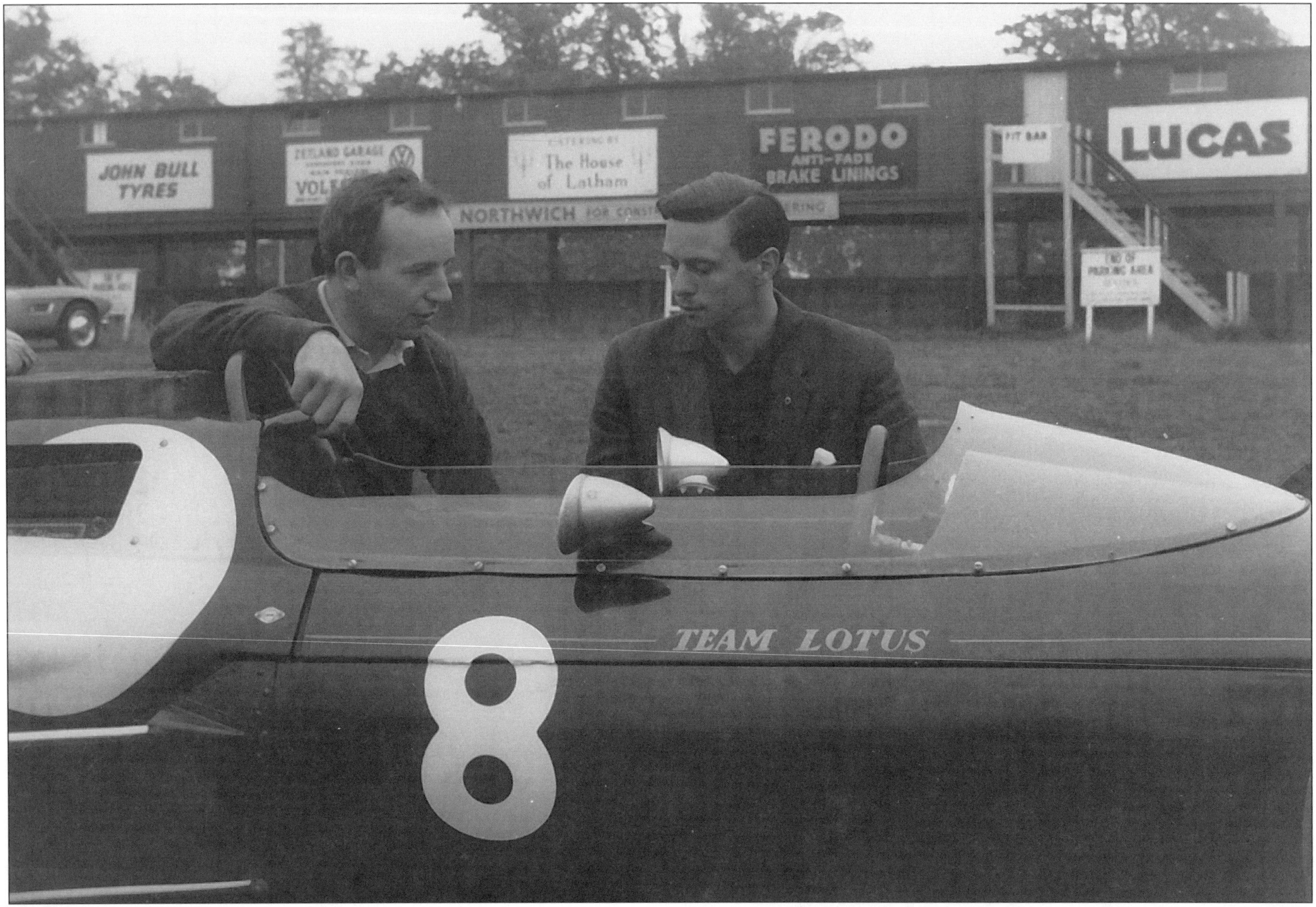

Jim Clark (right) and John Surtees in deep discussion behind a Lotus 25 in the paddock of Oulton Park during the 1962 Gold Cup Meet.

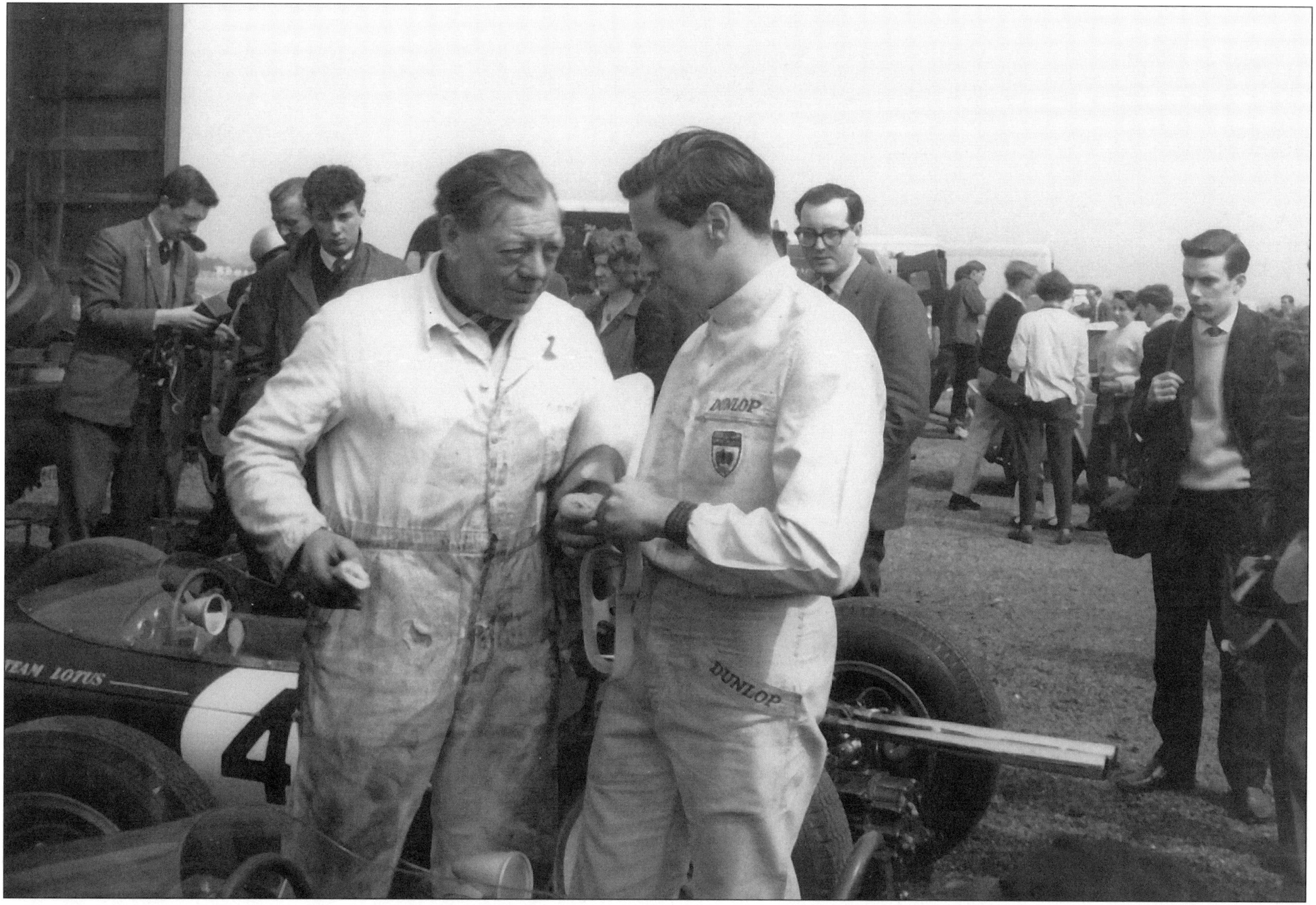

Jim Clark (right) talking to his chief mechanic in the pit area at the 1963 Aintree 200.

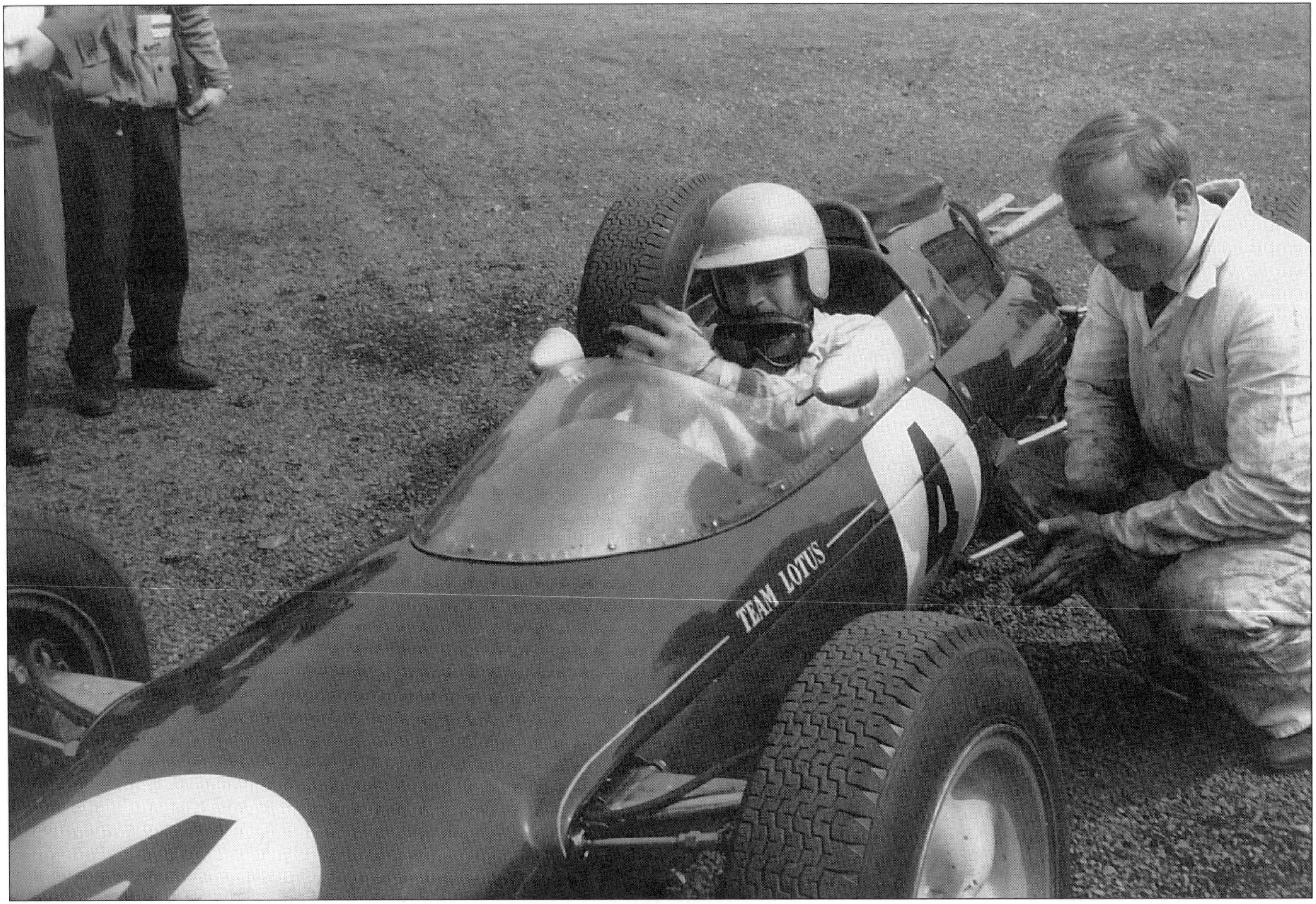

Trevor Taylor, seated in Lotus 25/R3, powered by a Climax V-8 engine, preparing for the 1963 Aintree 200.

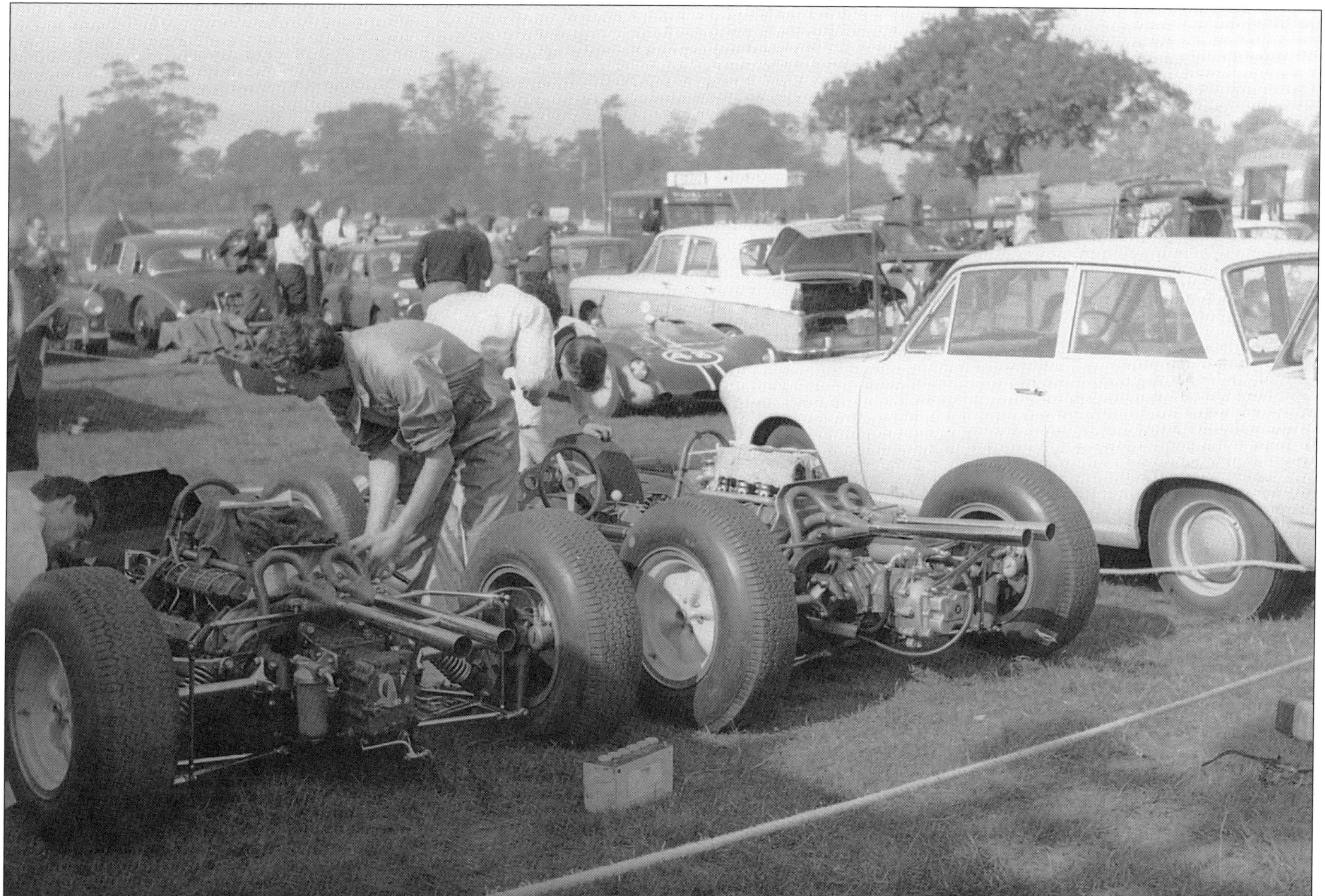

Lotus mechanics preparing the Lotus 25s of Jim Clark and Trevor Taylor for the 1963 Oulton Park Gold Cup Race.

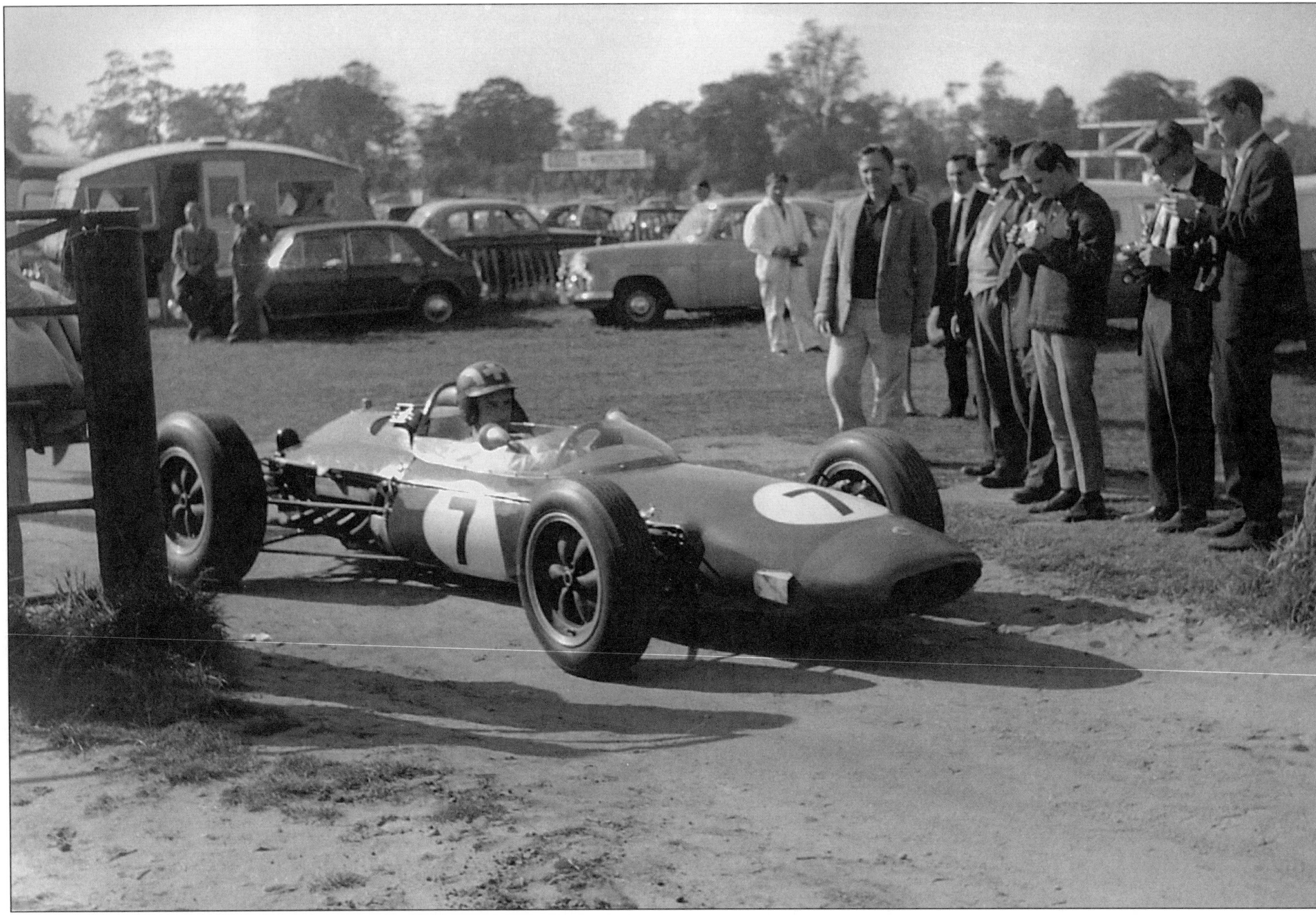

Jo Siffert entering the assembly area at Oulton Park before the 1963 Gold Cup Race. Siffert finished eleventh driving this BRM V-8 powered Lotus 24 - chassis 950.

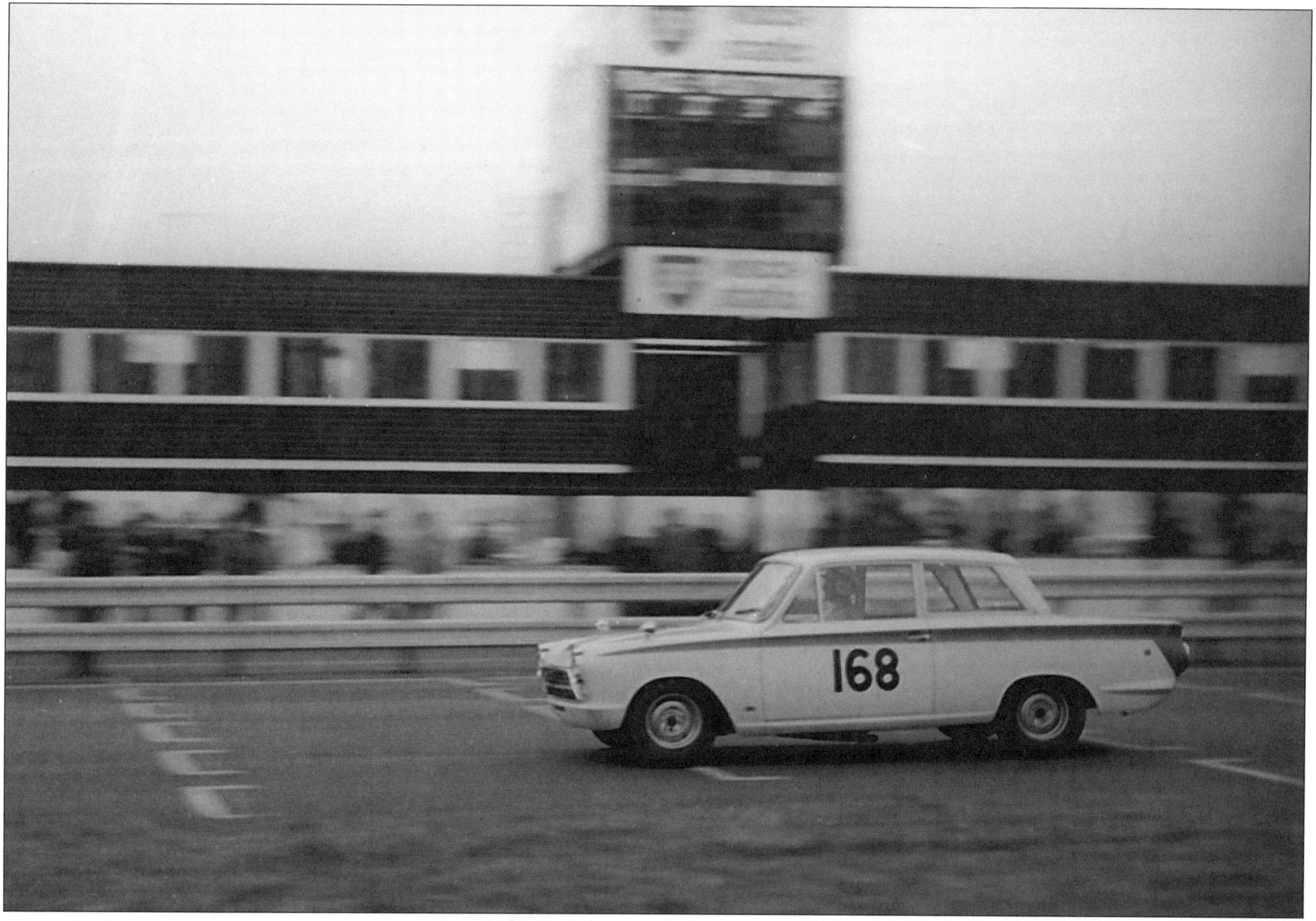

Jackie Stewart's Lotus Ford Cortina Type 28 winning the Saloon car race at Oulton Park in 1964.

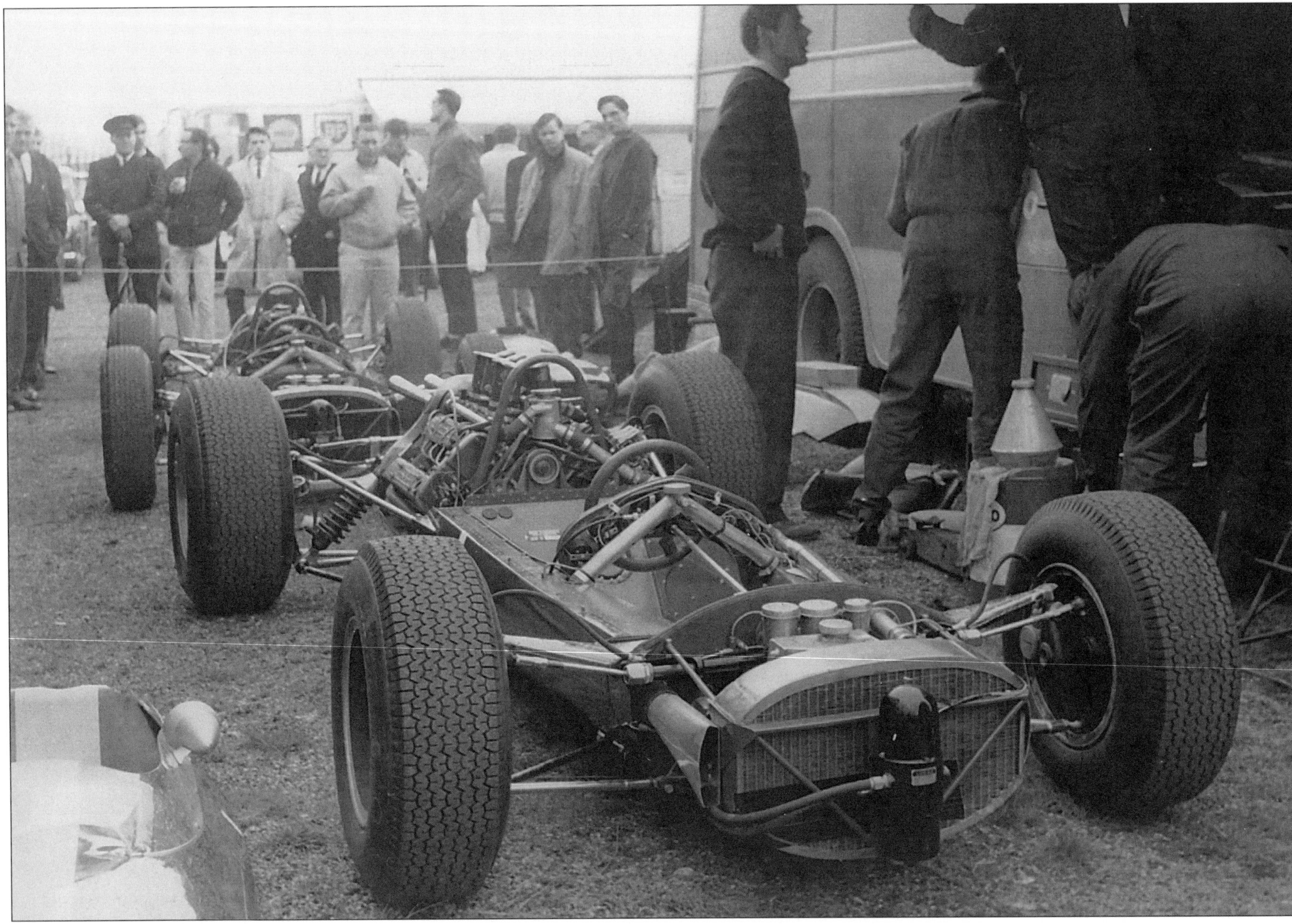

Jim Clark's Lotus 33/R8, with a Climax FWMV V-8, in the paddock before the 1964 Aintree 200.

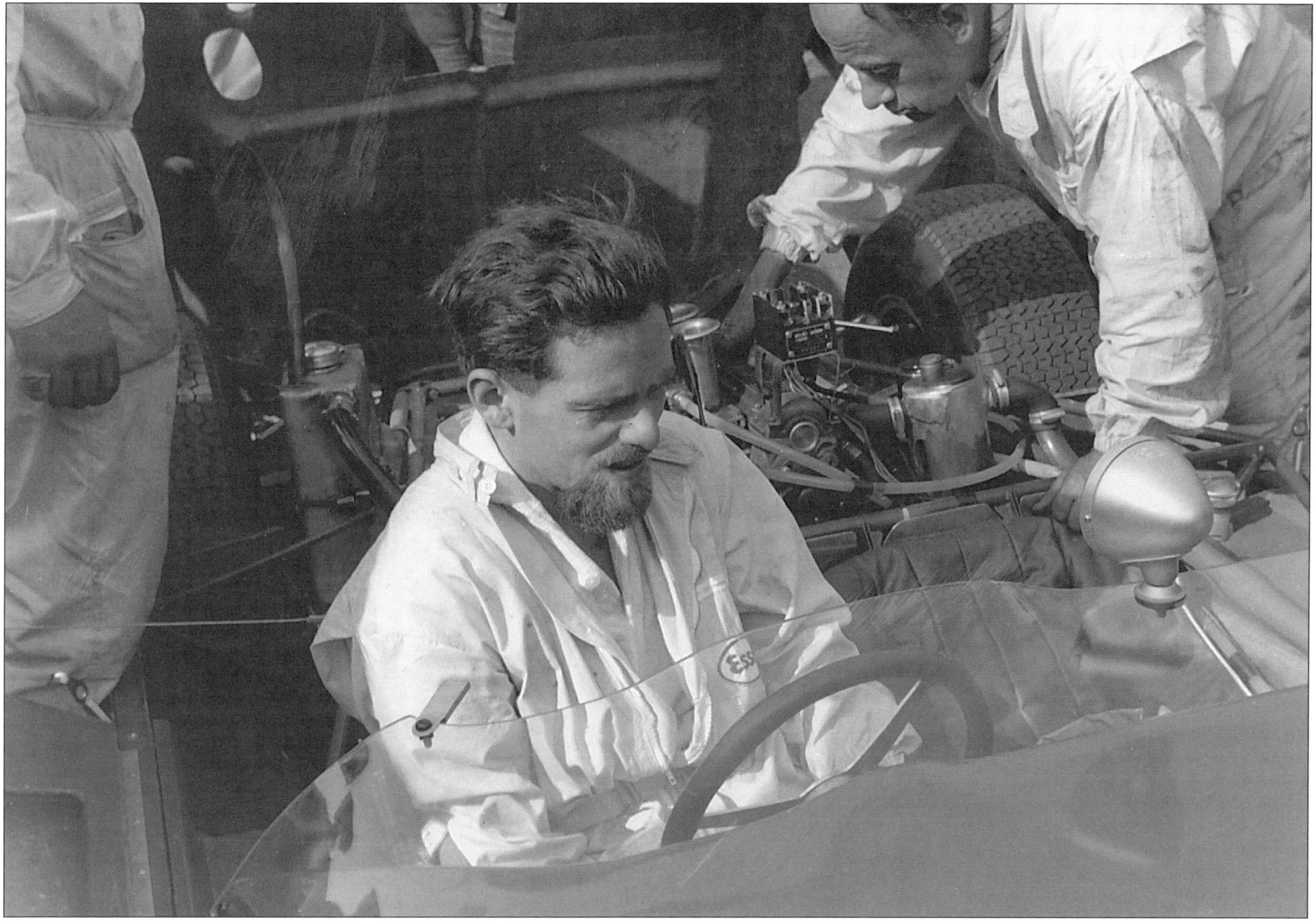

Waiting his turn at the 1964 Barbon Hill Climb is Peter Westbury in a Lotus 23 with 2-liter B.R.M. engine.

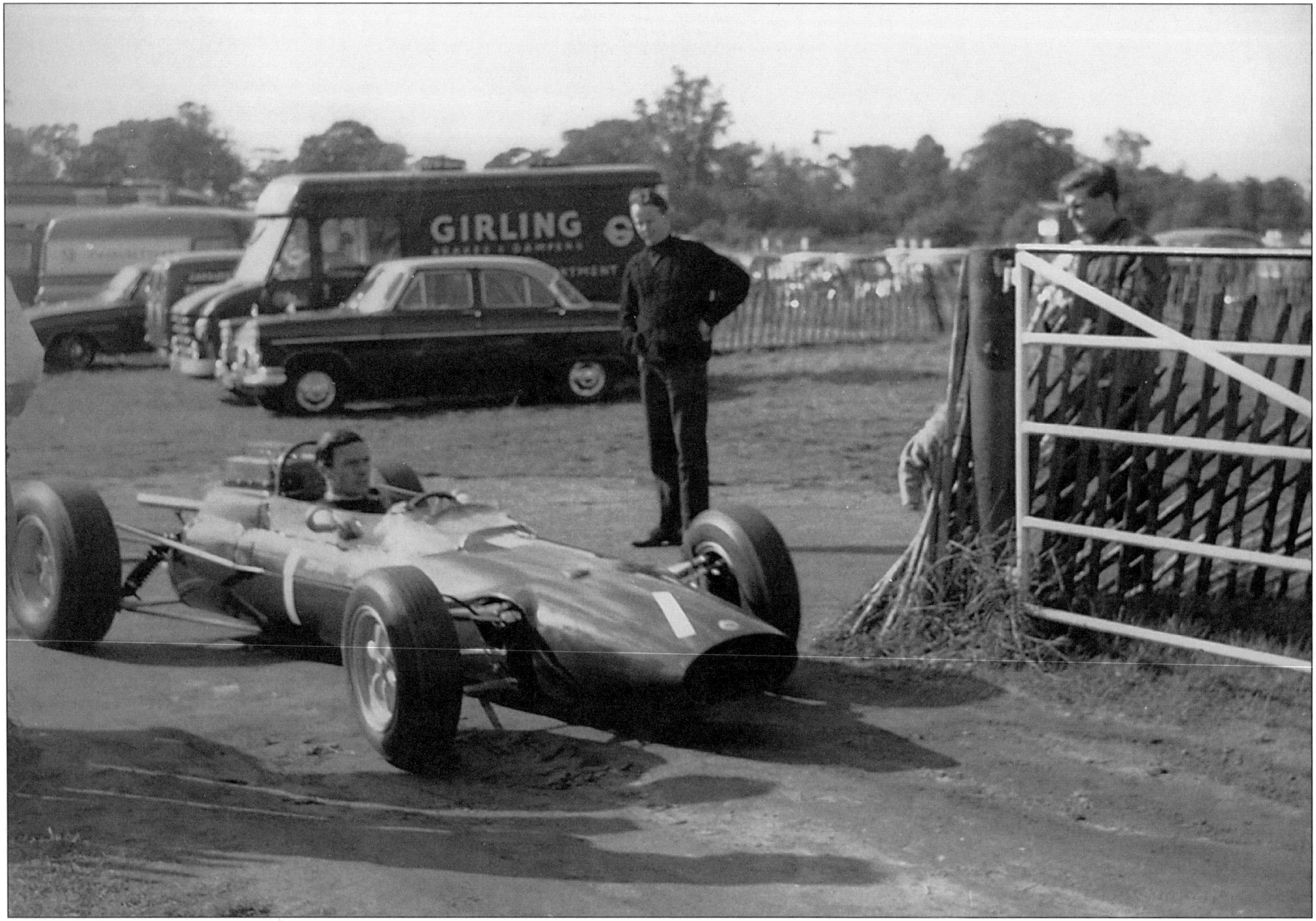

Jim Clark, driving a Lotus 32, entering the assembly area during practice session for the 1964 Oulton Park Gold Cup Meet.

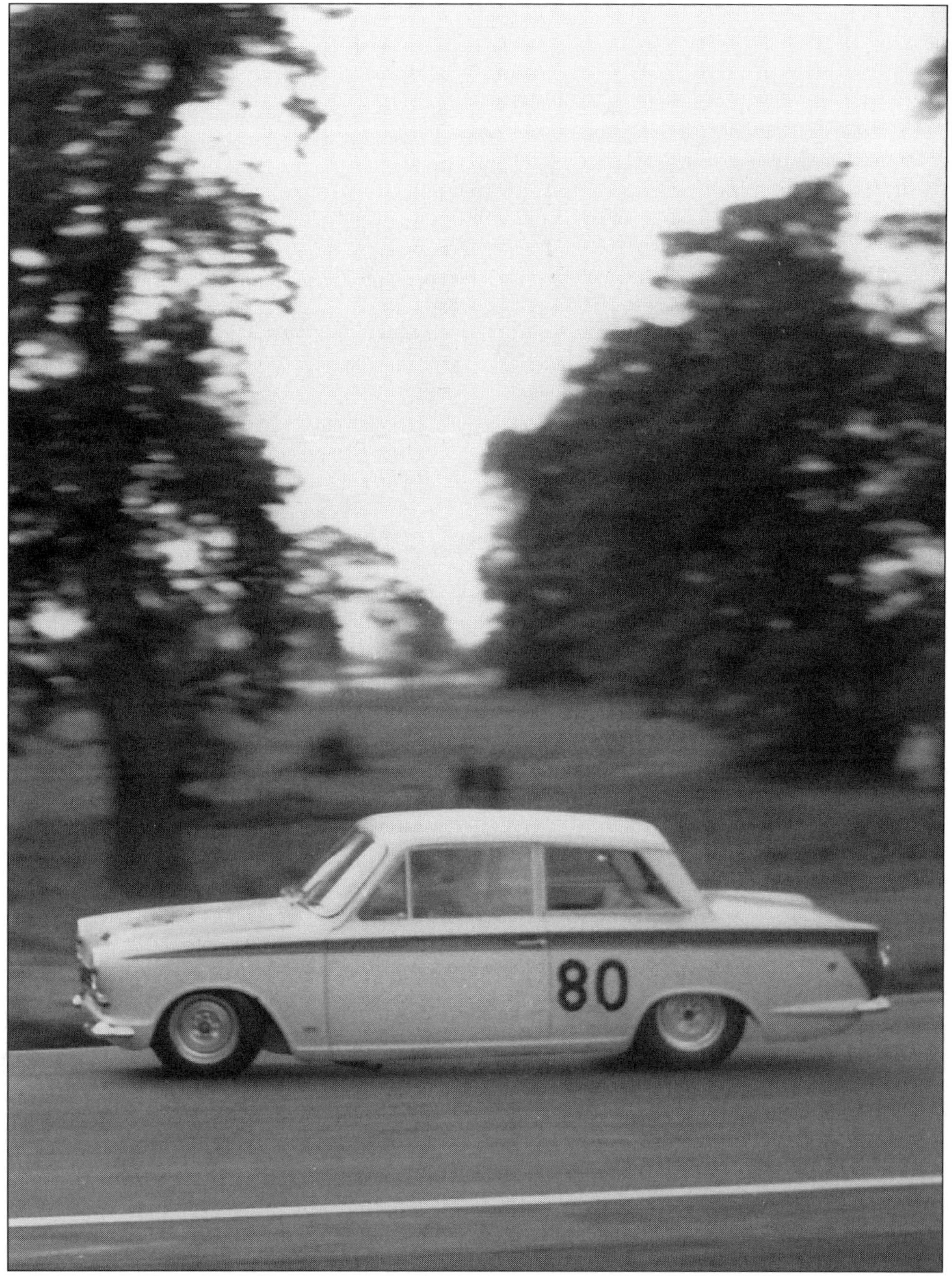

Driving a Lotus Ford Cortina, Jim Clark went on to win the 1964 Saloon Car race at the Oulton Park Gold Cup Meet.

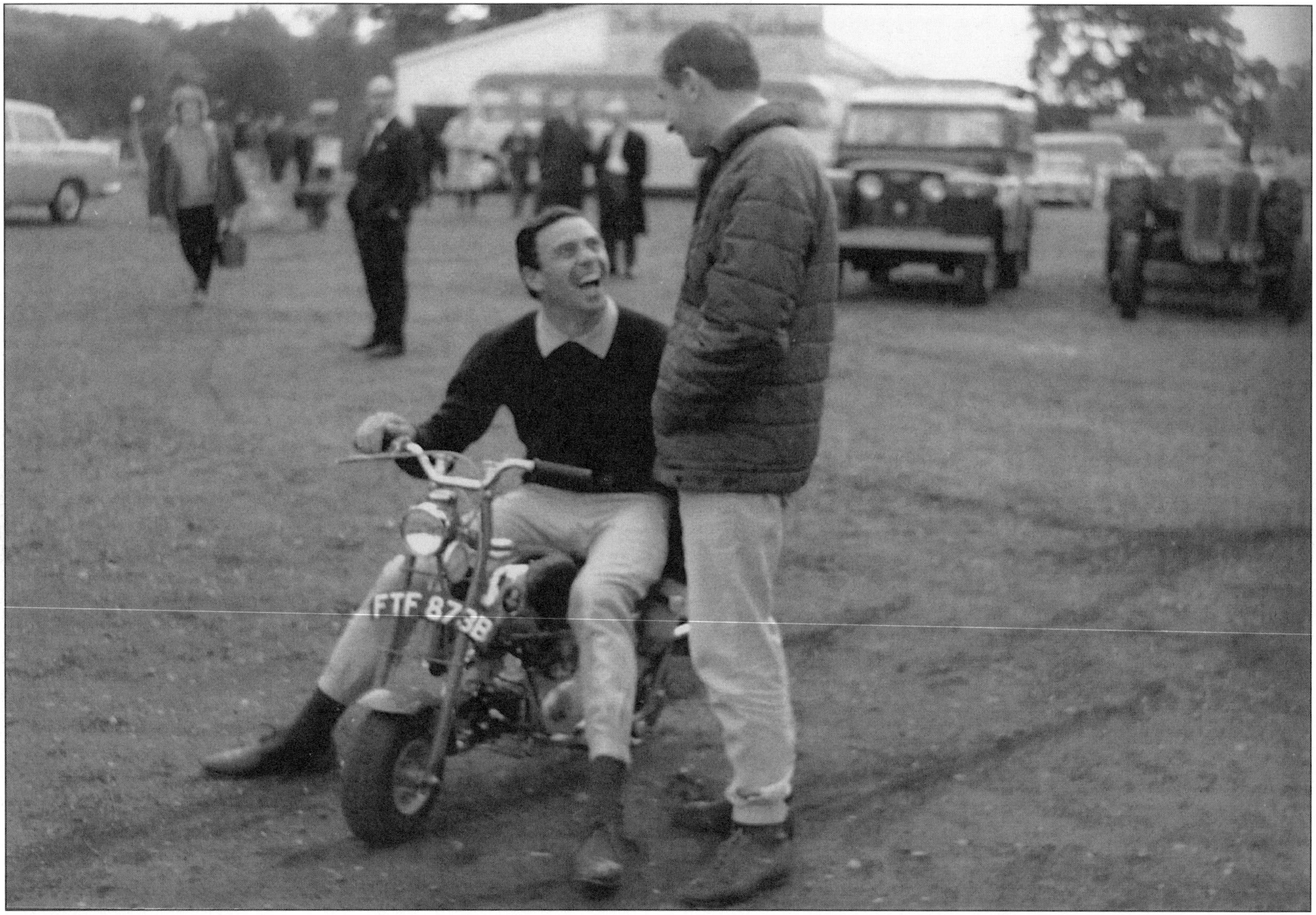

Jim Clark (seated) shares a joke with Jackie Stewart during the 1964 Oulton Park Gold Cup Meet.

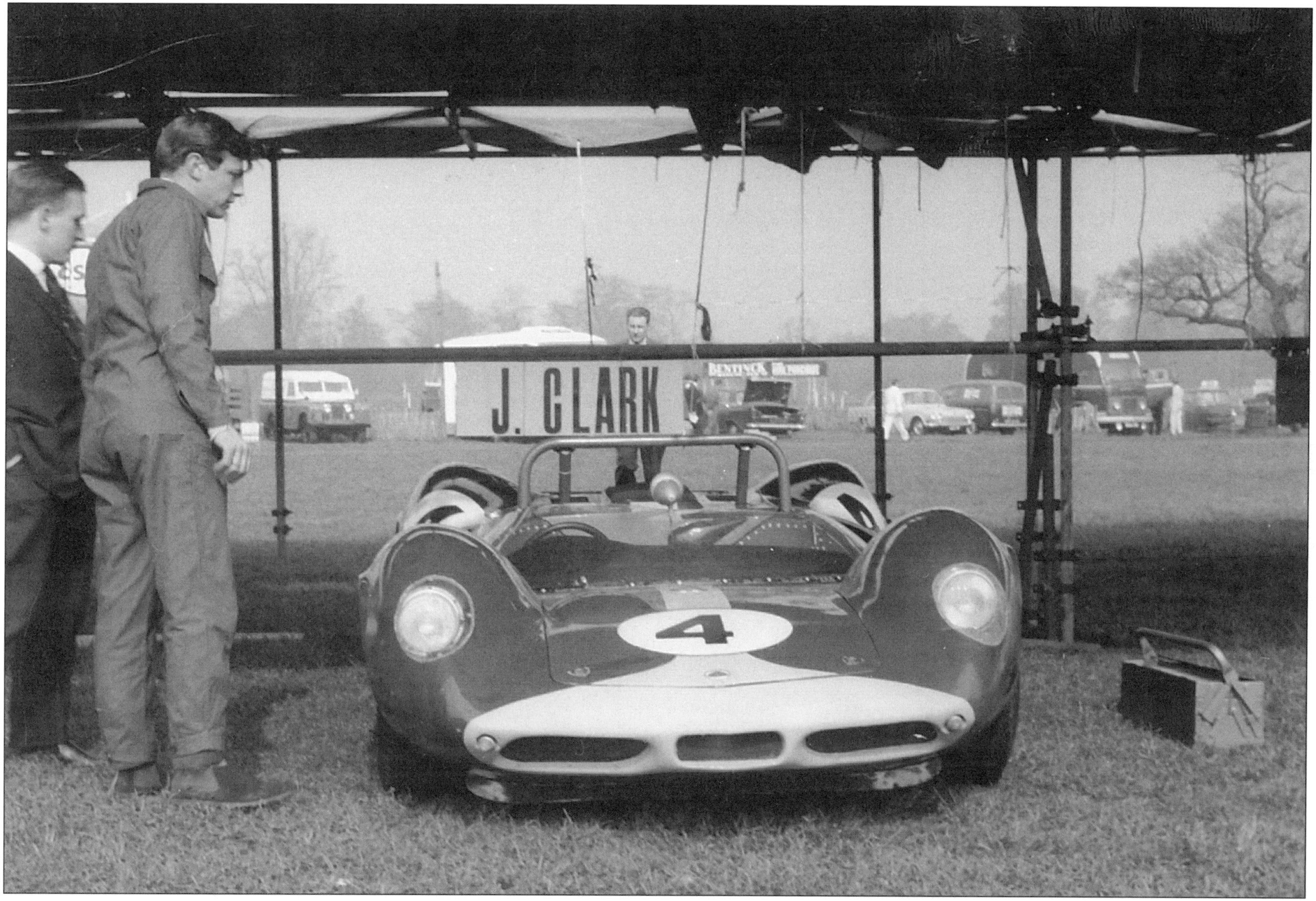

The Lotus 30 Jim Clark drove for Team Lotus in the paddock for the 1965 RAC Tourist Trophy race.

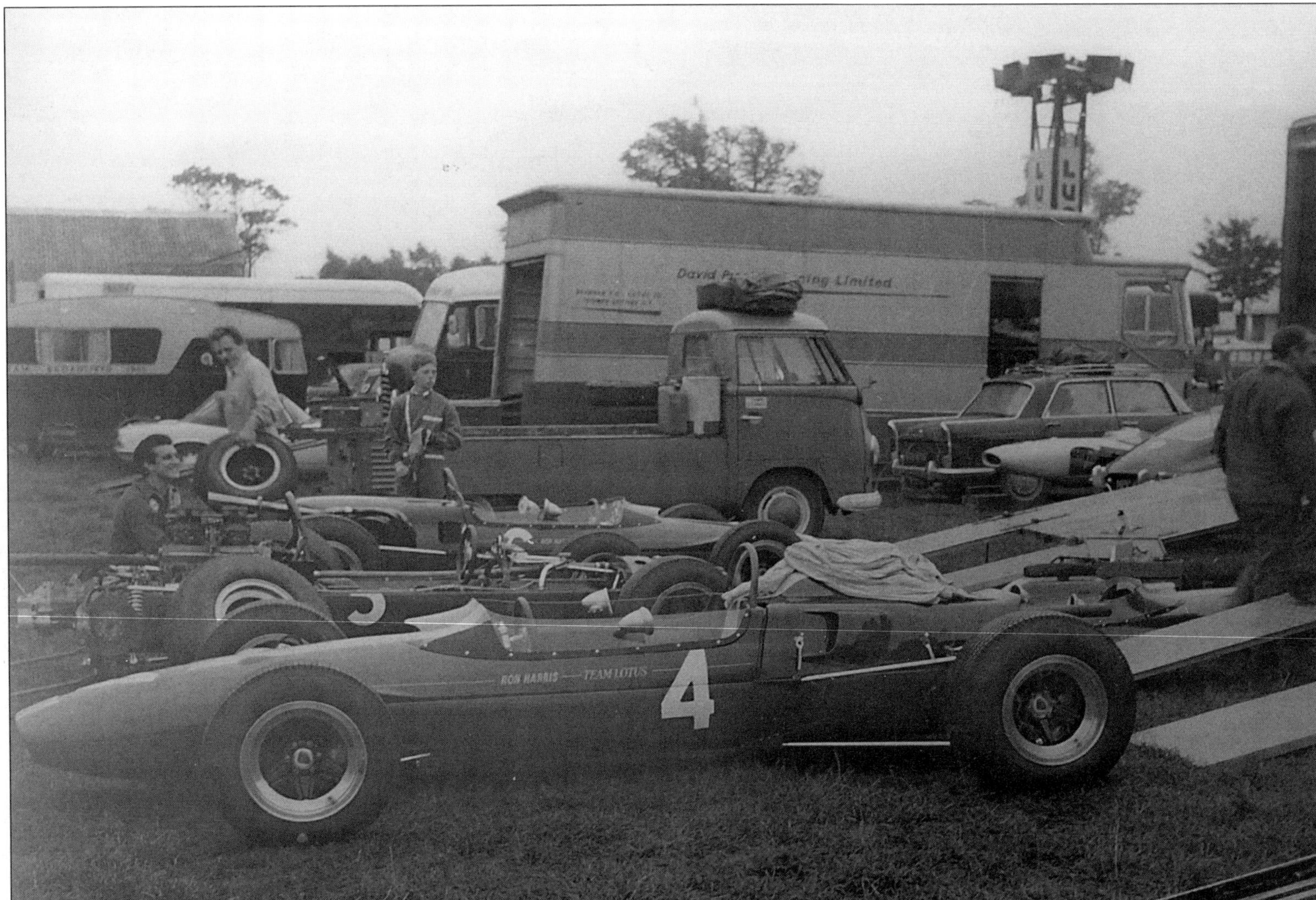

Lotus cars in the paddock at the 1965 Oulton Park Formula 2 Race.

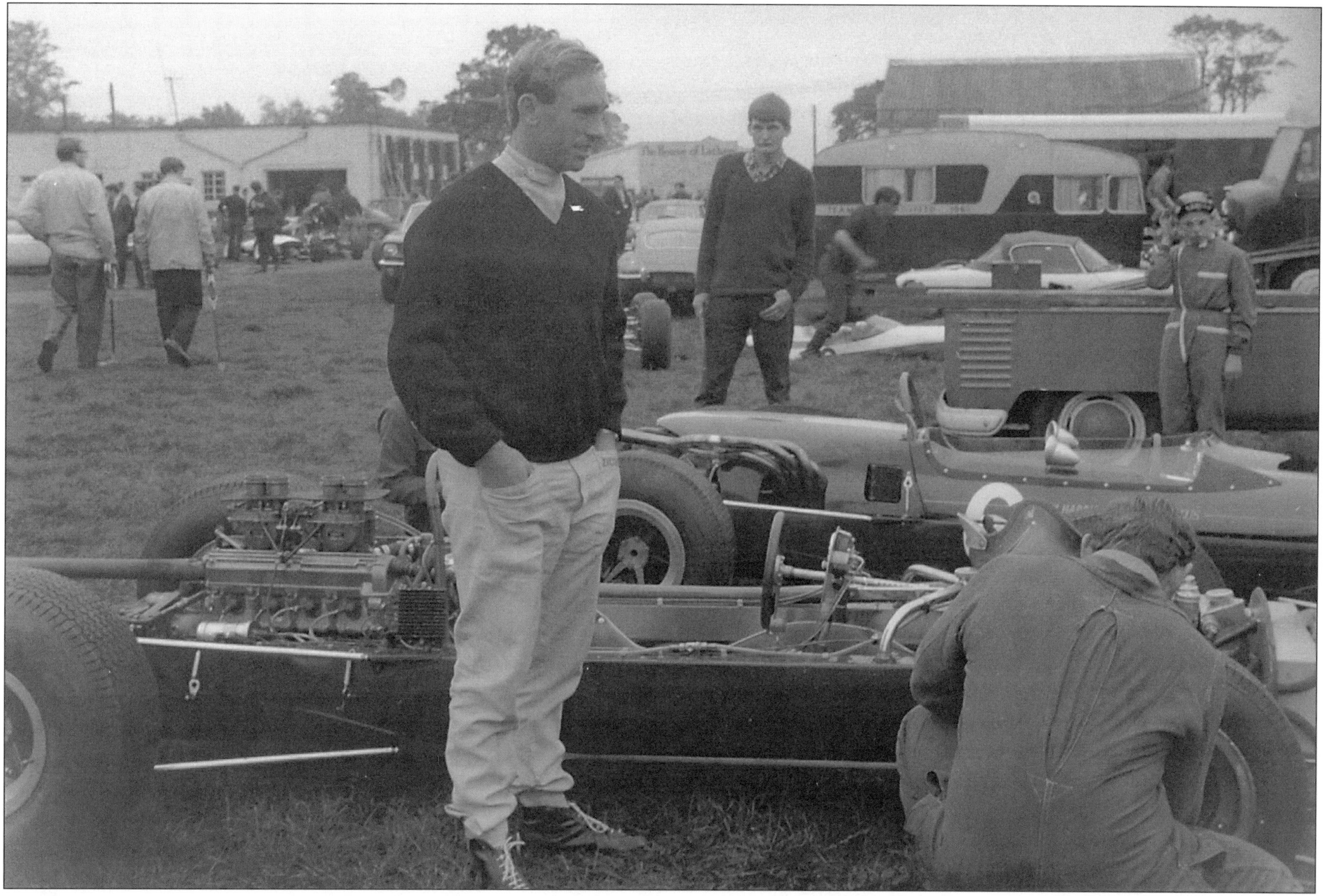

Mike Spence watches mechanics preparing his Lotus 35 for the 1965 International Gold Cup Race at Oulton Park.

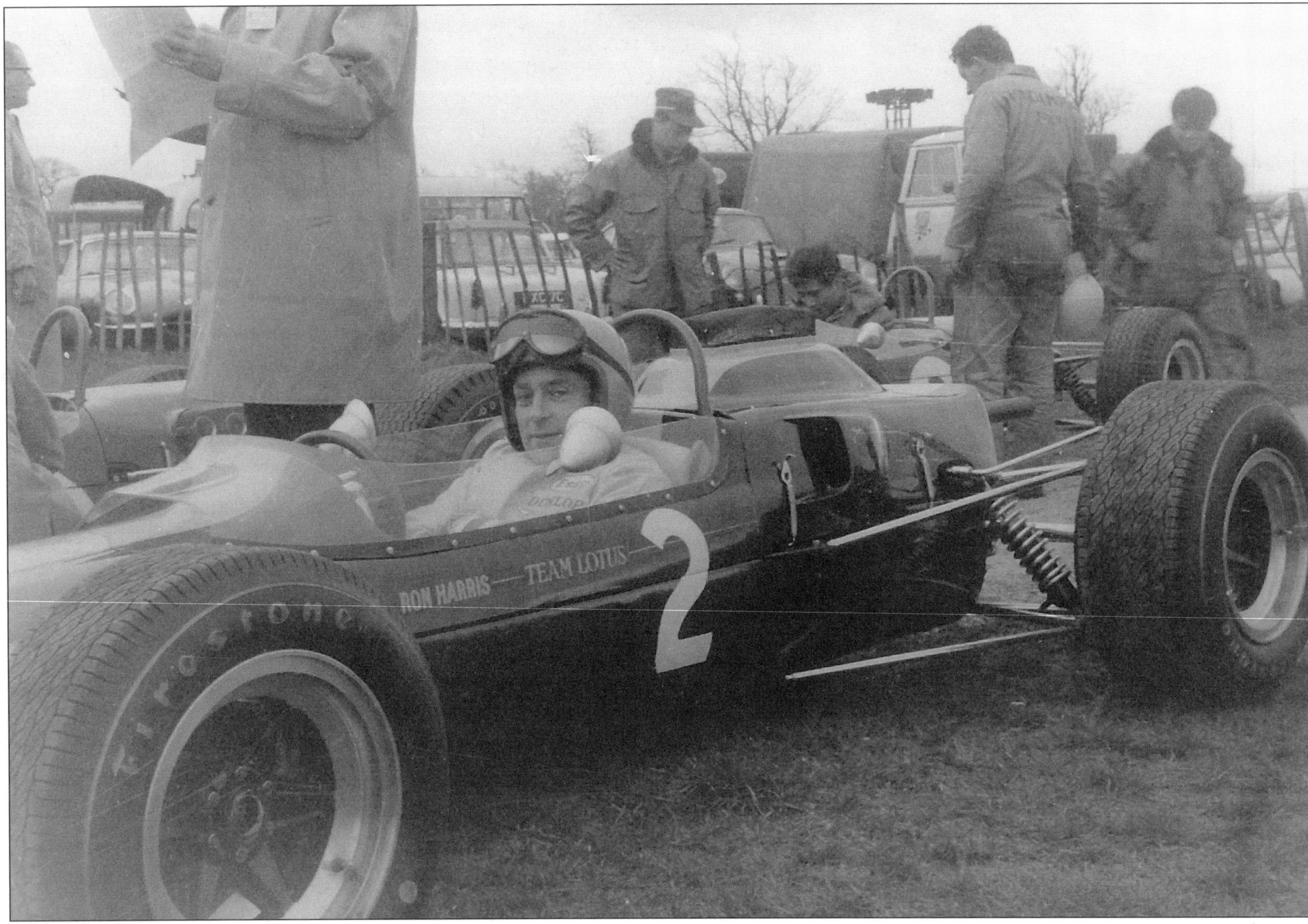

Peter Arundell in a Lotus 35 waiting for practice to begin at the 1966 Oulton Park International 200 Race.

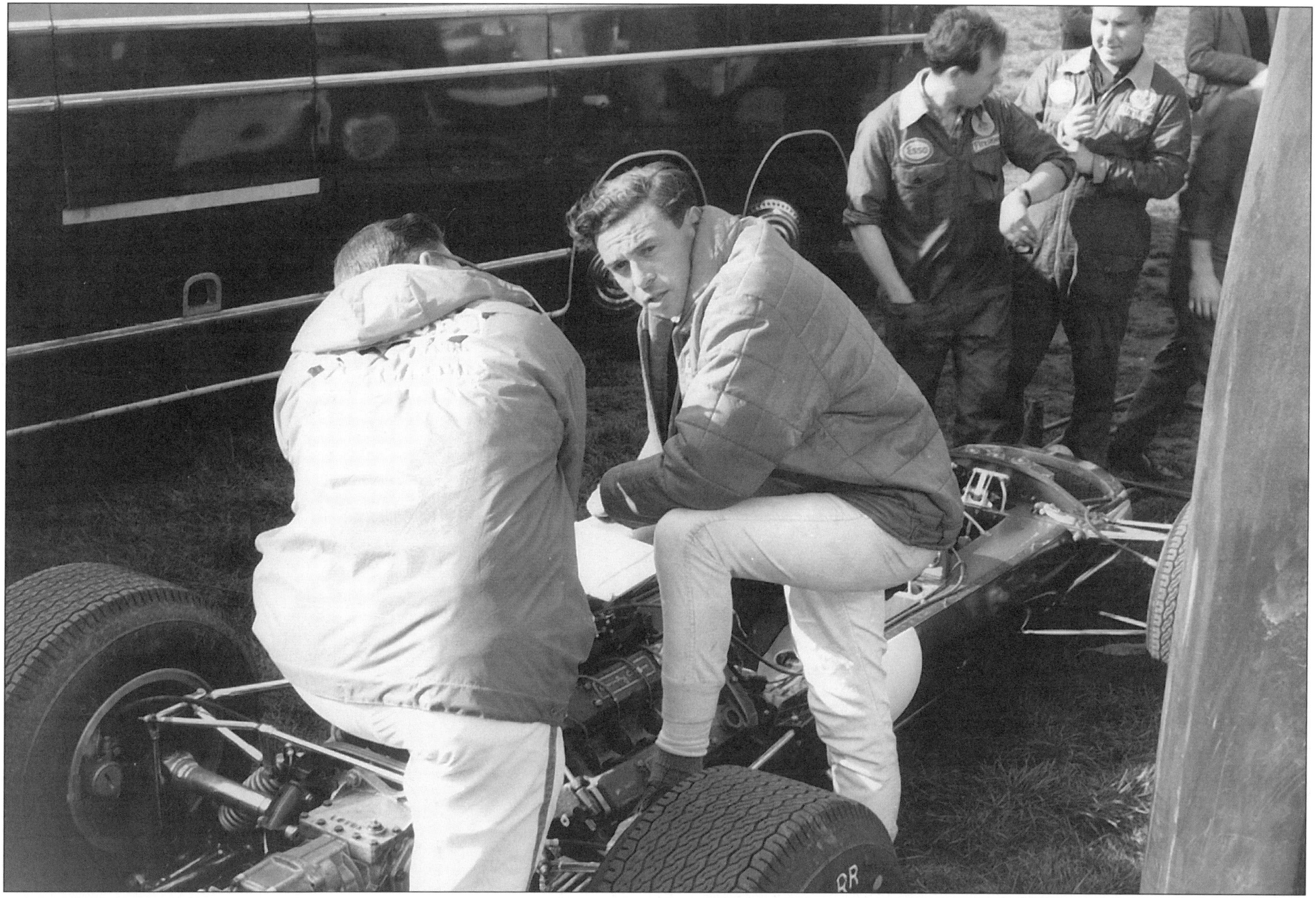

Jim Clark discusses tires with a Firestone technician at the 1966 Oulton Park Gold Cup Race.

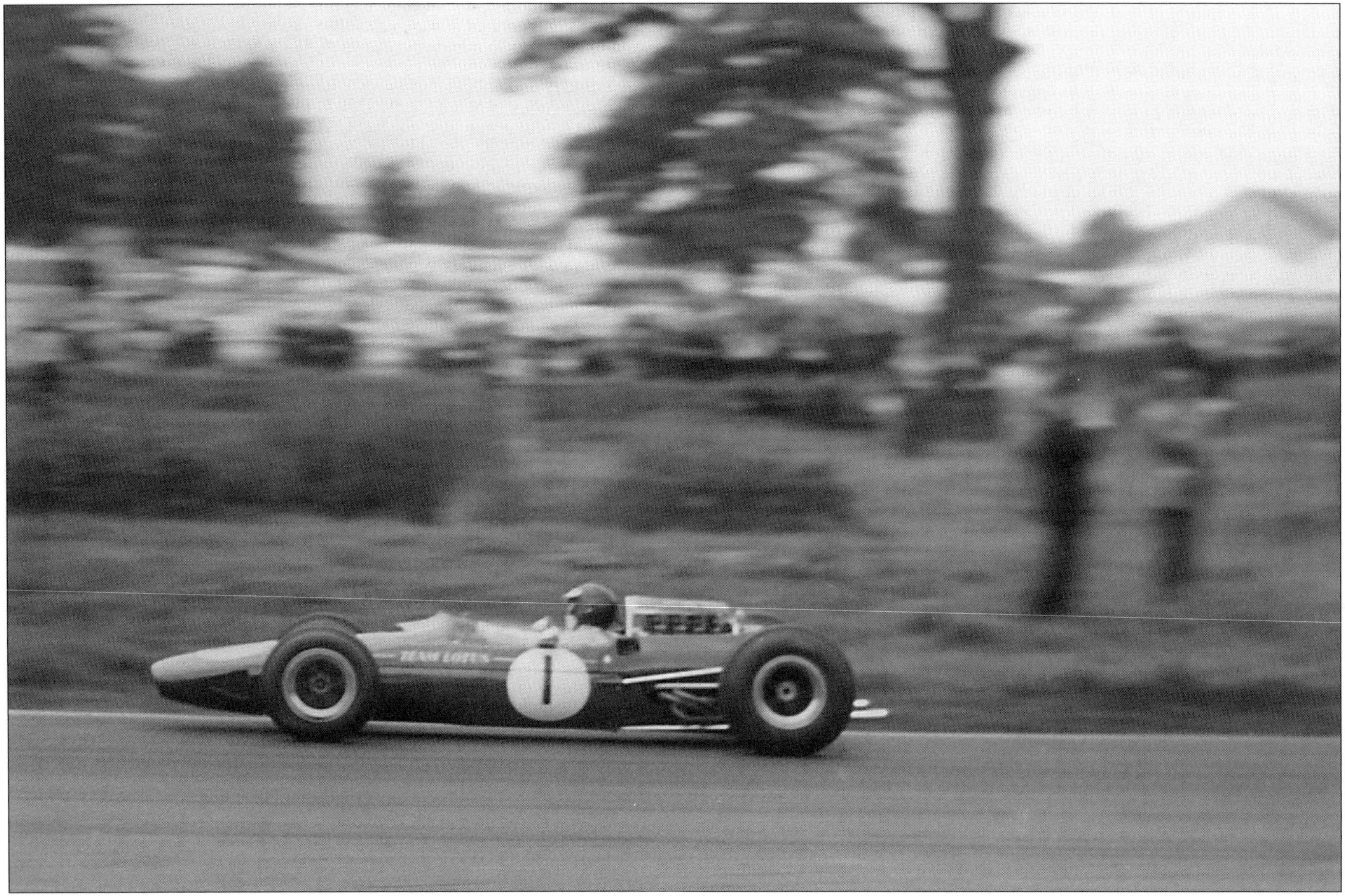

Jim Clark driving 2-liter Lotus 33/R14 at Oulton Park for the 1966 Gold Cup Race. Clark finished in third place.

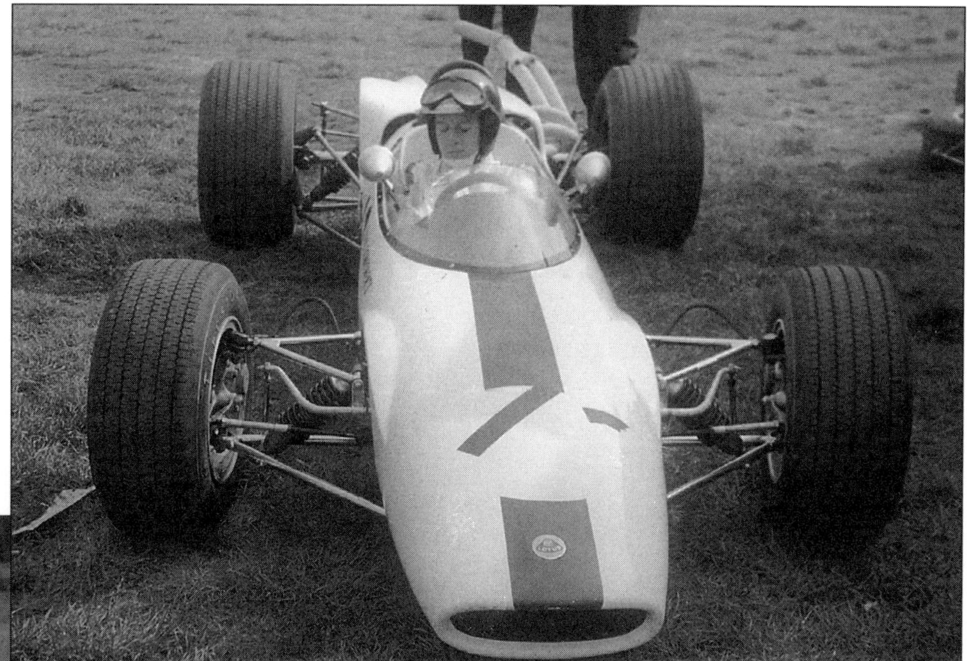

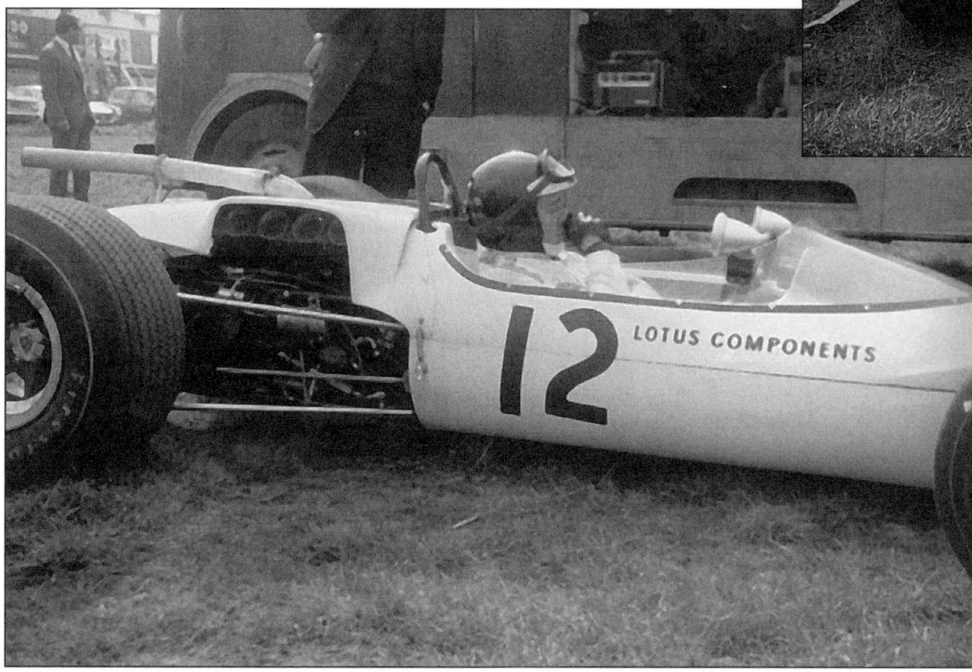

Two views of Jackie Oliver waiting in the assembly area before the start of the 1967 Oulton Park International Spring Cup Race. Oliver drove this Lotus Components-run 1.6-liter Lotus 41B Cosworth to fourth place overall.

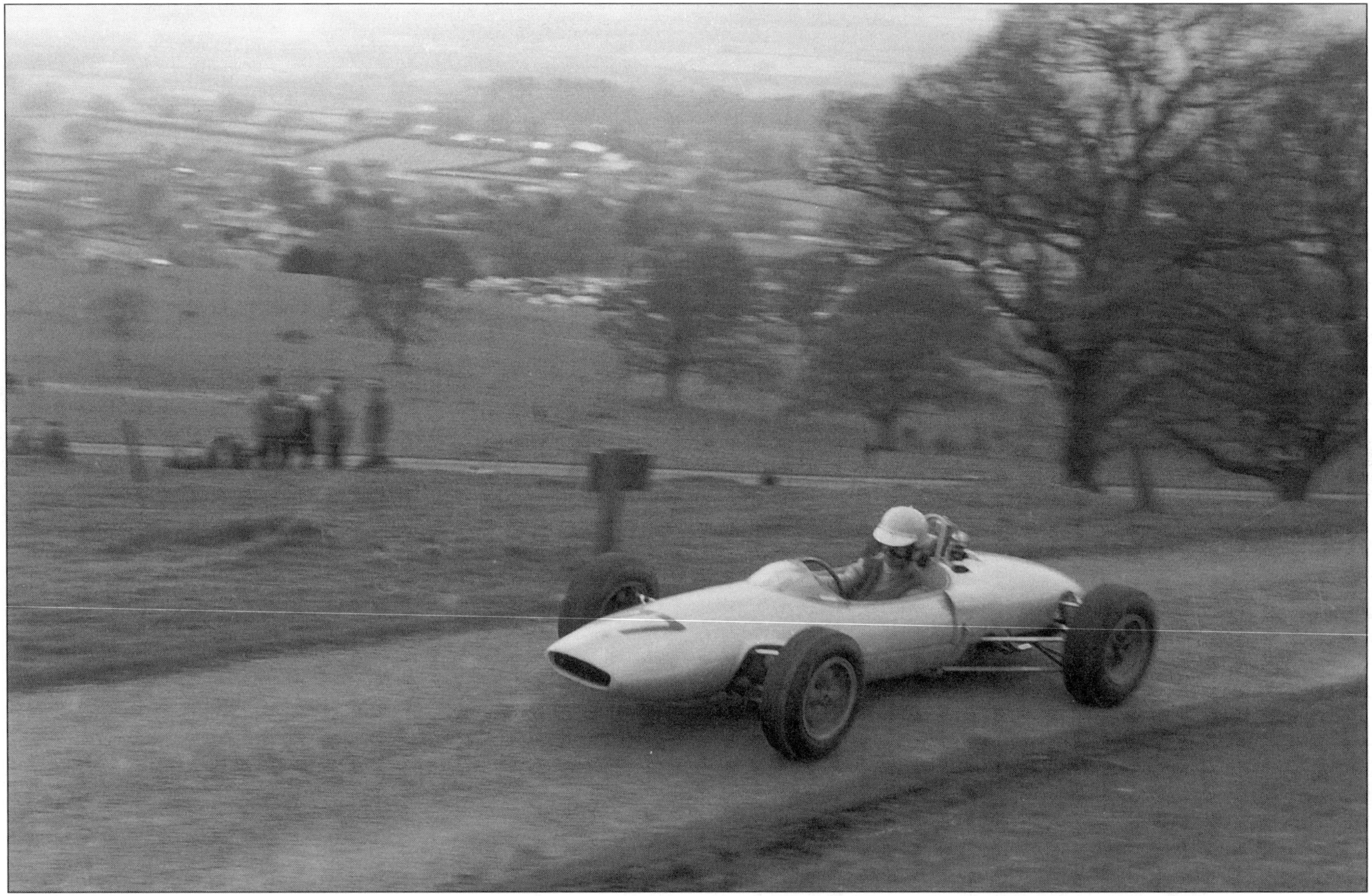

Peter Boshier-Jones takes his Lotus 22 to the top of Barbon Manor Hill-Climb in 1967.

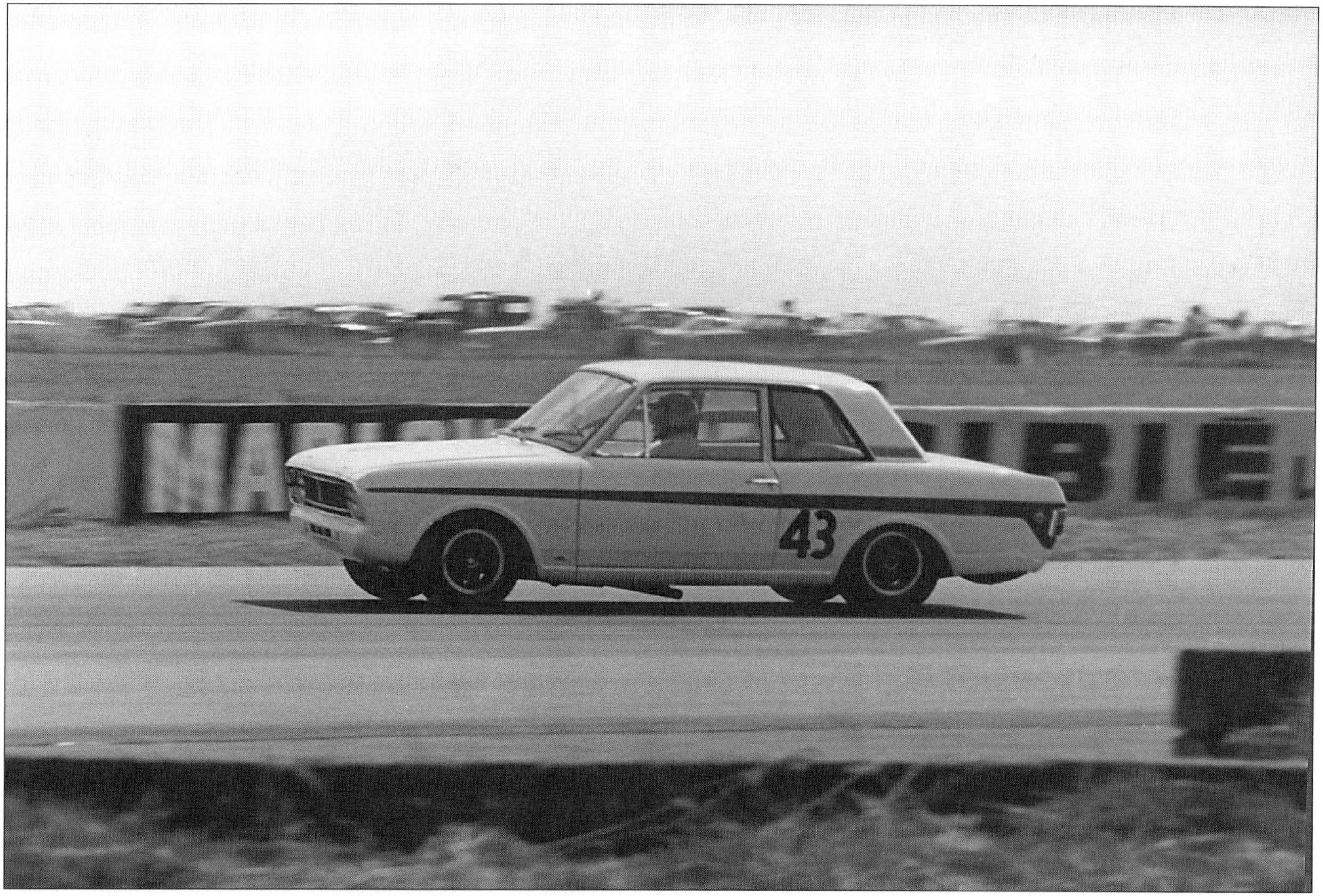

Paul Hawkins driving a Team Lotus-run 1.6-liter Ford Lotus Cortina powered by a Cosworth FVA in the 1967 British Grand Prix. Setting a new class record, Hawkins easily won the 2-liter category, finishing fourth overall.

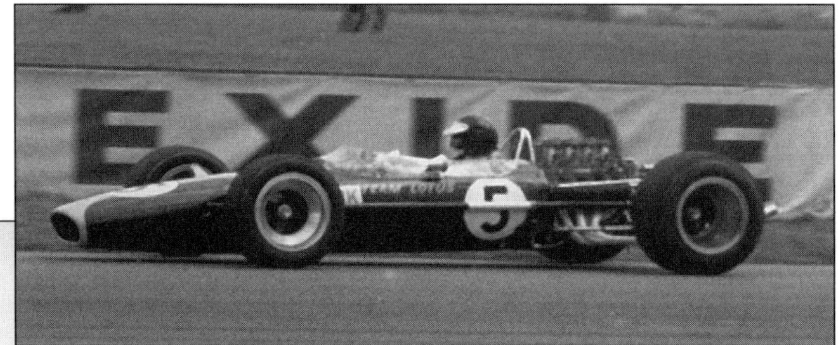

Clark driving a Ford Cosworth V-8 DFV powered Lotus 49. Clark remained in the lead for most of the race.

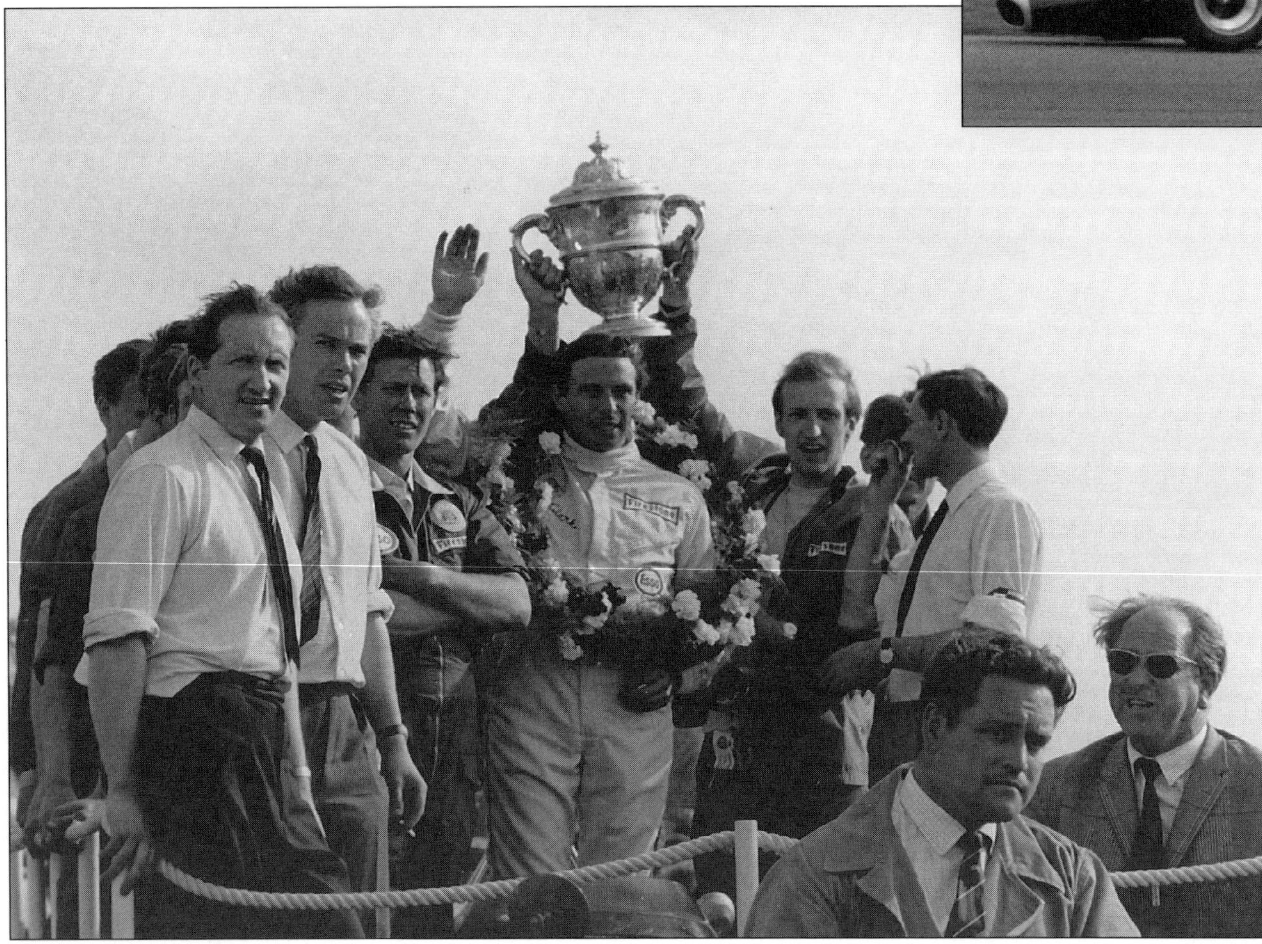

Jim Clark parades around the Silverstone circuit after winning the 1967 British Grand Prix.

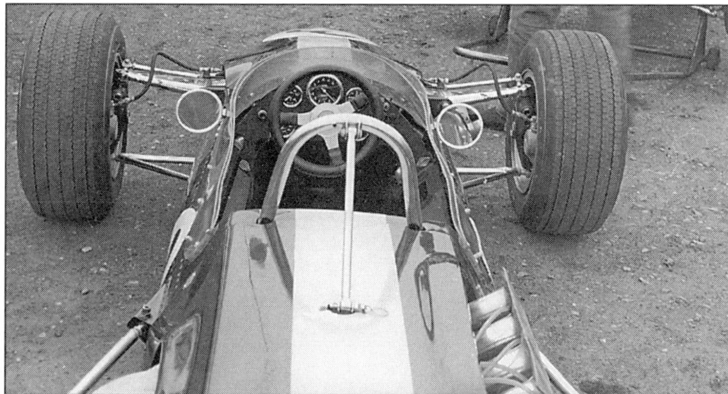

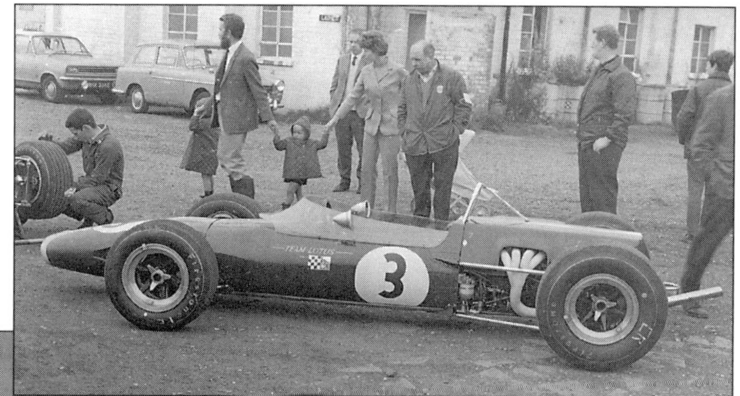

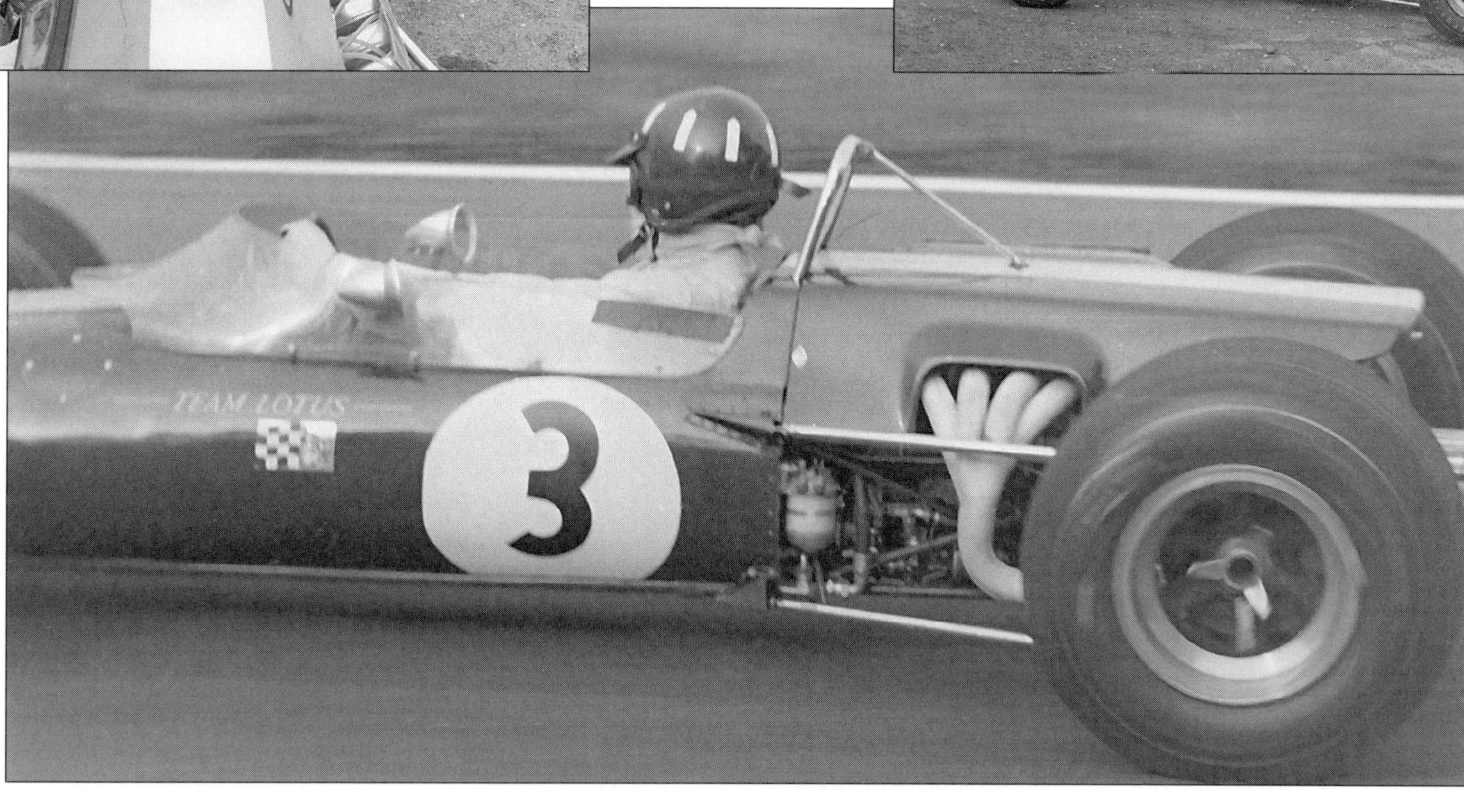

Graham Hill's 1.6-liter Cosworth powered Formula 2 Lotus 48 at the 1967 Oulton Park International Gold Cup Race. The car is pictured in the paddock (top right) and with a close-up of the cockpit (top left.) Bottom is a close-up at Lodge Corner of Hill in the Lotus 48.

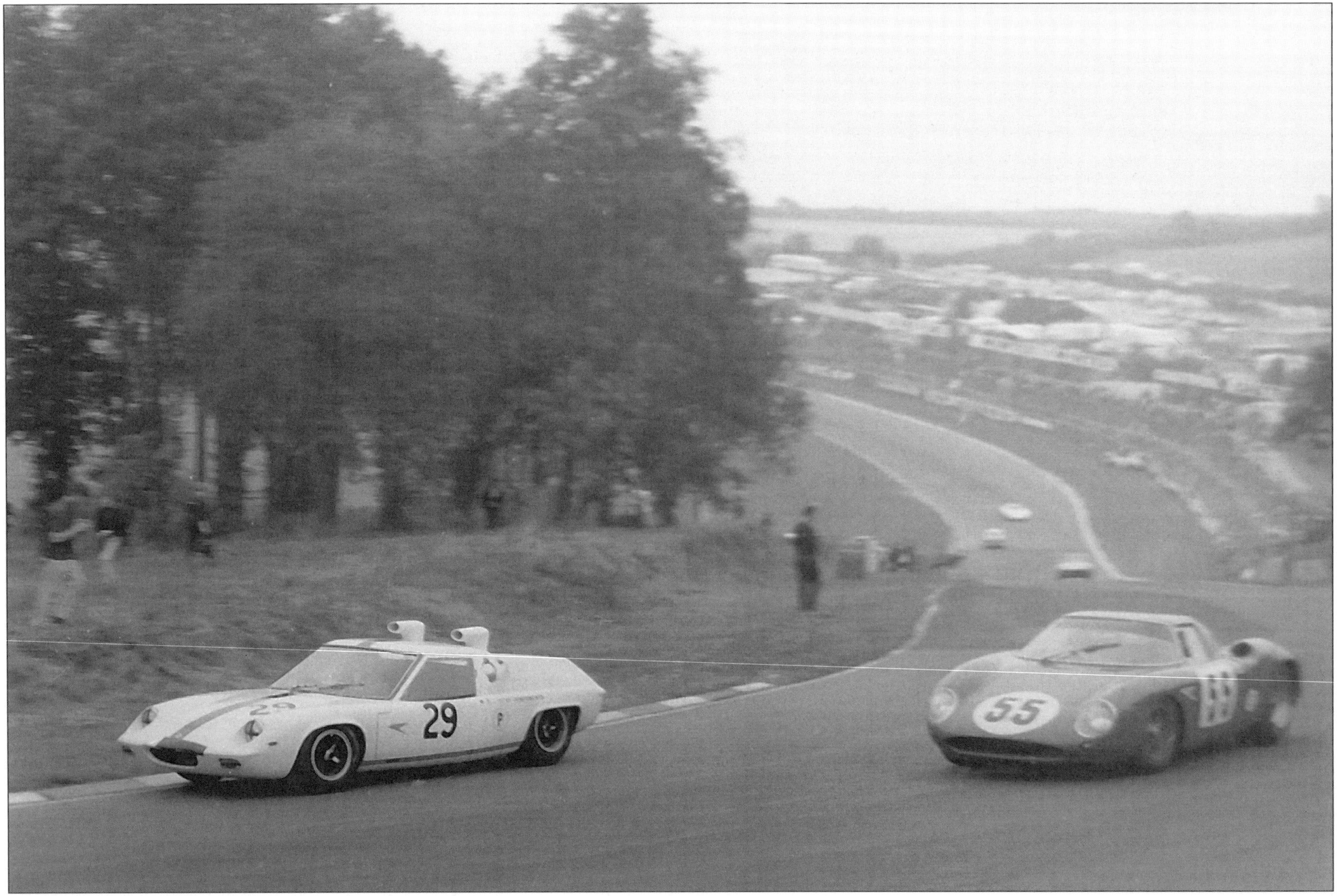

John Miles' and Jackie Oliver's 1.6 liter Lotus 47 Cosworth Ford Group 4 Sports Car passing a Ferrari 250 LM at Brands Hatch in the 1967 BOAC International 500 Race. They went on to finish in fourth place overall.

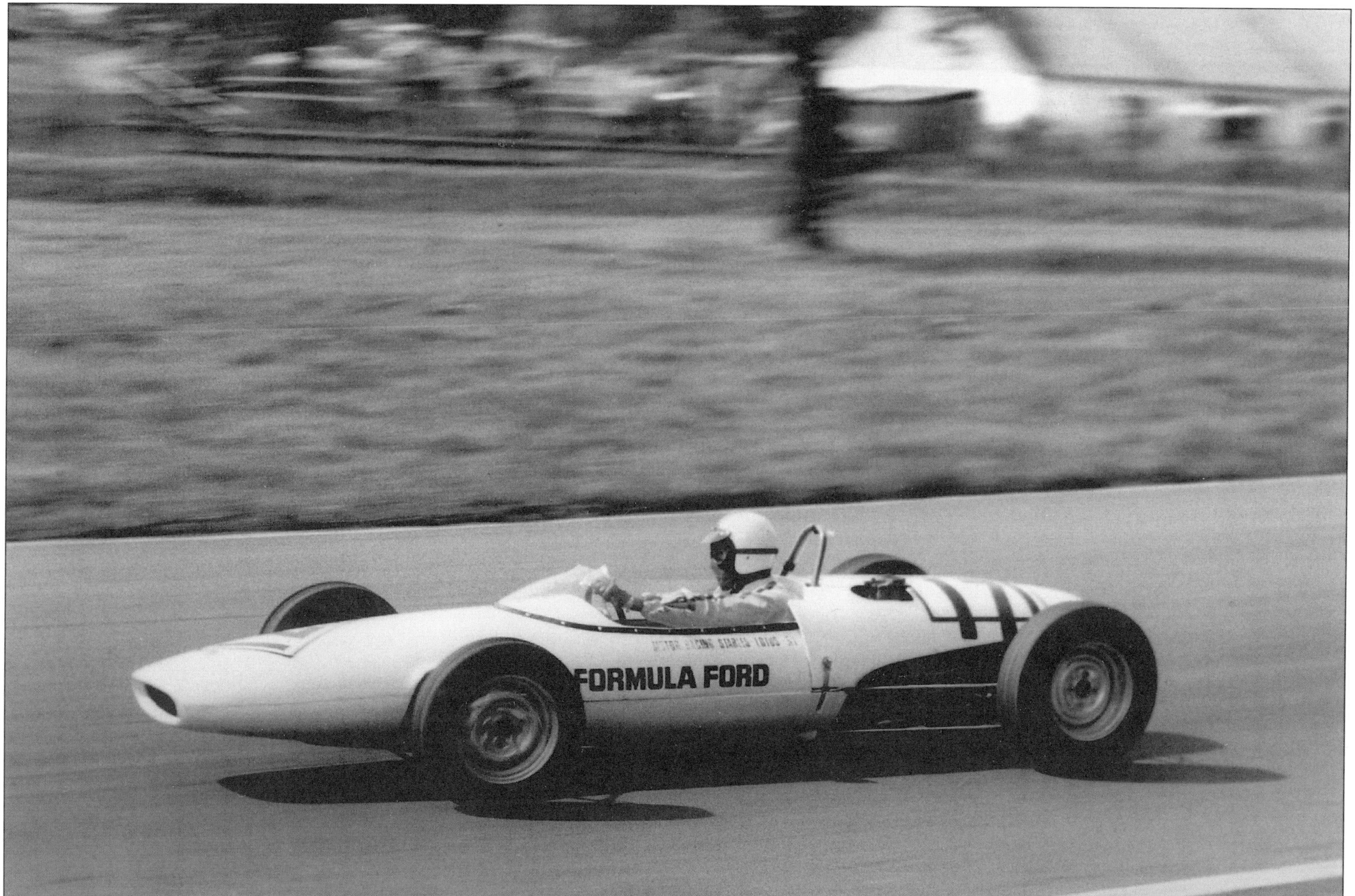

Doug Hack driving a Lotus 51 1.6-liter Formula Ford to third place, in the first Formula Ford Race to run at Oulton Park, in 1967.

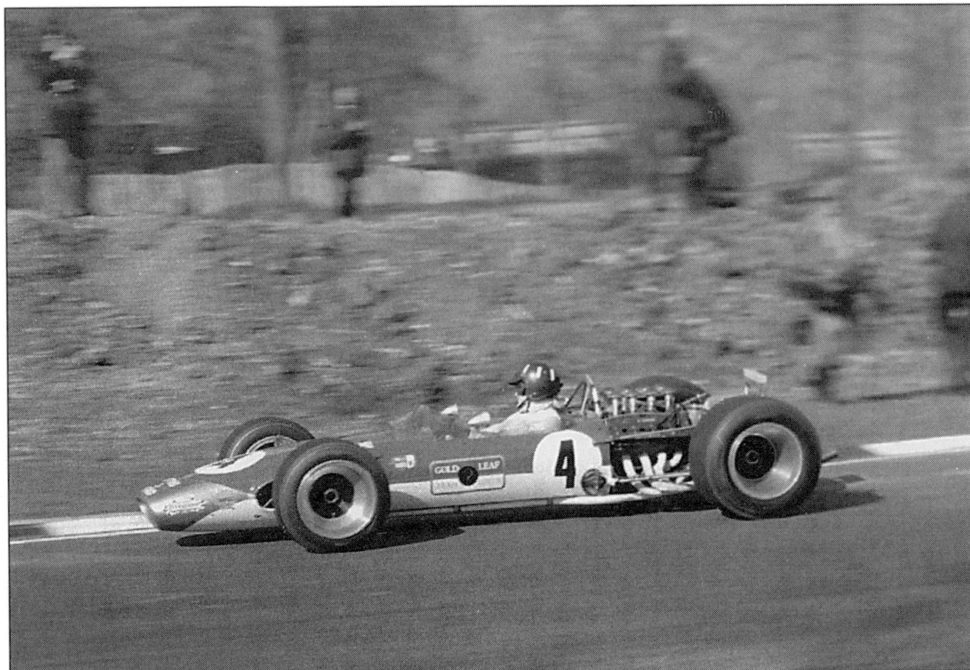

Gold Leaf Team Lotus fielded the new 3-liter Ford Cosworth DFV V-8 powered Lotus 49B/R5 for Graham Hill at the 1968 Race of Champions at Brands Hatch.

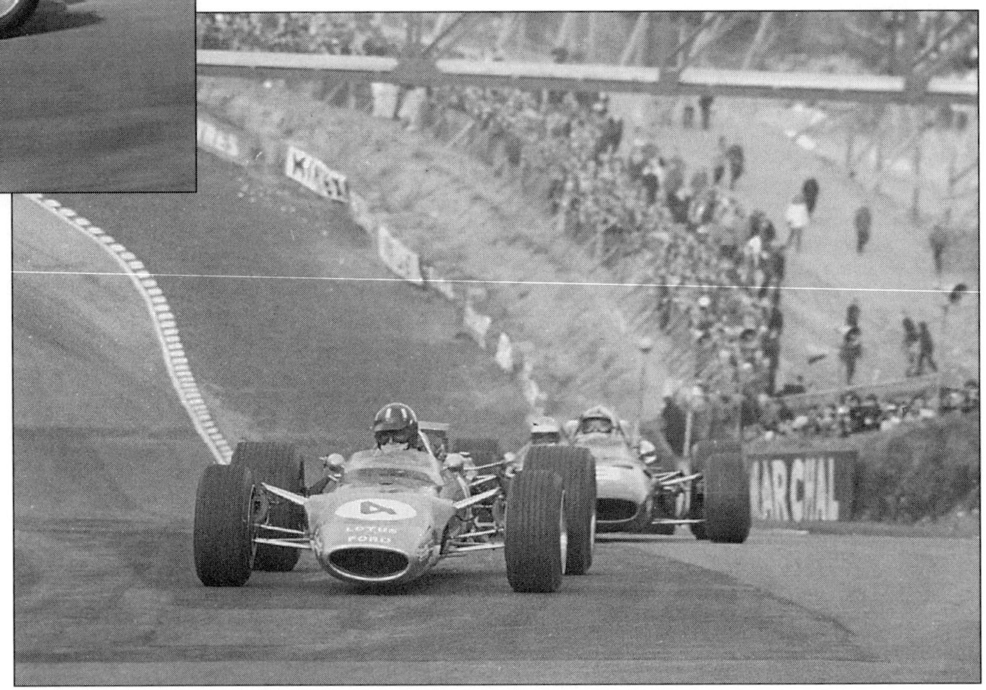

Hill leads Chris Amon in a Ferrari 312 and Denny Hulme in a McLaren. Unfortunately, Hill retired in the tenth lap with a broken drive shaft.

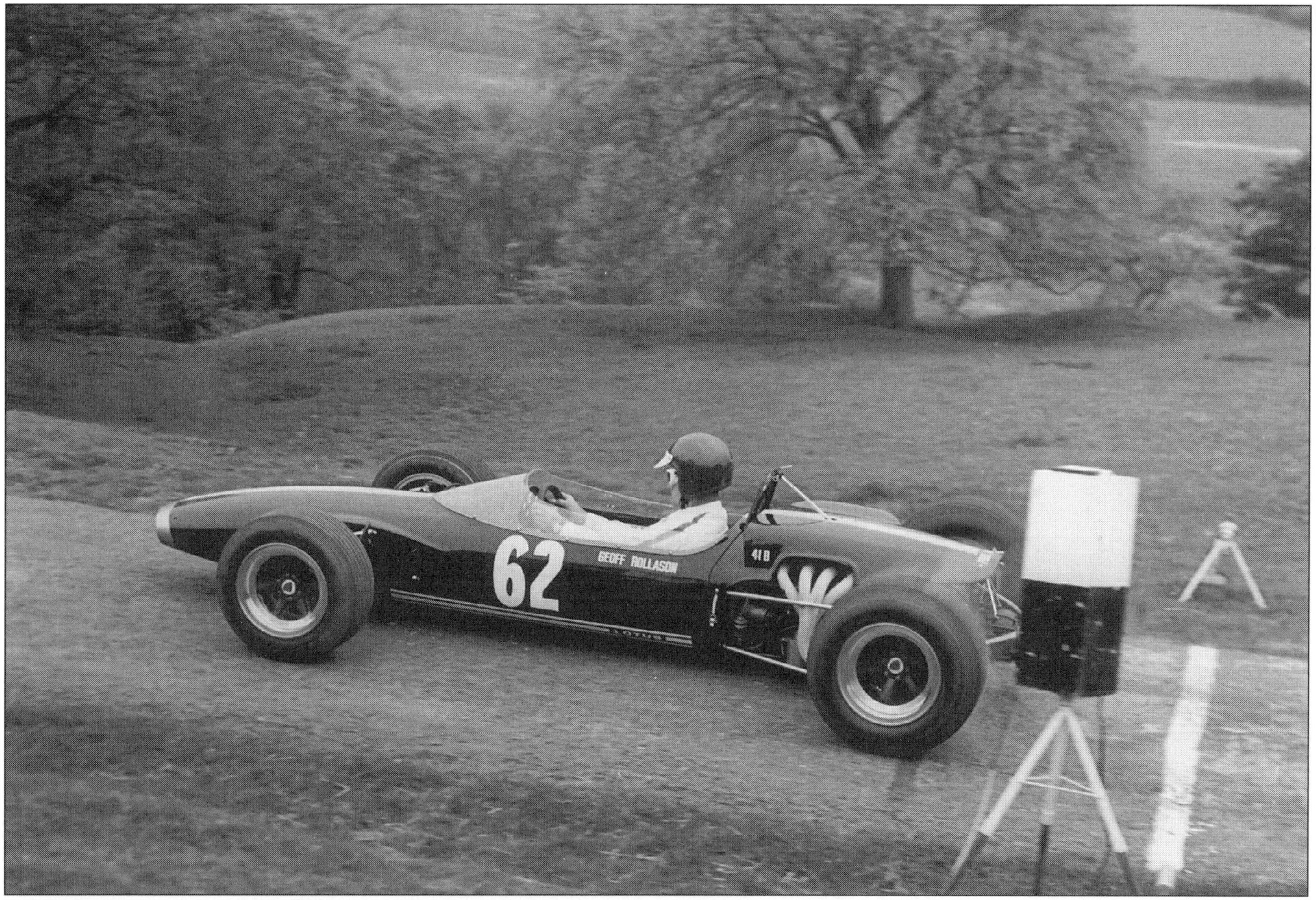

Geoff Rollason accelerating away from the start line in a Lotus 41B at the 1968 Barbon Manor Hill-Climb. Rollason achieved the sixth fastest time of the day.

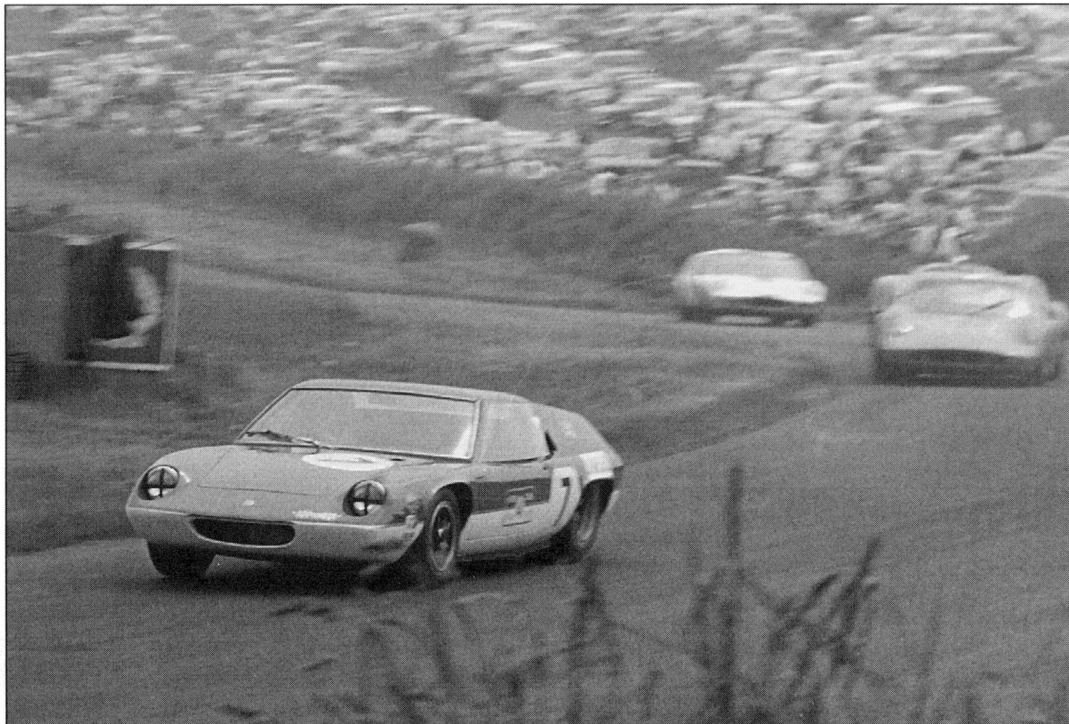

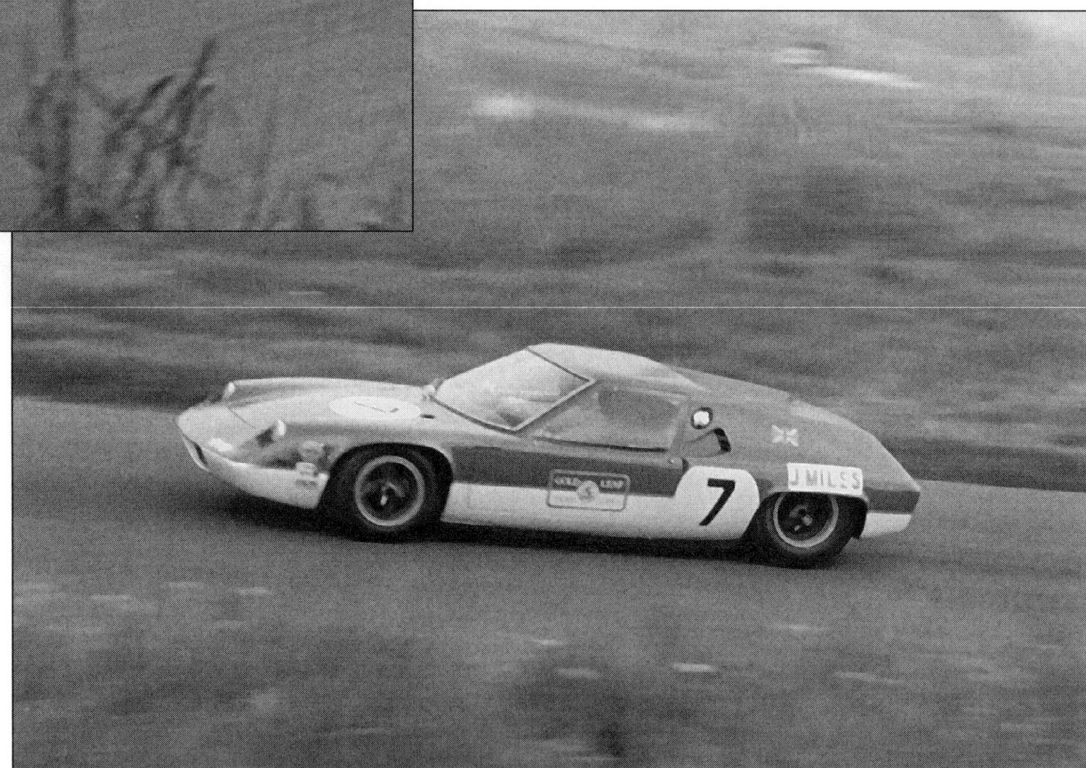

Two shots of John Miles driving a 1.6-liter Lotus 47 Europa Ford twin cam in the 1968 RAC Tourist Trophy Race at Oulton Park. A late entry from Gold Leaf Team Lotus, the car finished a creditable tenth place overall.

1968 British Grand Prix at Brands Hatch. Three Lotus 49s, powered by 3-liter Ford Cosworth DFV V-8s. Graham Hill driving 'R5' for Gold Leaf Team Lotus. Hill won 100 bottles of champagne after setting the fastest lap time during qualifying. Hill led the race but retired in lap 26 with a broken universal joint.

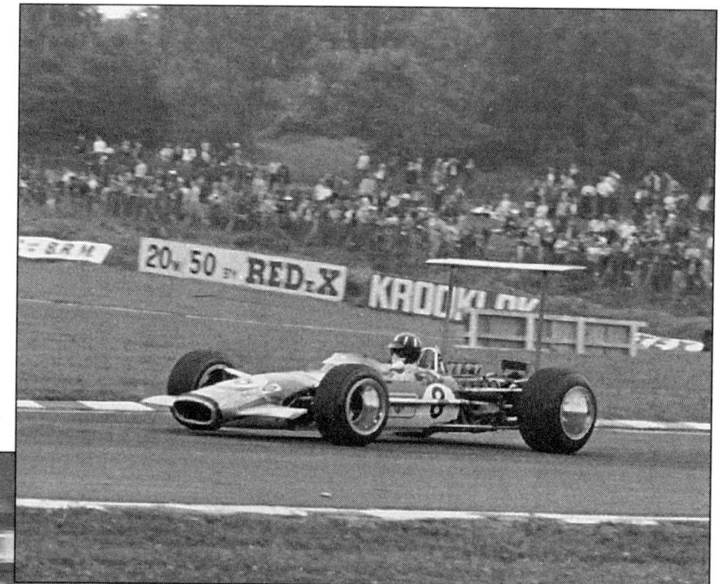

Jackie Oliver in Gold Leaf Team Lotus 'R1' took over the lead when Hill retired. Oliver also retired when the transmission failed.

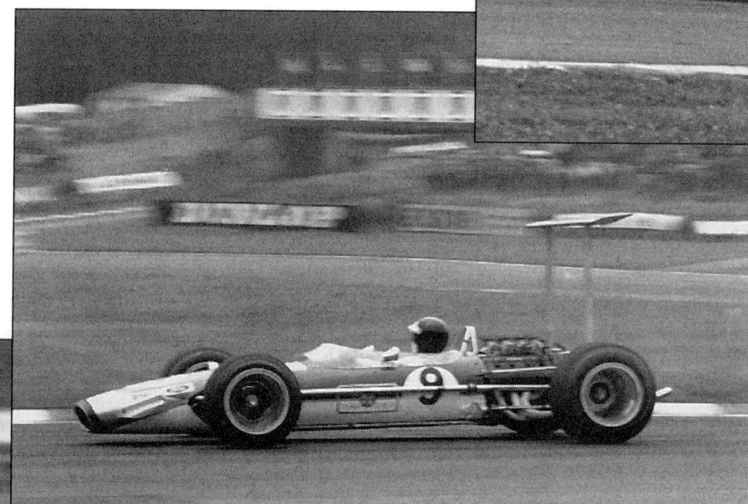

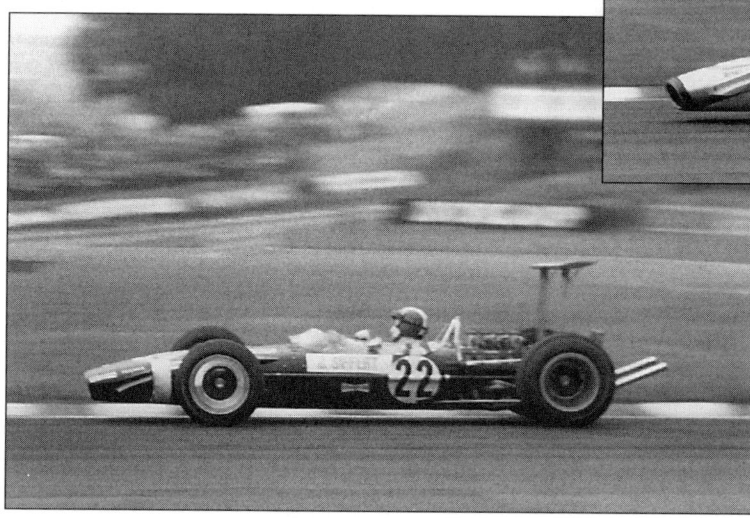

Jo Siffert driving the brand new 'R7' for Rob Walker's team went on to his first World Championship win.

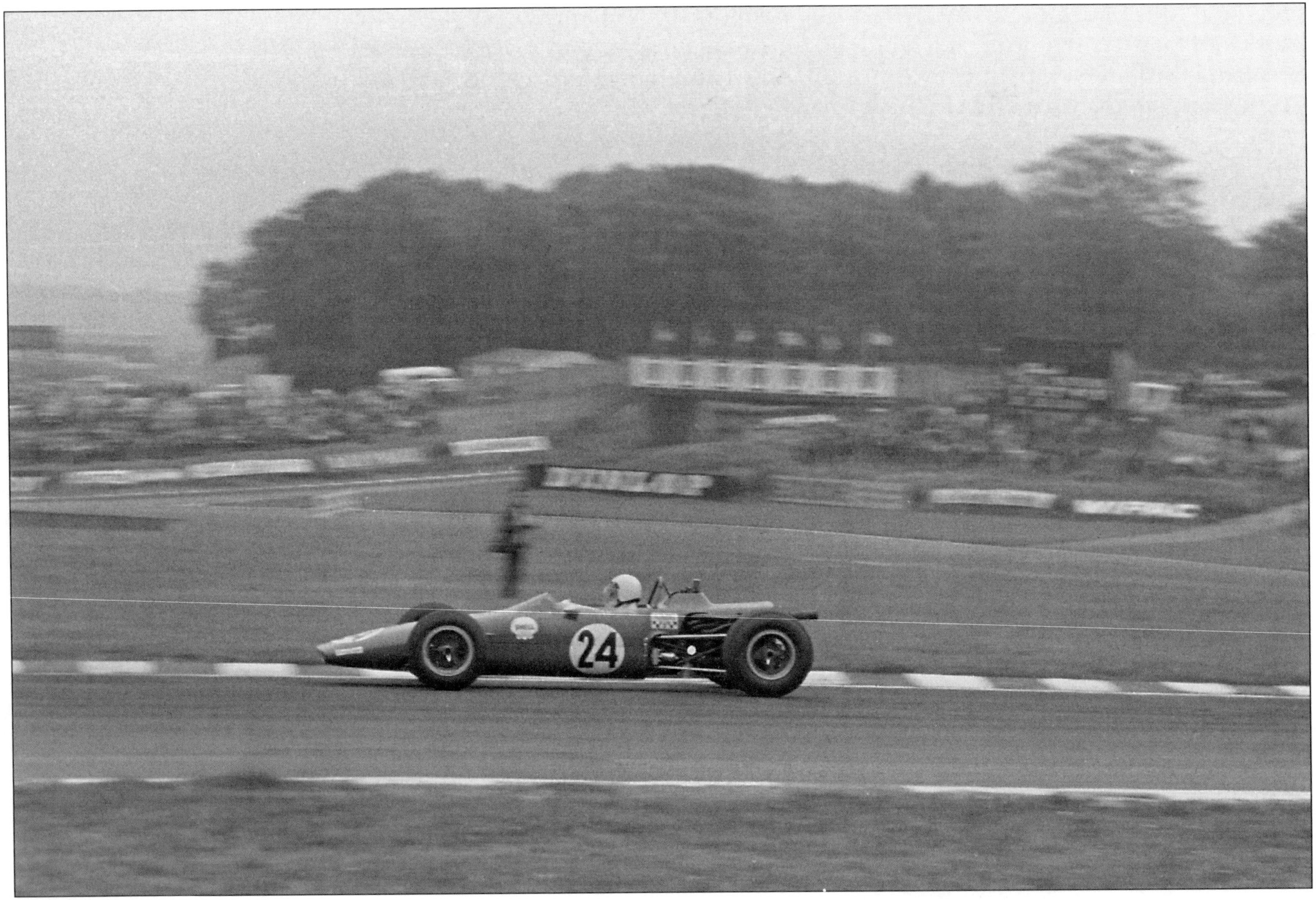

John Miles won the Formula 3 support race for the 1968 British Grand Prix at Brands Hatch in a 1-liter Lotus 41X Ford, he also set a new lap record of 97.34 mph.

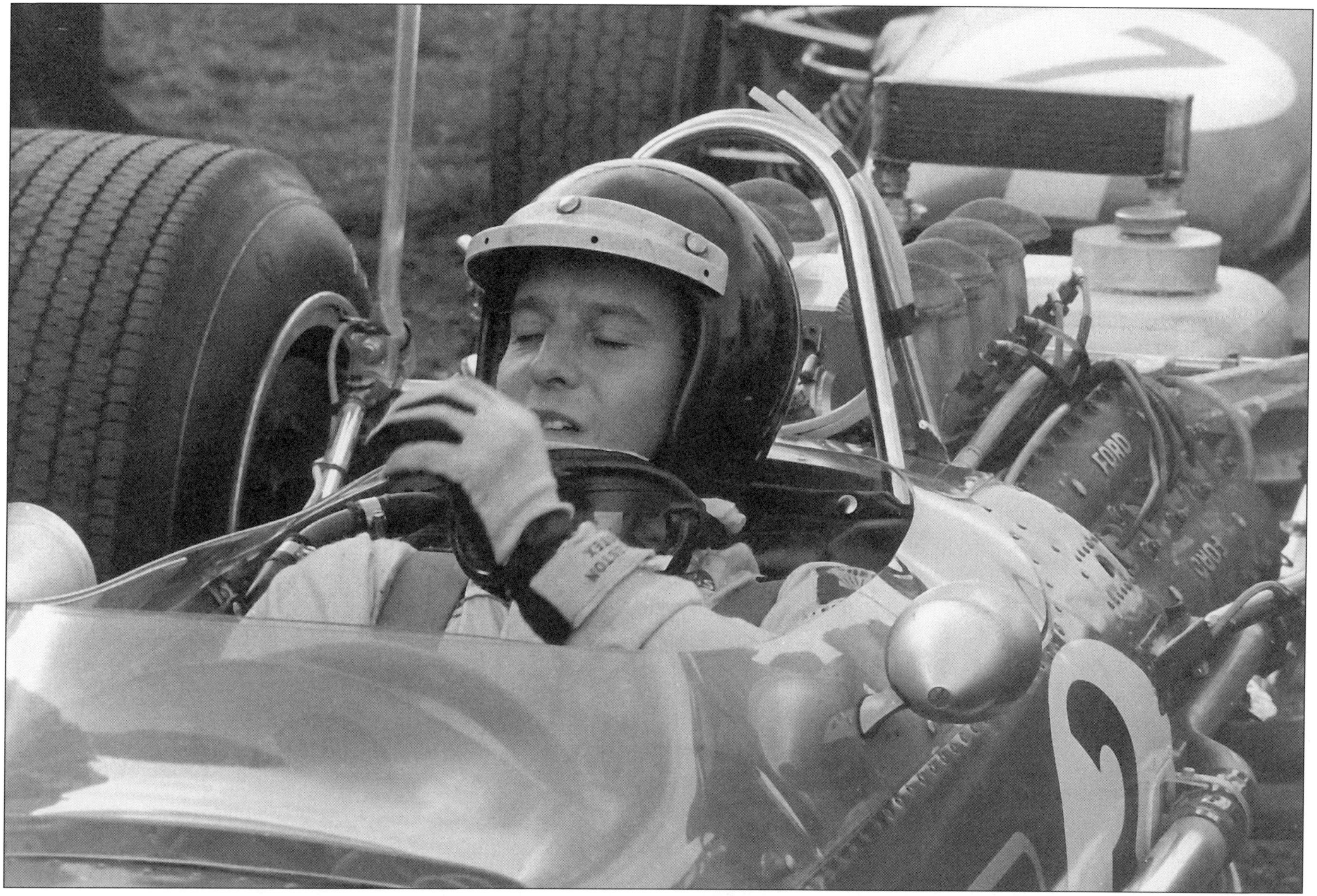

Jackie Oliver waits in his 3-liter Ford Cosworth DFV V-8 powered Lotus 49B/R2, before moving onto the starting grid at the 1968 Oulton Park Gold Cup.

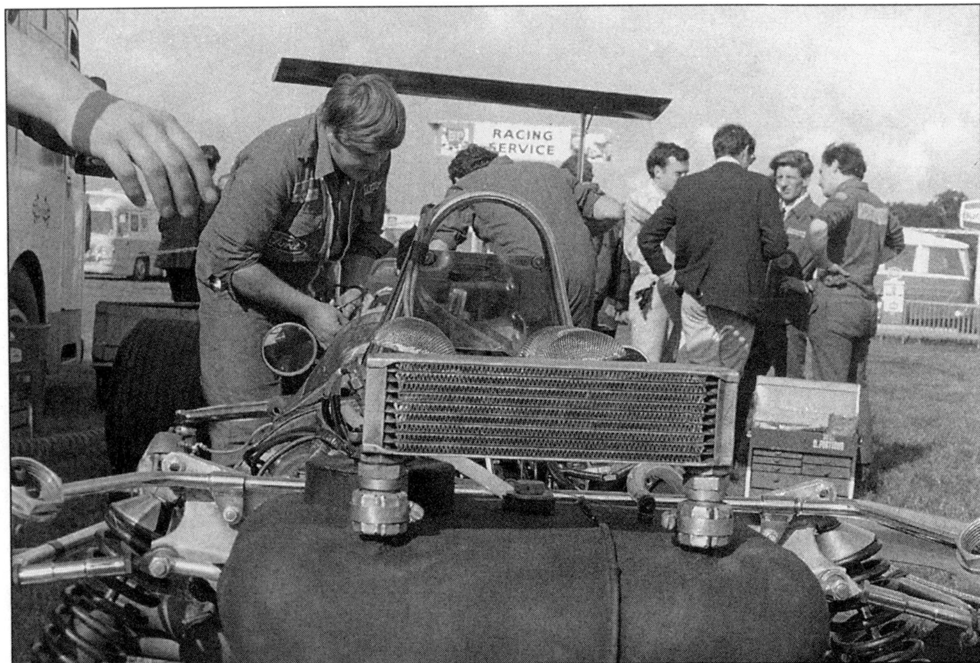

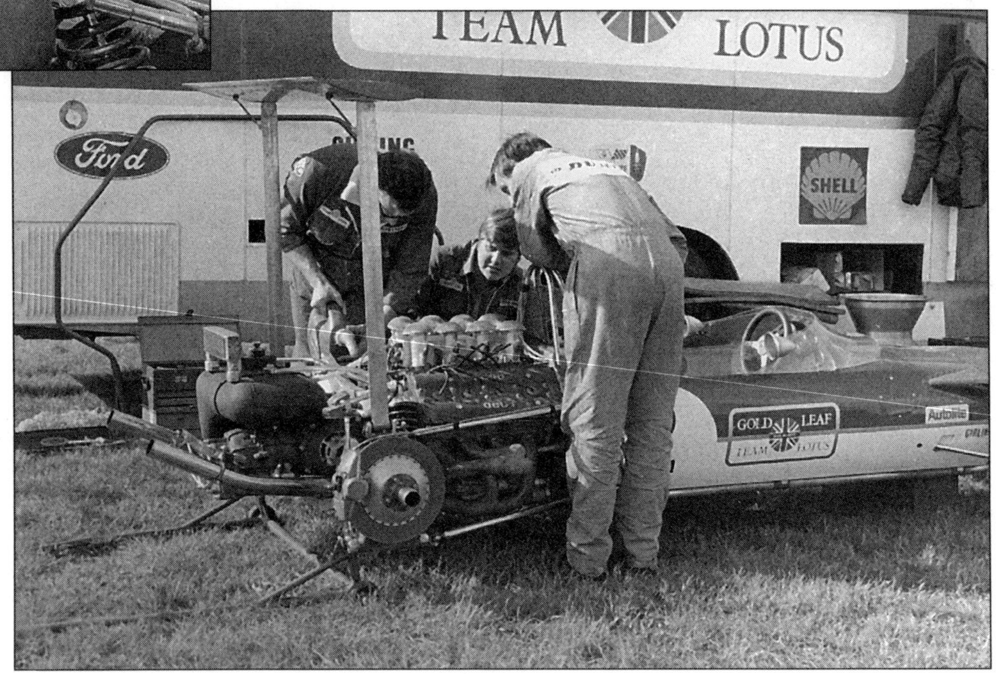

Two views of a Gold Leaf Team Lotus 49B at the 1968 Oulton Park Gold Cup.

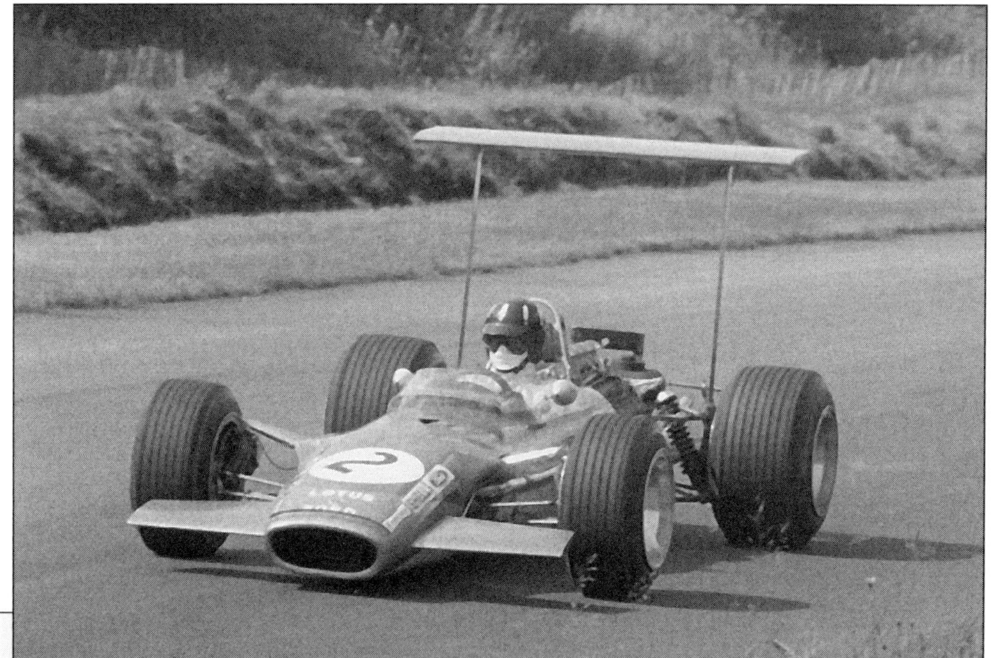

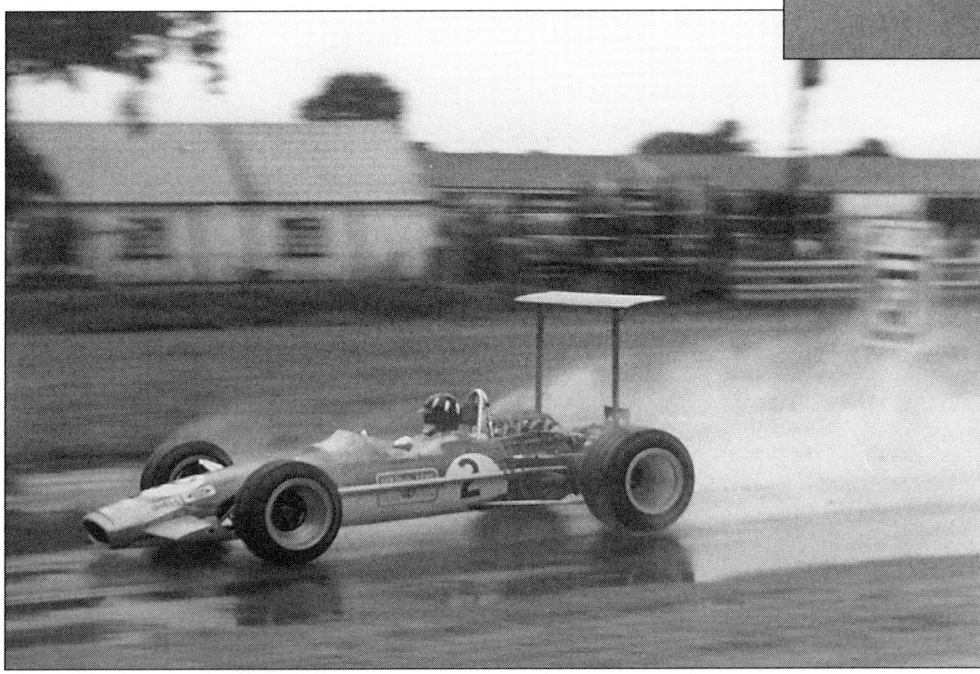

Two shots of Graham Hill driving Lotus 49B/R5 powered by a 3-liter Ford Cosworth DFV V-8 at the 1968 Oulton Park Guards Gold Cup. Left - Hill during a practice session in heavy rain. Hill set a new lap record during qualifying. He led the race from the start, but by lap 7 the crown wheel and pinion broke and he coasted into the pits to retire.

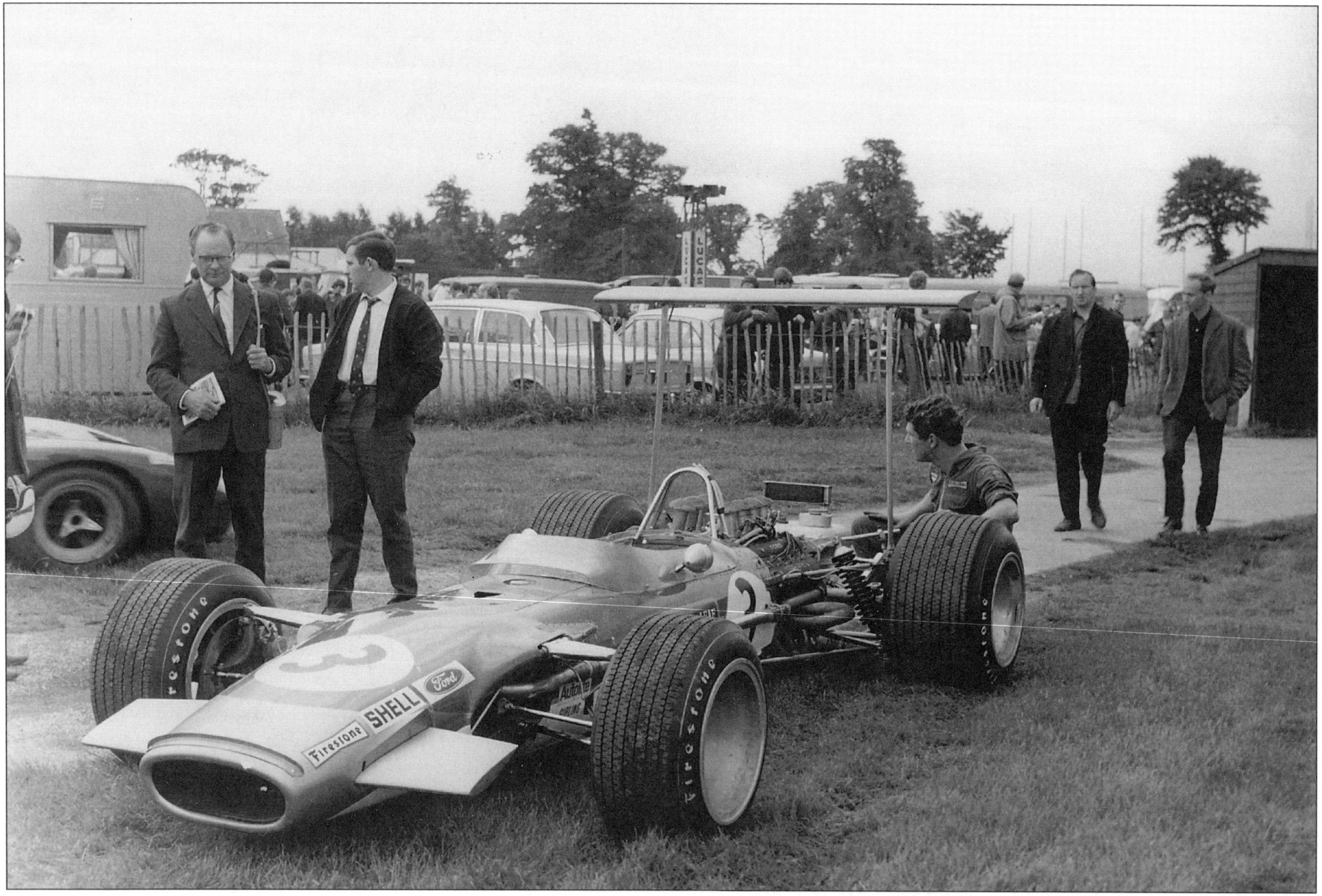

Jackie Oliver's Gold Leaf Team Lotus car in the paddock at Oulton Park for the 1968 Guards Gold Cup Meeting.

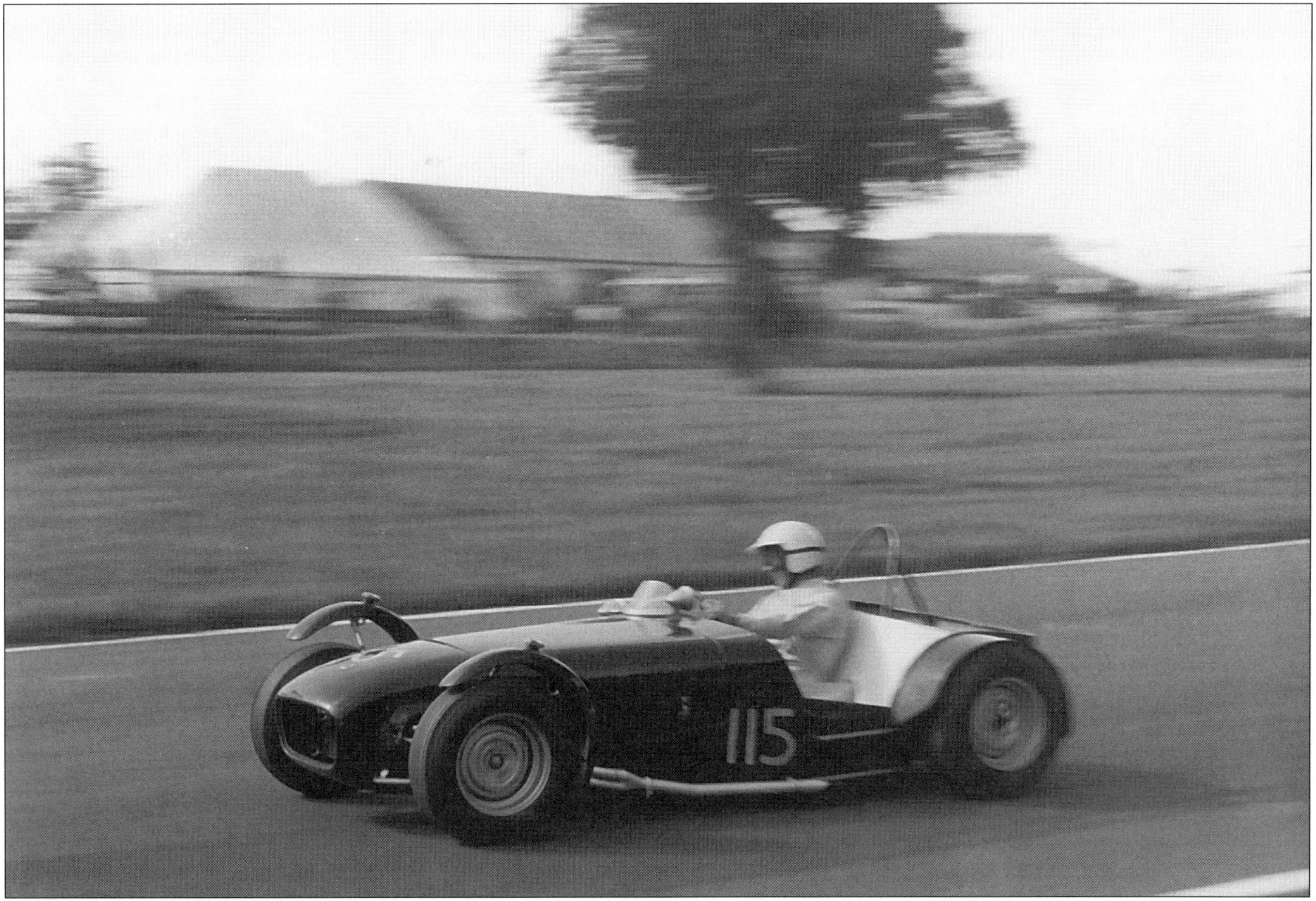

John Moulds' Lotus 7 at Old Hall corner Oulton Park during the 1968 Peco Trophy race.

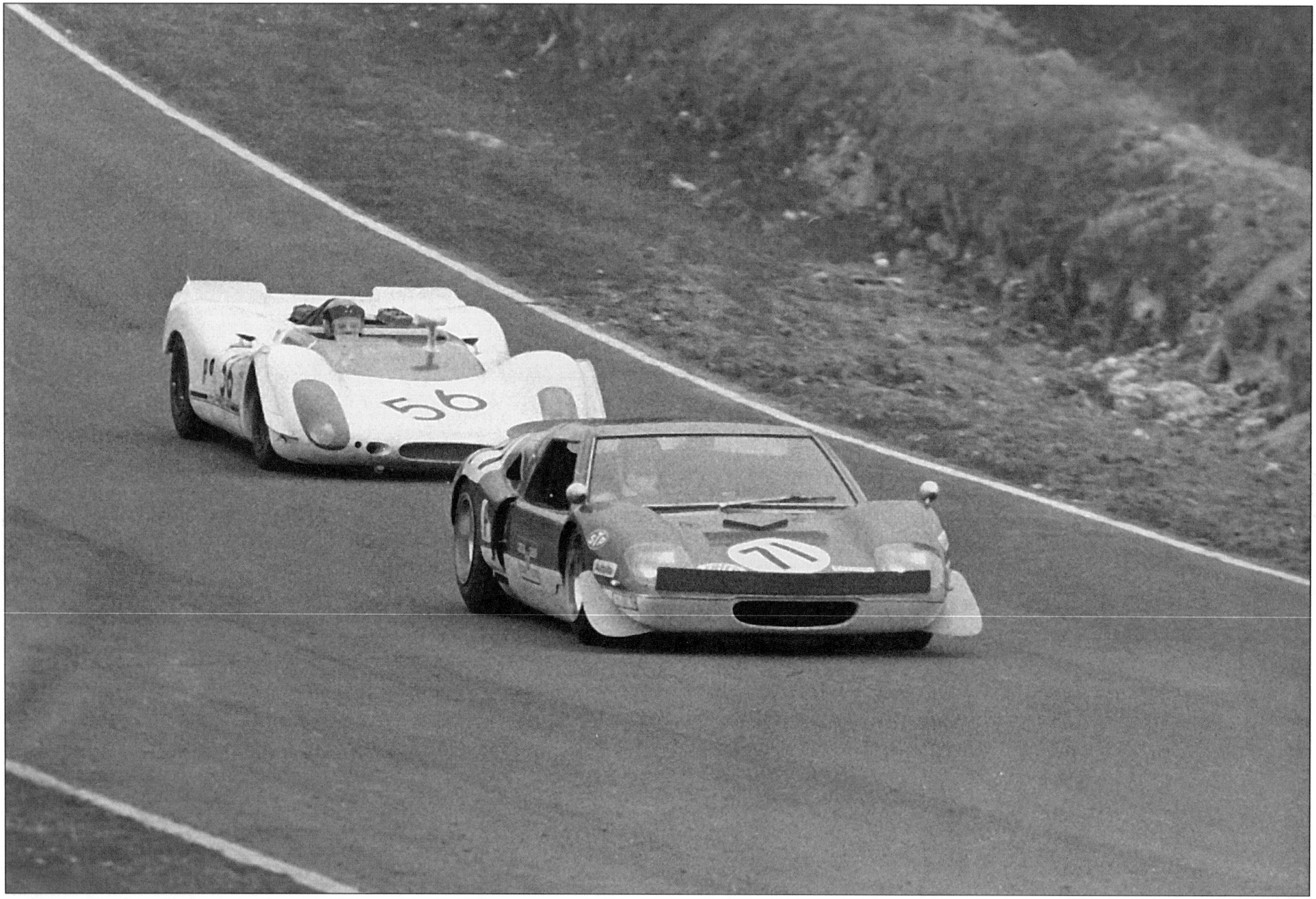

Car No 71 of John Miles/Brian Muir, a 2-liter Lotus Europa 62 Lotus Vauxhall, leading a Porsche 908 of Hermann/ Stommelen during the 1969 BOAC 500 Sports Car Race at Brands Hatch.

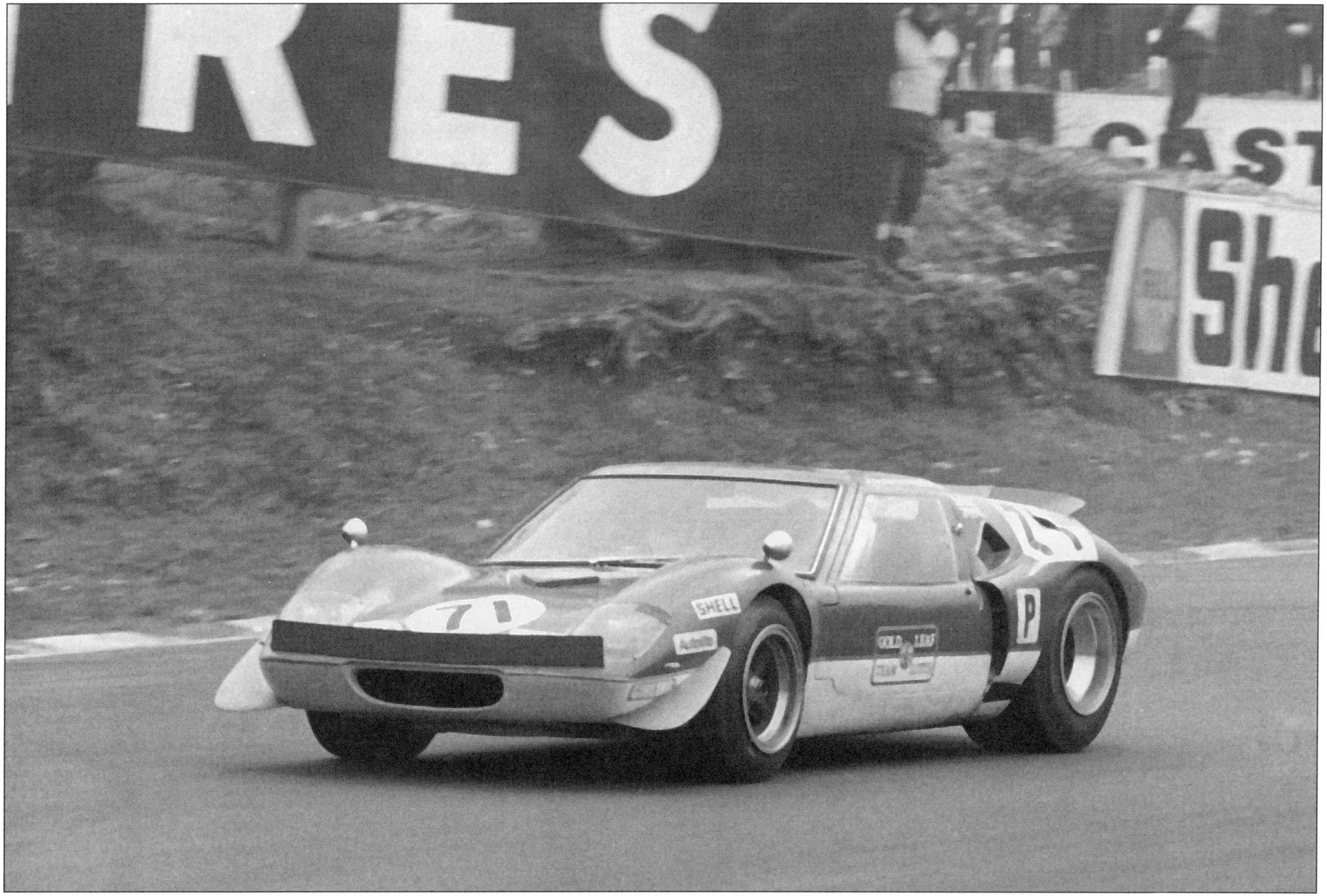

In spite of a few problems with their 2-liter Lotus 62 during the 1969 BOAC 500 Brands Hatch, Miles and Muir went on to finish the race in thirteenth position overall.

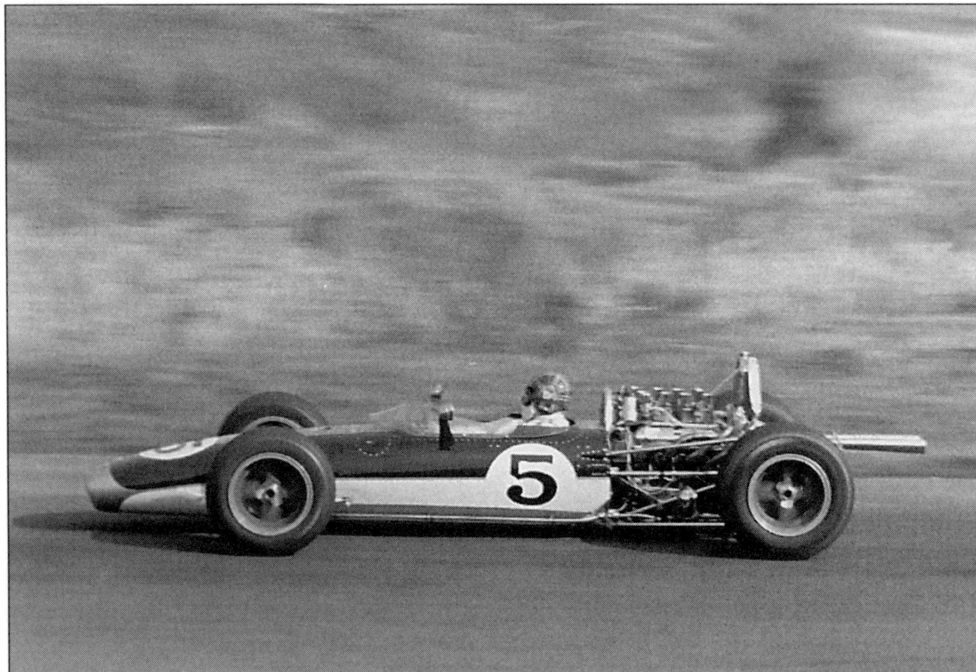

Two shots of Jock Russell driving Lotus 43/1, a 4.7 Shelby-Ford, during the 1969 Oulton Park Guards 5000.

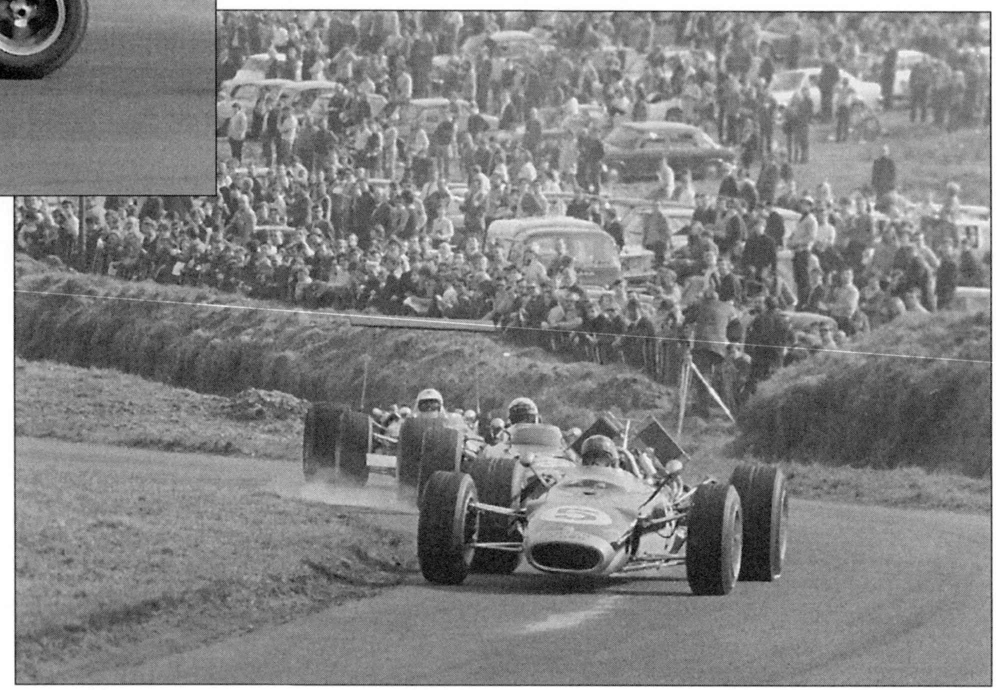

Russell leading two other cars through Knicker Brook corner. Russell's car was the first car to retire, with a split gearbox casing.

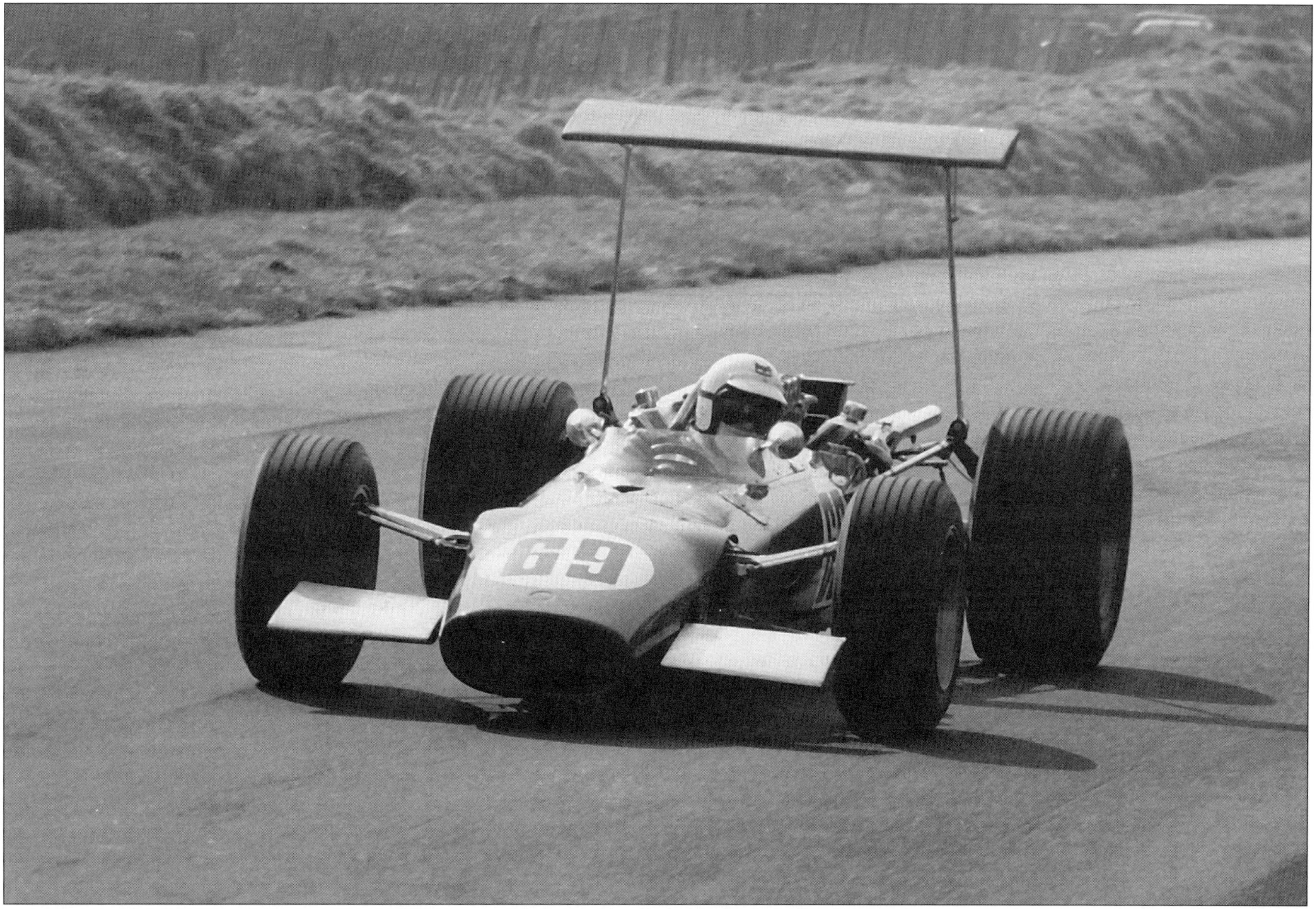

Robert Lamplough in 43/2, a 4.7 Lotus Shelby-Ford - this car had much of the monocoque renewed after a work shop fire. Lamplough retired the car with a blown engine in lap 6 of the 1969 Guards 5000 Race at Oulton Park.

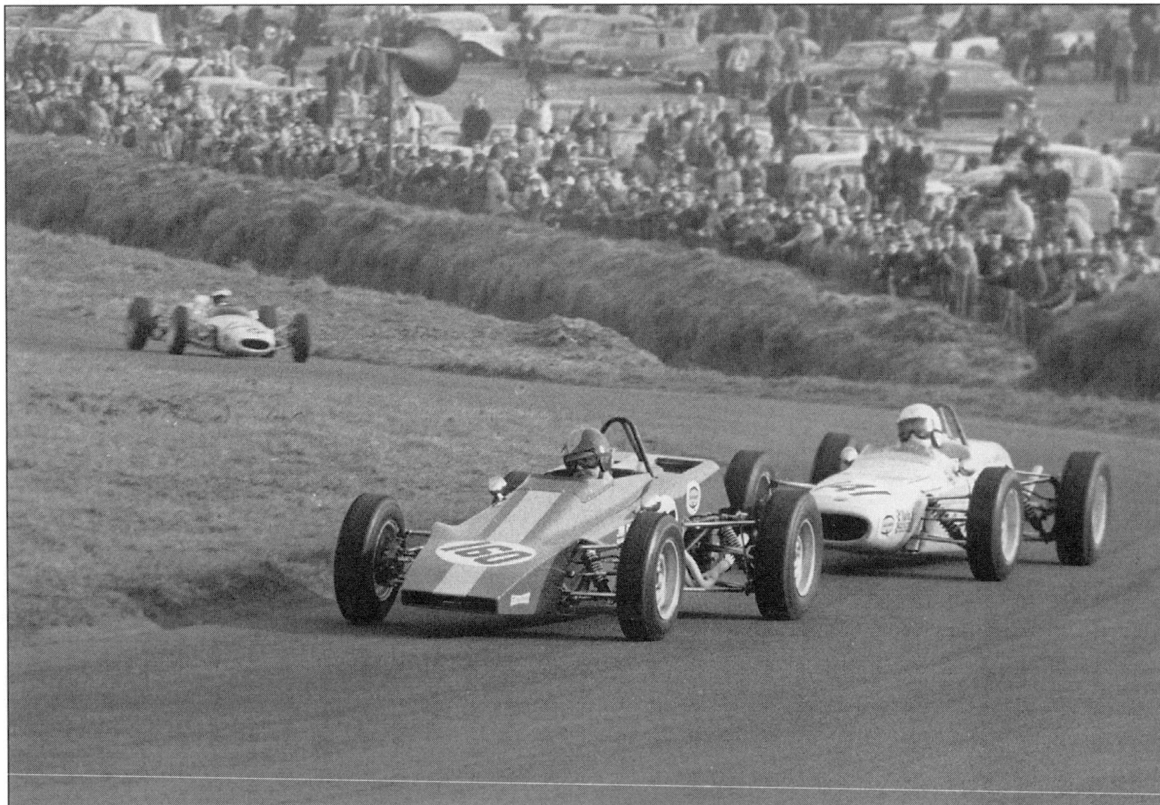

Two Lotus 61s in the Formula Ford support race during the 1969 Oulton Park Guards 5000. Dave Walker finished third in his 1600cc Holbay Ford powered car.

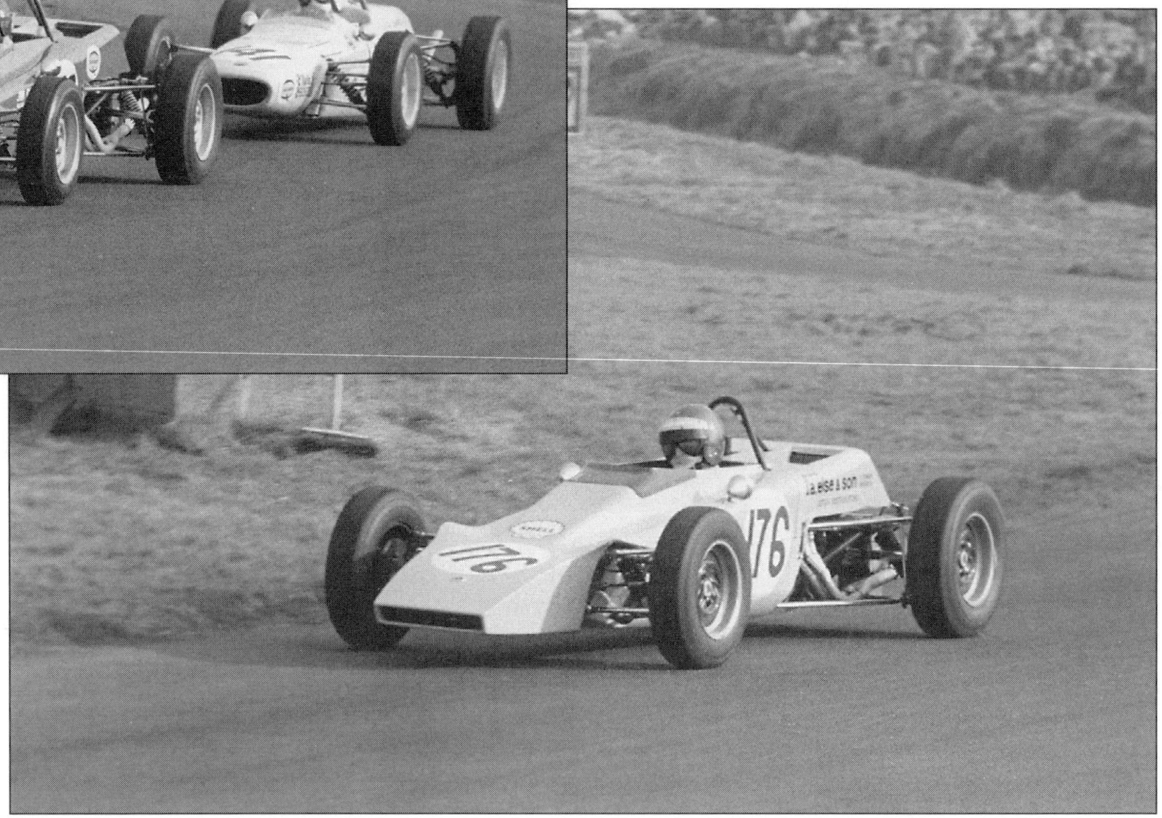

Chris Oates driving car number 176.

Three shots of John Miles driving a Gold Leaf Team Lotus during the 34th RAC Tourist Trophy Race at Oulton Park in 1969. Miles, with the fastest 2-liter car of the race, finished third overall.

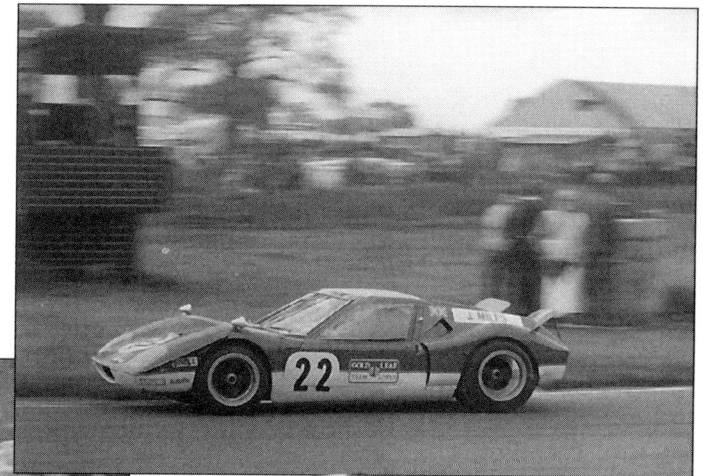

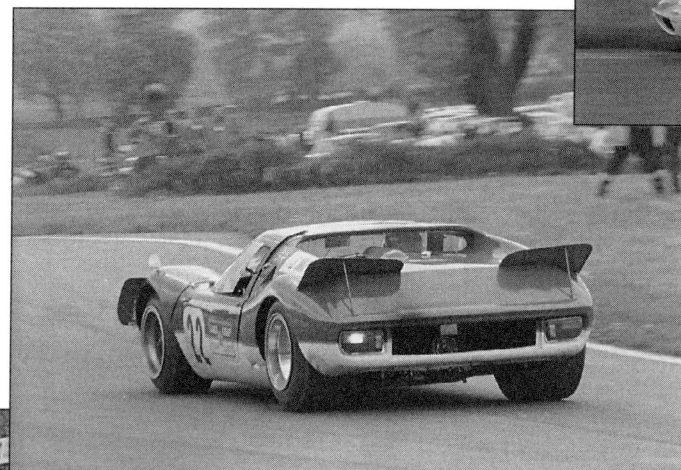

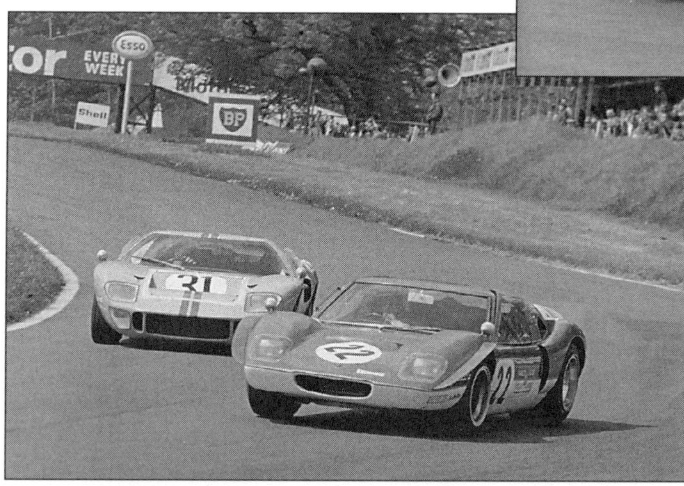

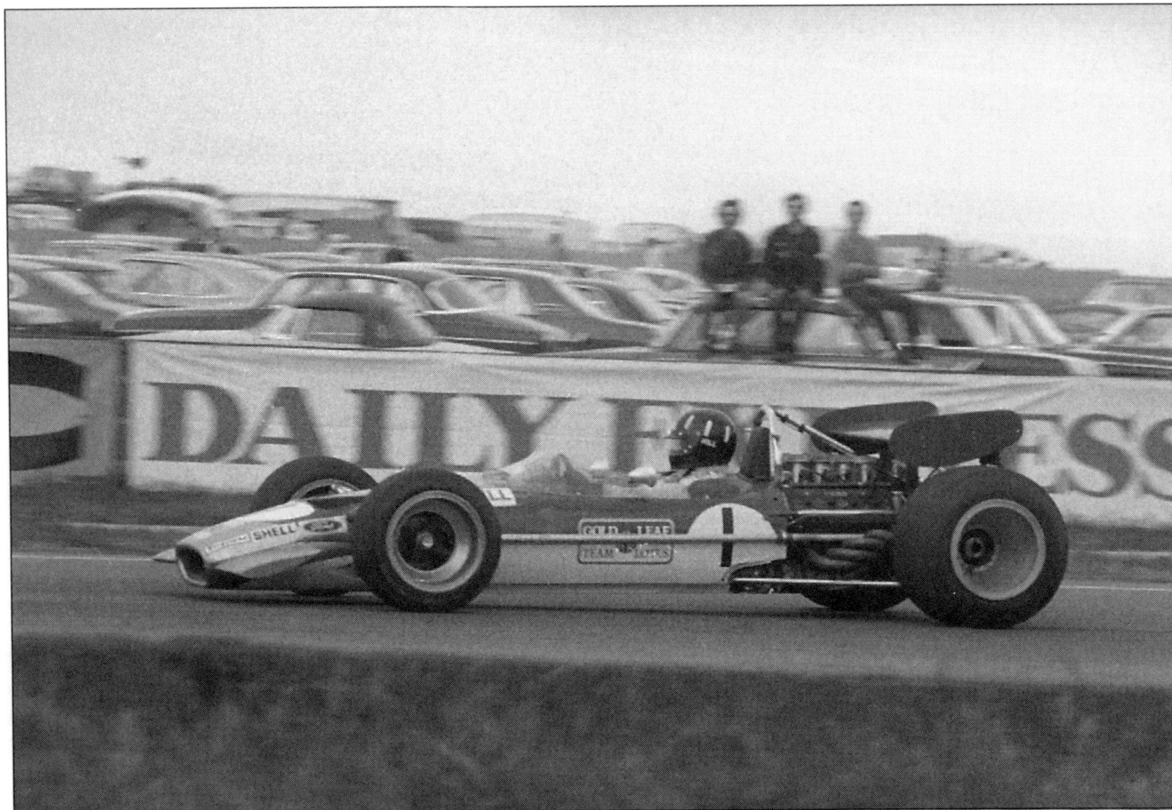

1969 British Grand Prix at Silverstone. Graham Hill driving Lotus 49B/8, with a 3-liter Ford Cosworth DFV V-8. Hill ran out of fuel on the last lap, and was classified in seventh place.

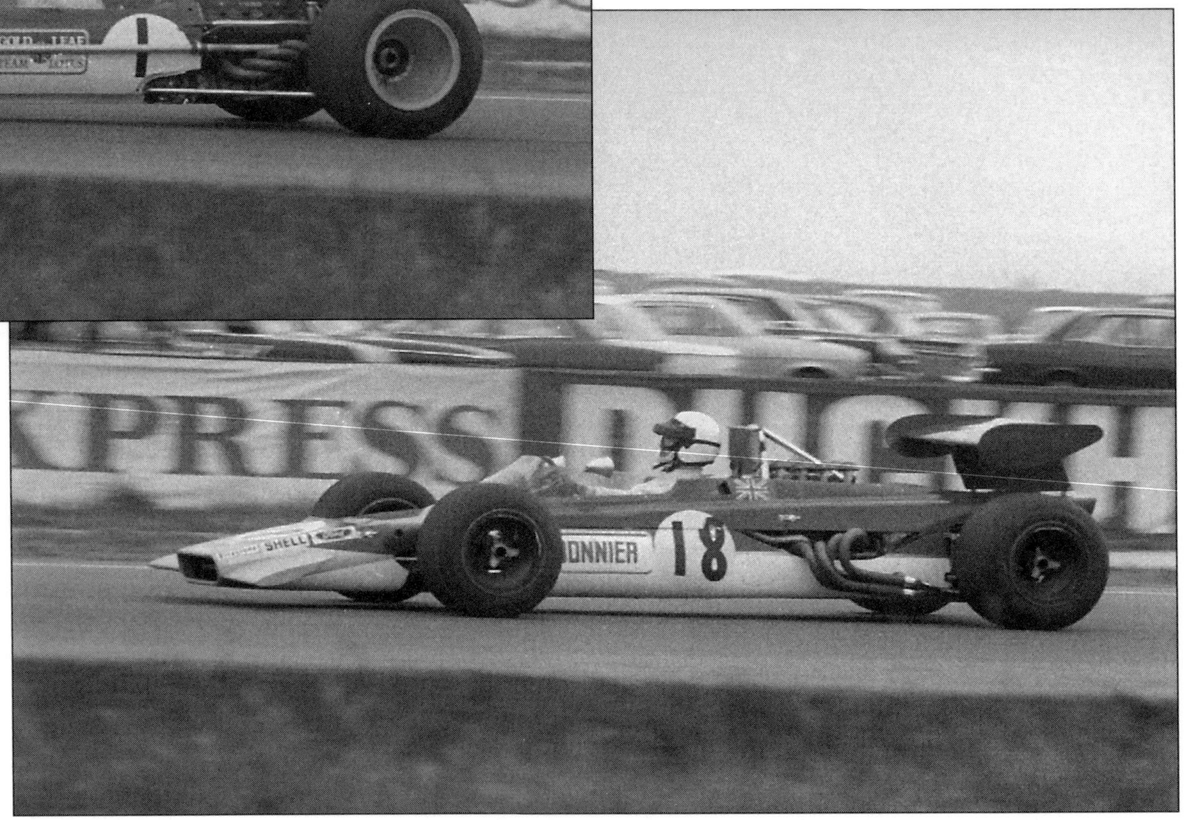

John Miles in Lotus R63/2, an experimental four wheel drive car, also with a 3-liter Ford Cosworth DFV V-8. Miles finished in tenth place overall, with only third gear remaining.

1969 British Grand Prix at Silverstone. Jo Siffert driving the Rob Walker/Jack Durlacher Racing Team Lotus 48B/7 ran out of gas and was classified in eighth place.

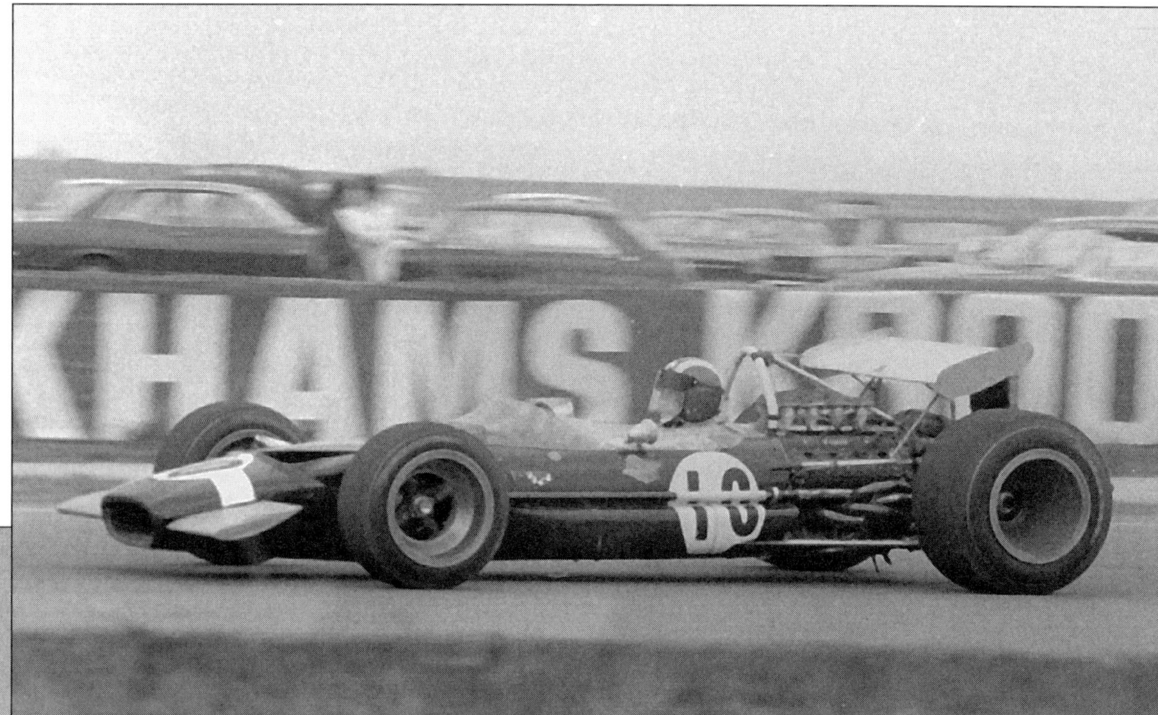

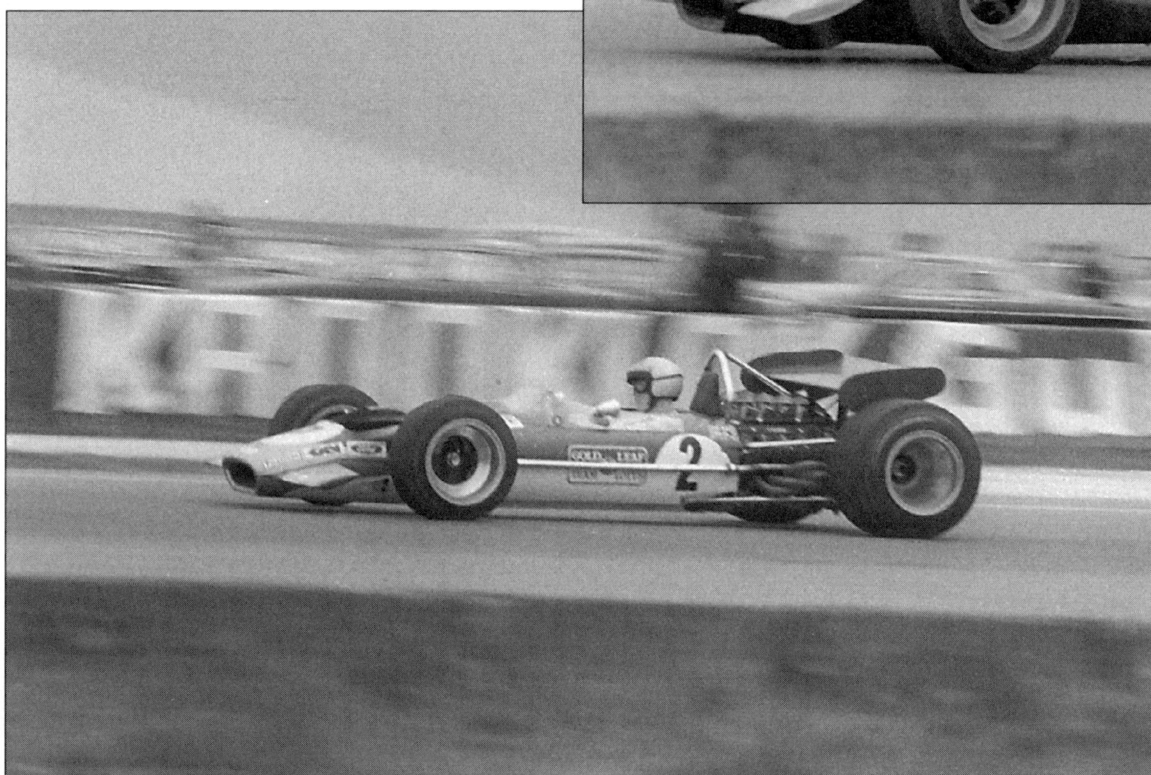

Jochen Rindt finished in fourth place in Lotus 49B/6.

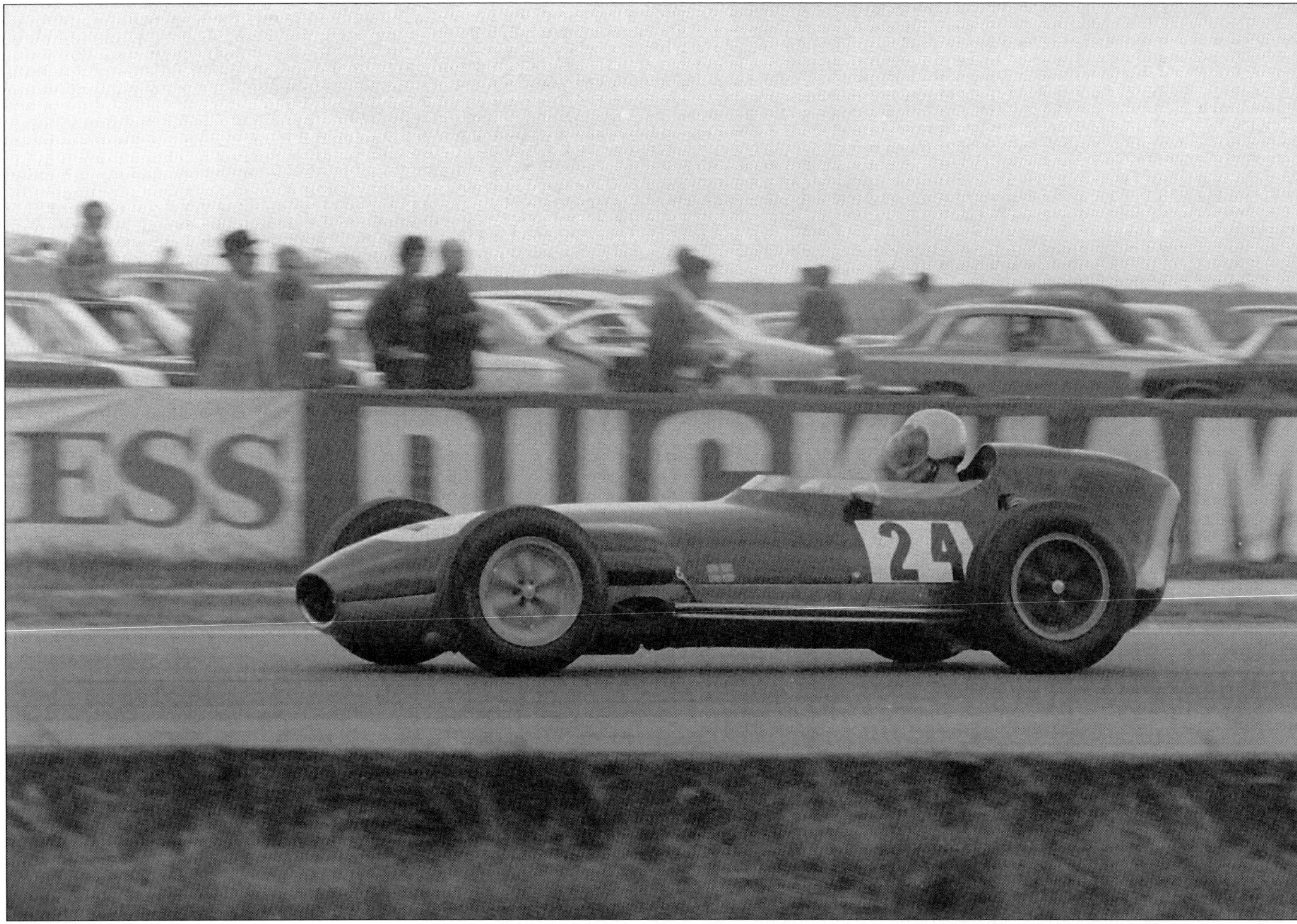

A 1959 4 cylinder 2-liter Lotus 16 during a demonstration lap at the 1969 British Grand Prix at Silverstone.

Three views of Jochen Rindt driving Lotus 63/1, a 4WD with 3-liter Ford Cosworth DFV V-8 during the 1969 Oulton Park Guards Gold Cup. Rindt finished in second place.

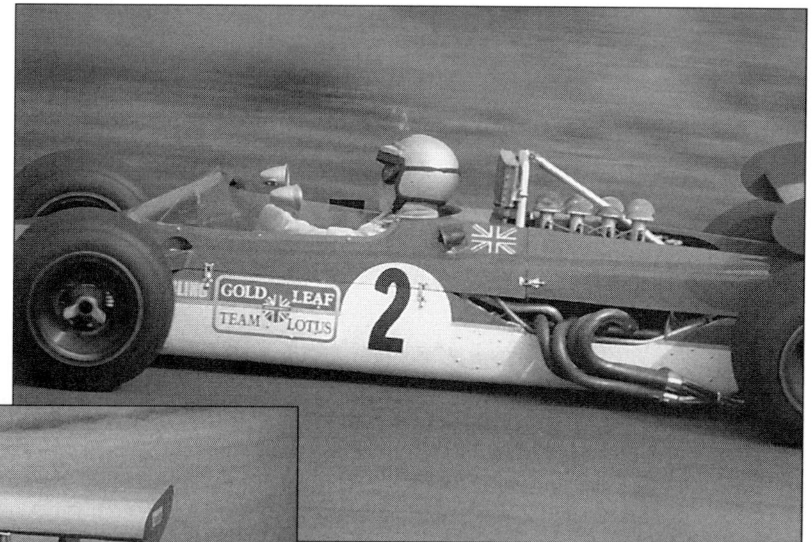

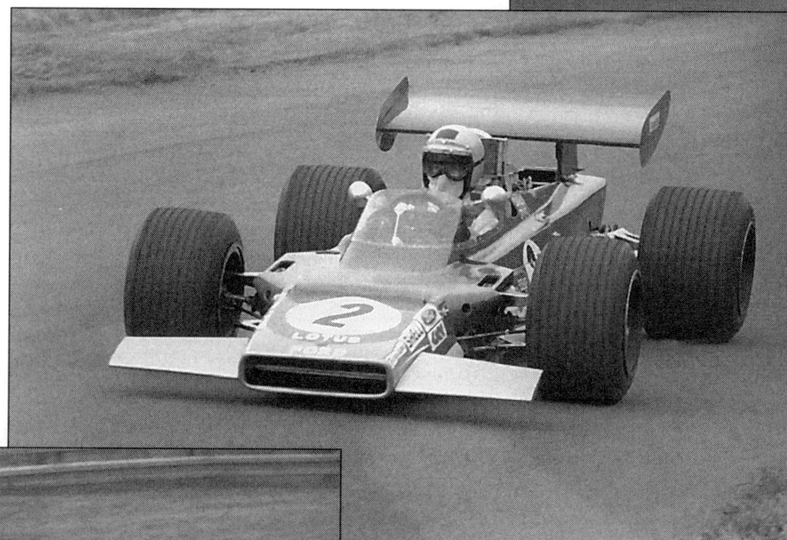

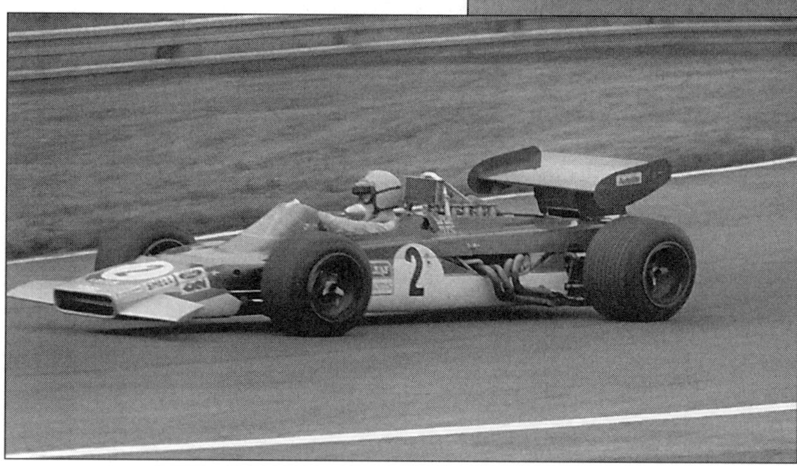

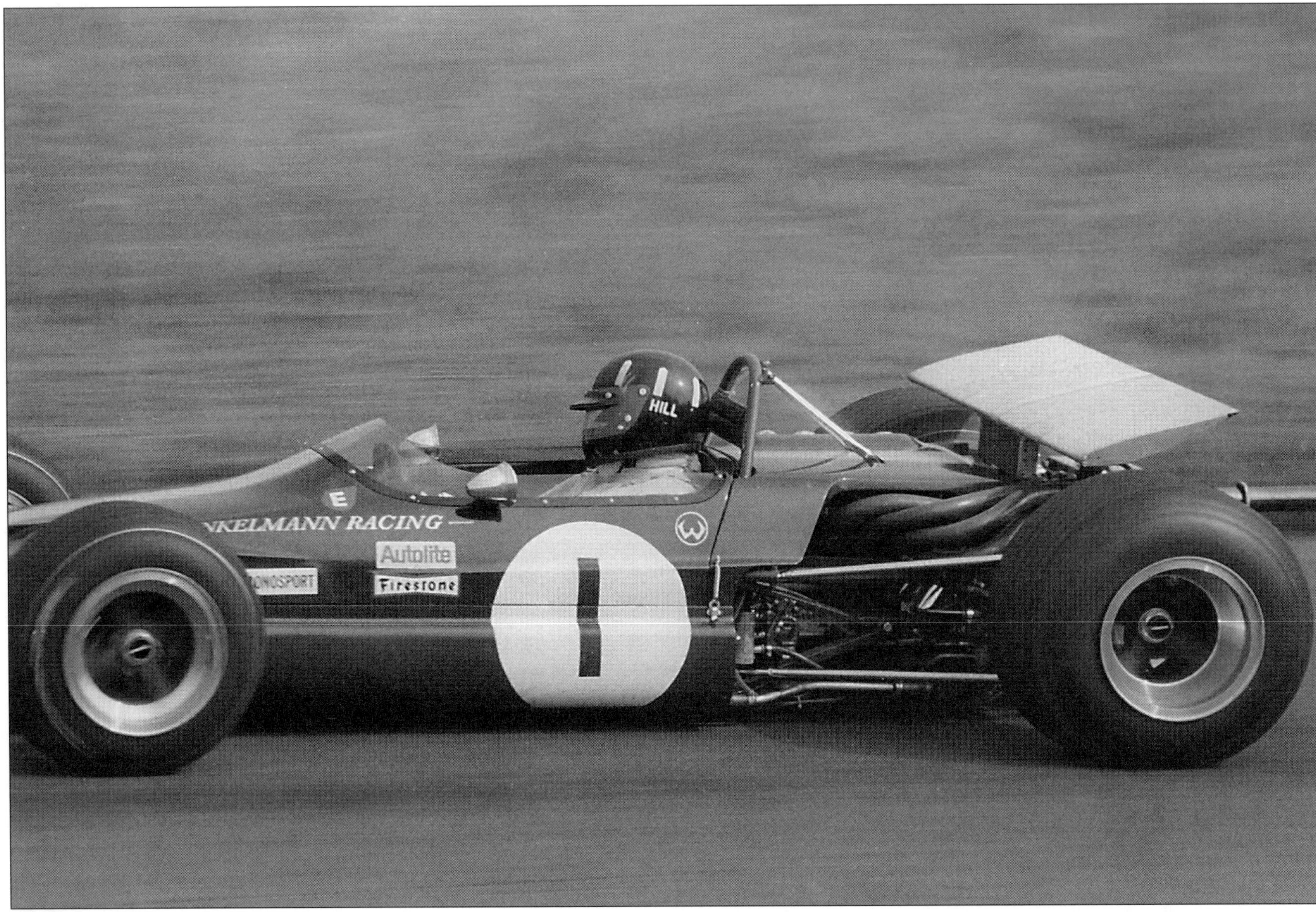

Graham Hill driving a Formula 2 Lotus 59 Ford during 1969 Guards Gold Cup at Oulton Park. After working his way to fifth place, Hill's engine blew-up on lap 36.

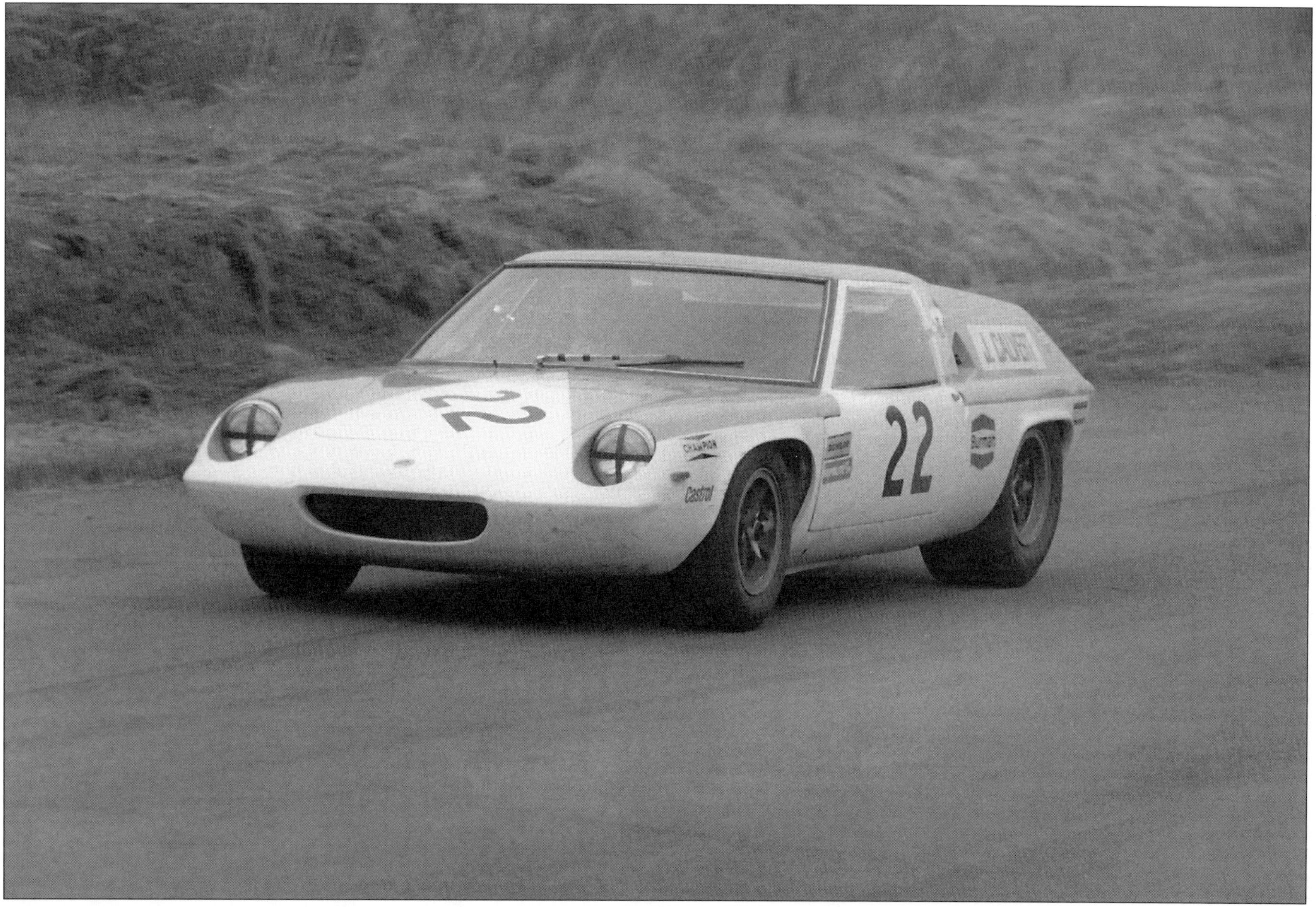

John S. Calvert's 1598cc Lotus Europa 47 finished in tenth place overall during a supporting race for the 1969 Guards Gold Cup at Oulton Park.

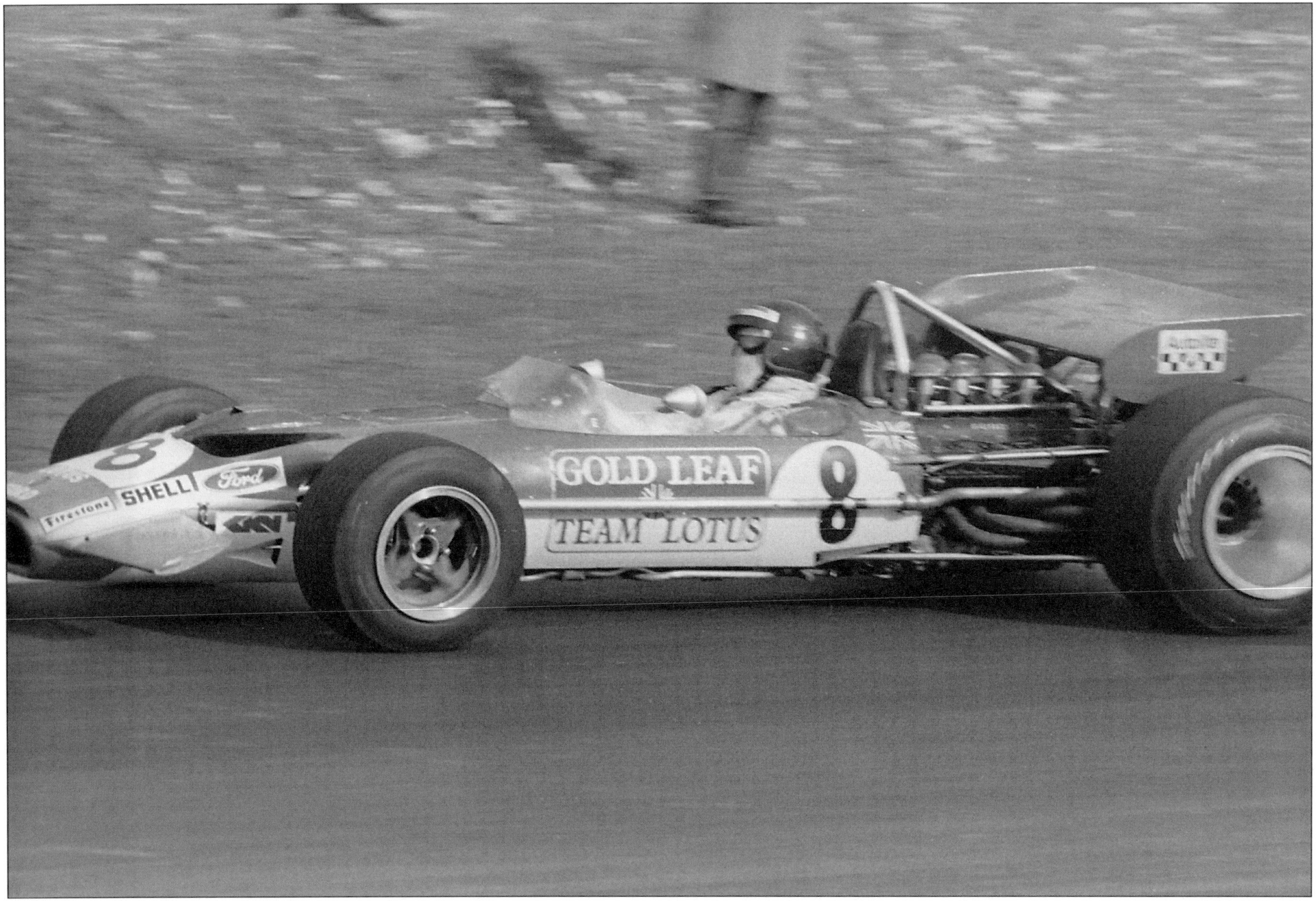

Jochen Rindt driving Lotus 49C/6, with a 3-liter Ford Cosworth DFV V-8, finished in second place during the 1970 Race of Champions at Brands Hatch.

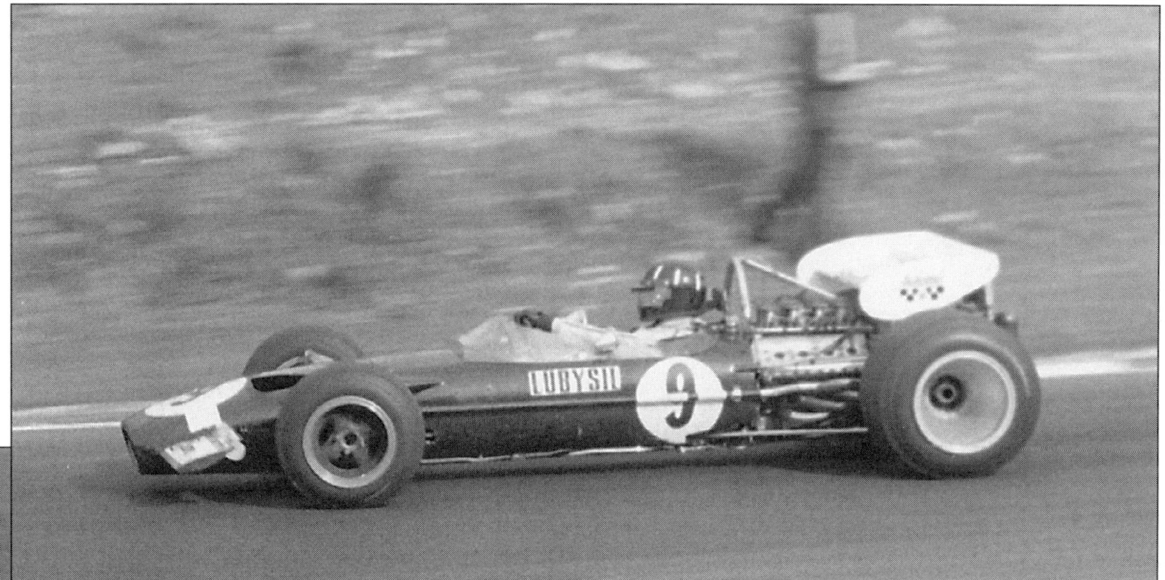

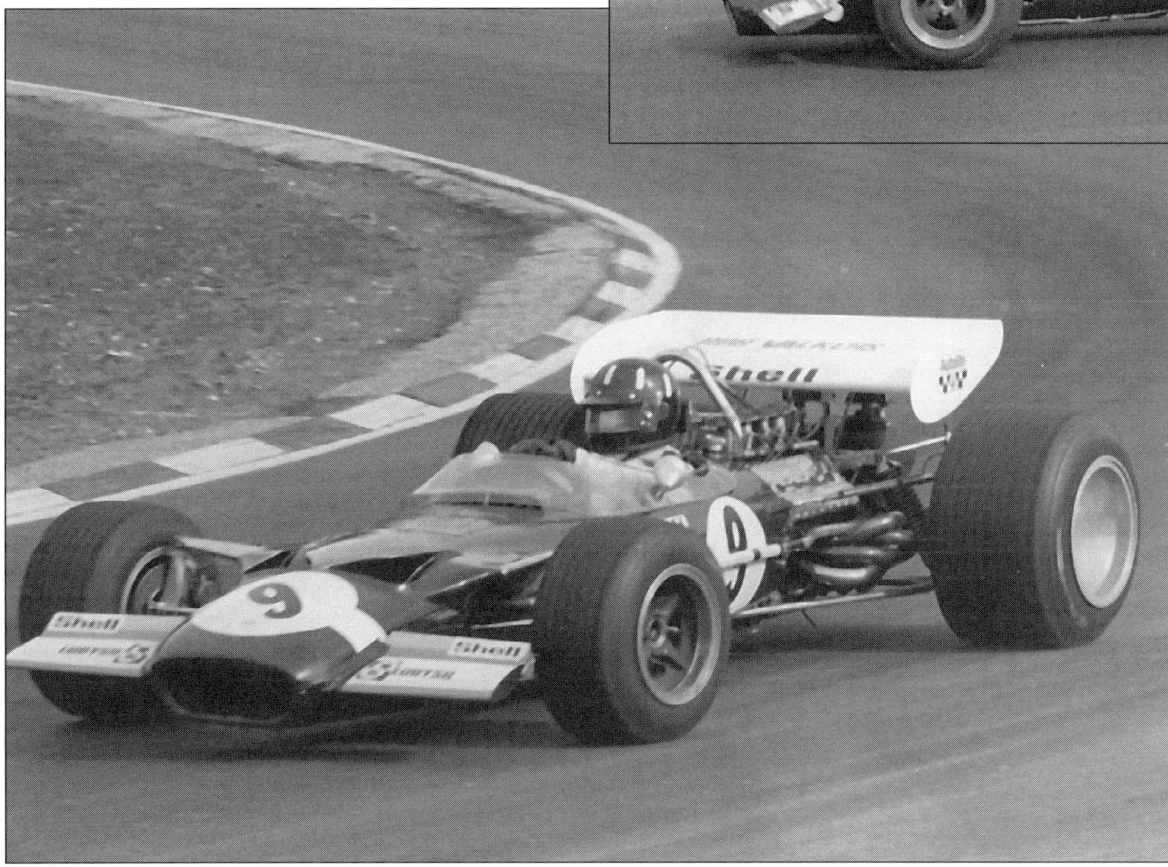

Graham Hill driving Rob Walker's Lotus 49C/7, powered by a Ford Cosworth DFV V-8 during the 1970 Race of Champions at Brands Hatch. Hill had a troublesome Hewland gearbox and finally finished fifth overall.

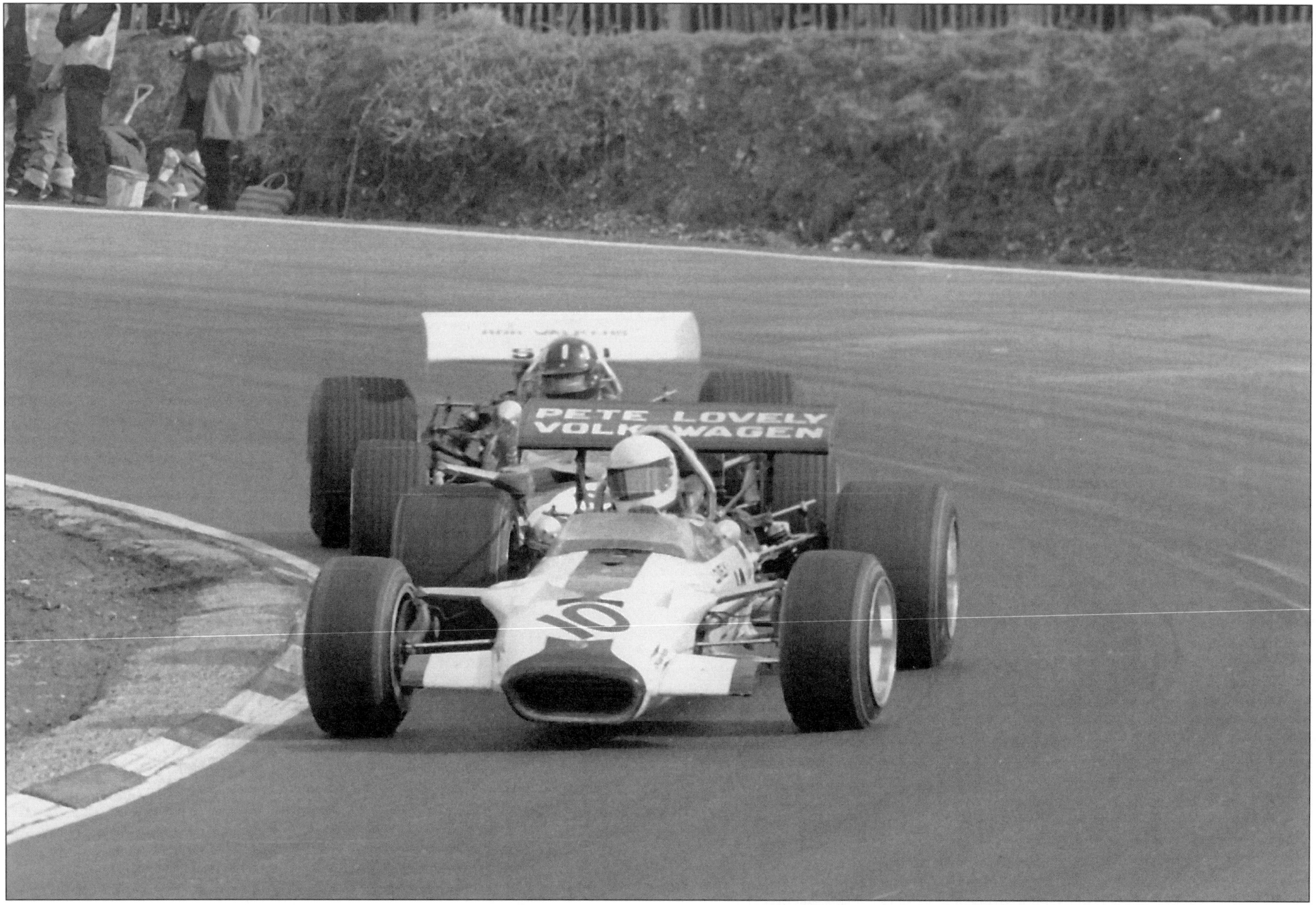

Pete Lovely in Lotus 49B/11, with a Ford Cosworth DFV V-8, holds up Hill at Druids Corner during the 1970 Race of Champions at Brands Hatch. Lovely went off the track at Paddock Bend. After the race he said it was due to "brain fade."

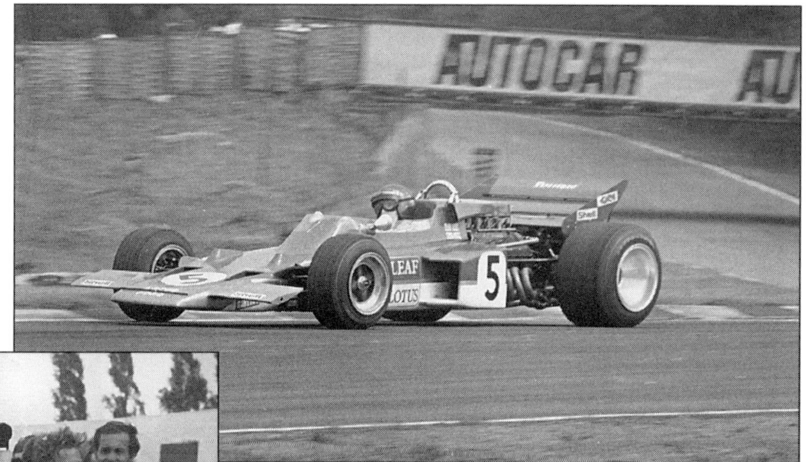

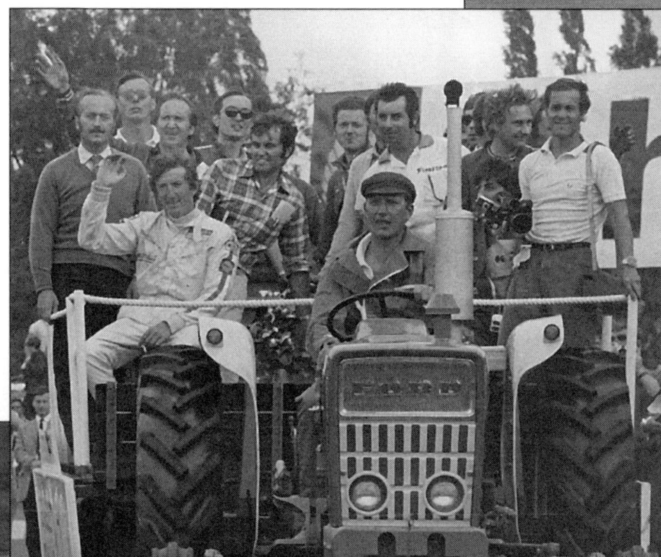

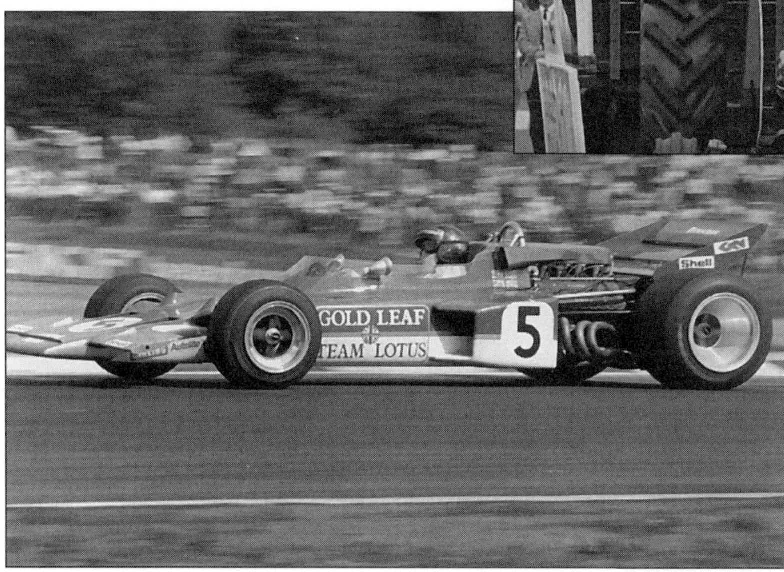

Jochen Rindt drove Gold Leaf Team Lotus 72C/2 to win the 1970 British Grand Prix on the last corner of the last lap. Rindt took the lead in the seventh lap but was overtaken by Jack Brabham. Brabham ran out of fuel in the last lap, allowing Rindt the victory.

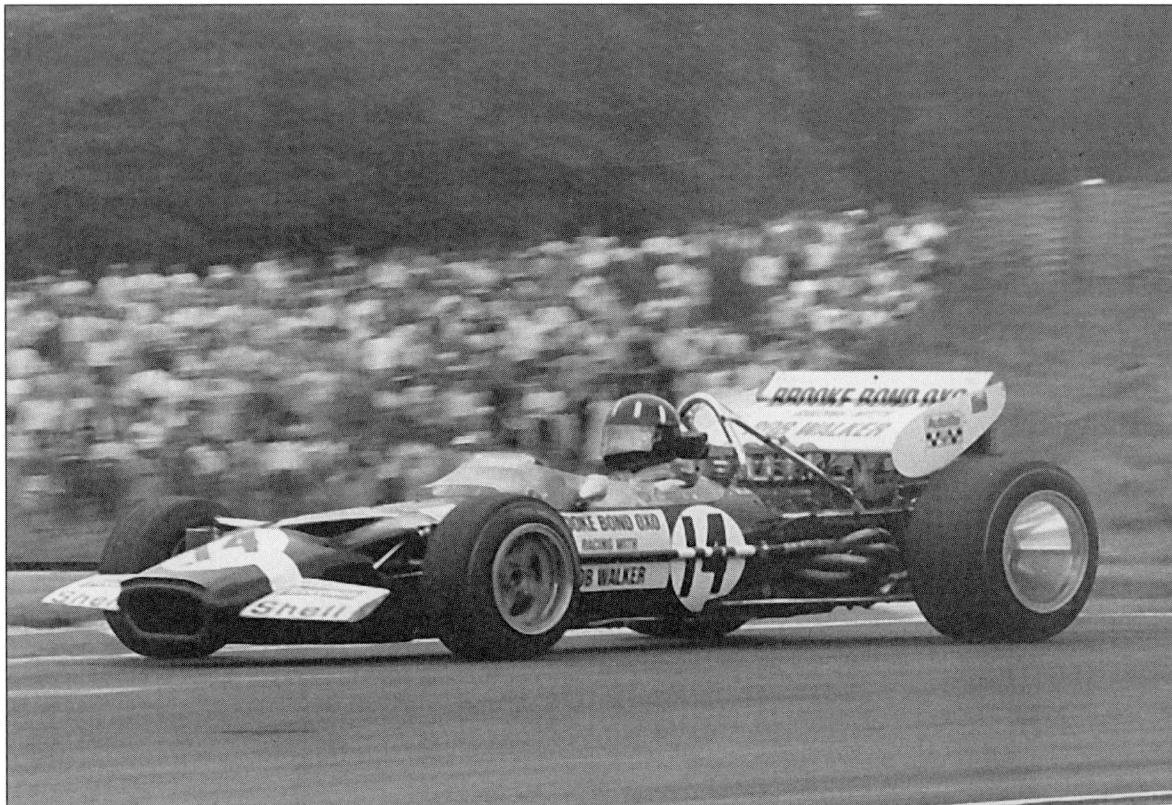

1970 British Grand Prix at Brands Hatch. Graham Hill driving Lotus 49C/7 to sixth place.

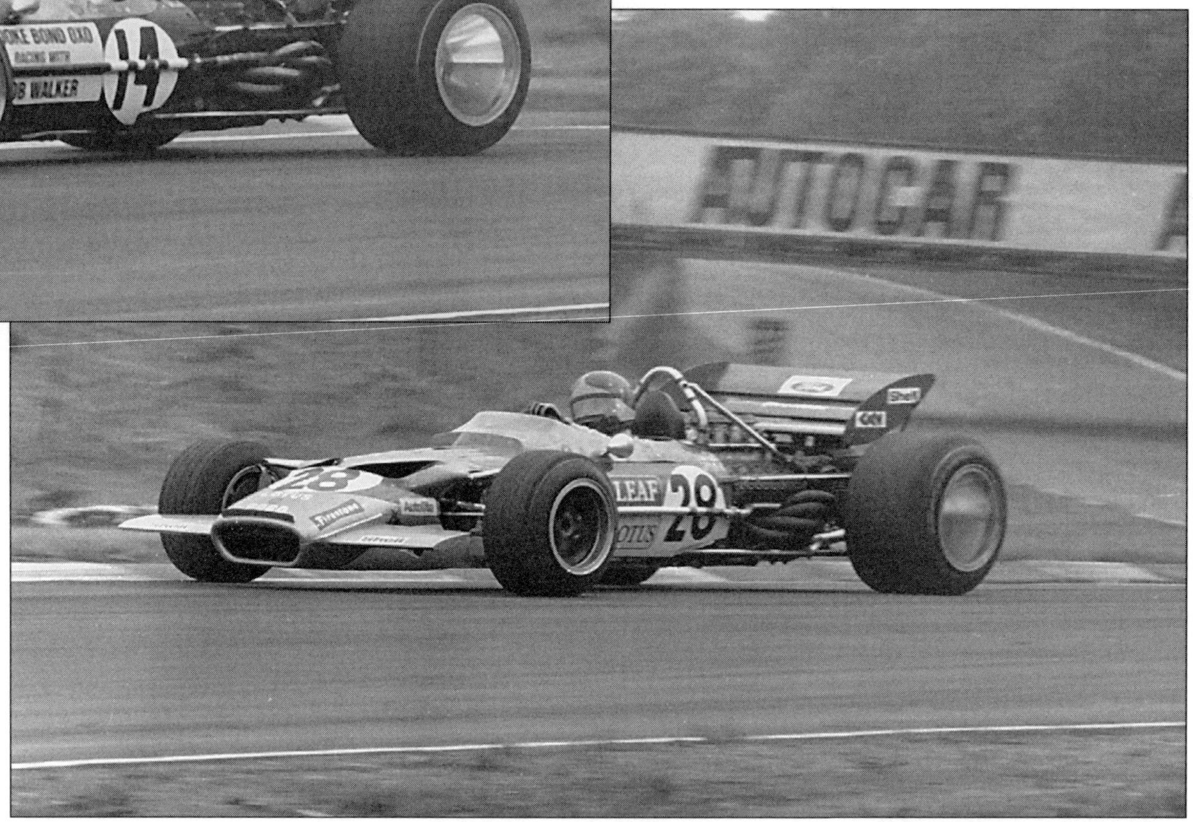

Emerson Fittipaldi driving Lotus 49C/10 to finish eighth. Both cars were powered by 3-liter Ford Cosworth DFV V-8s.

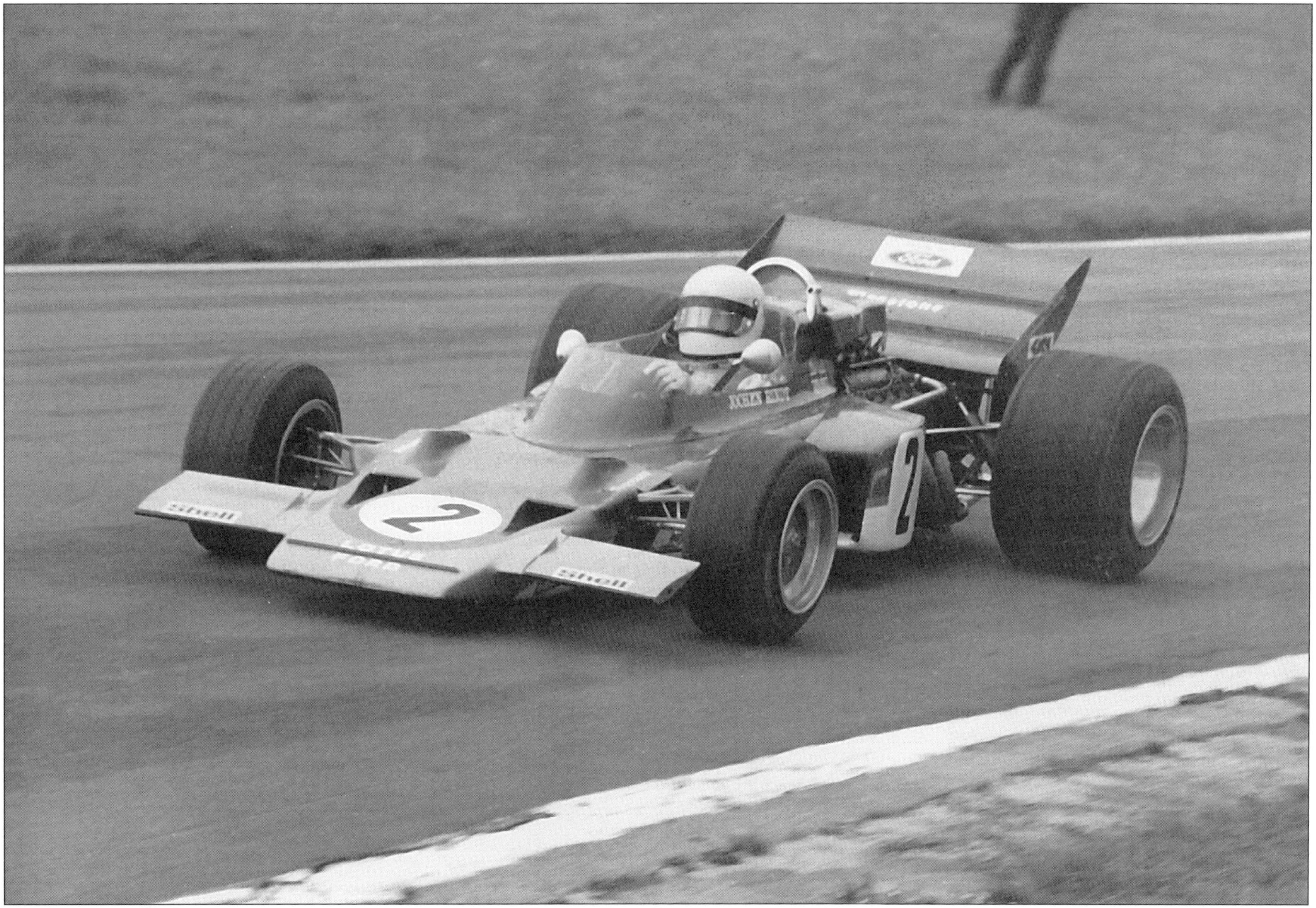

Jochen Rindt finished the 1970 Daily Express Gold Cup at Oulton Park second overall driving Lotus 72C/2 with 3-liter Ford Cosworth DFV V-8.

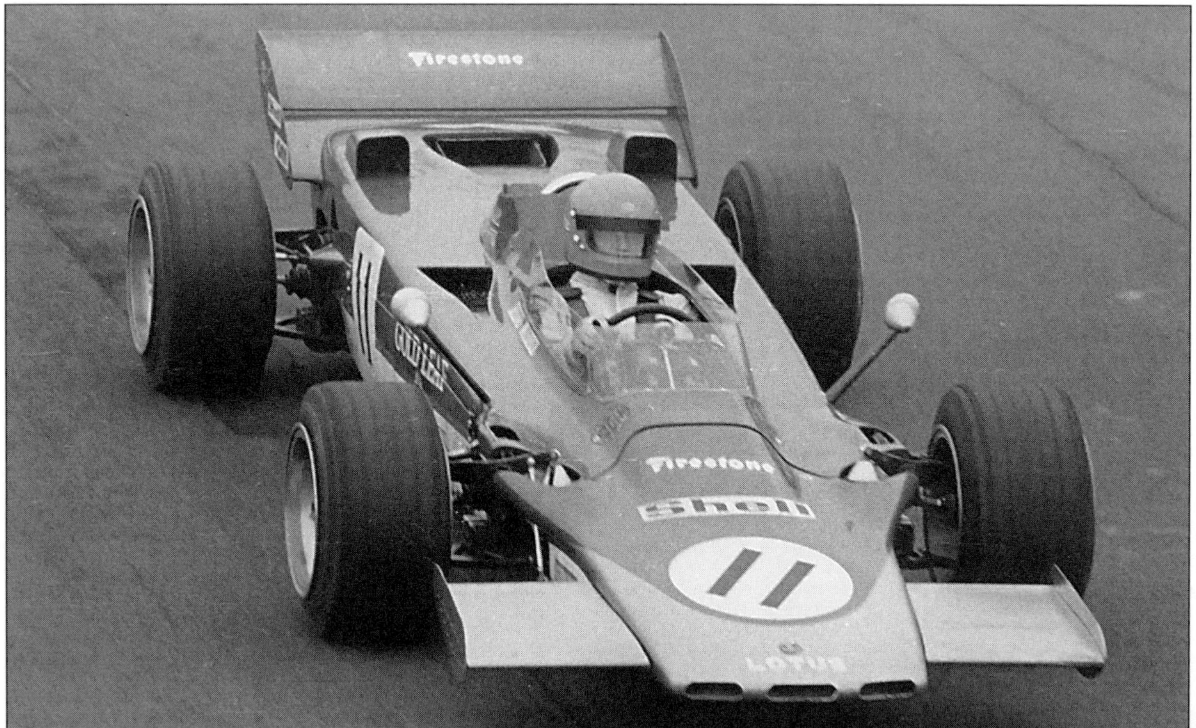

Rothmans Formula 1 Race, Oulton Park, 1971. Reine Wisell's Lotus 56B/1, with Pratt & Whitney Turbine. The second outing for the car, it was retired in lap 17 with a blowout that damaged the suspension.

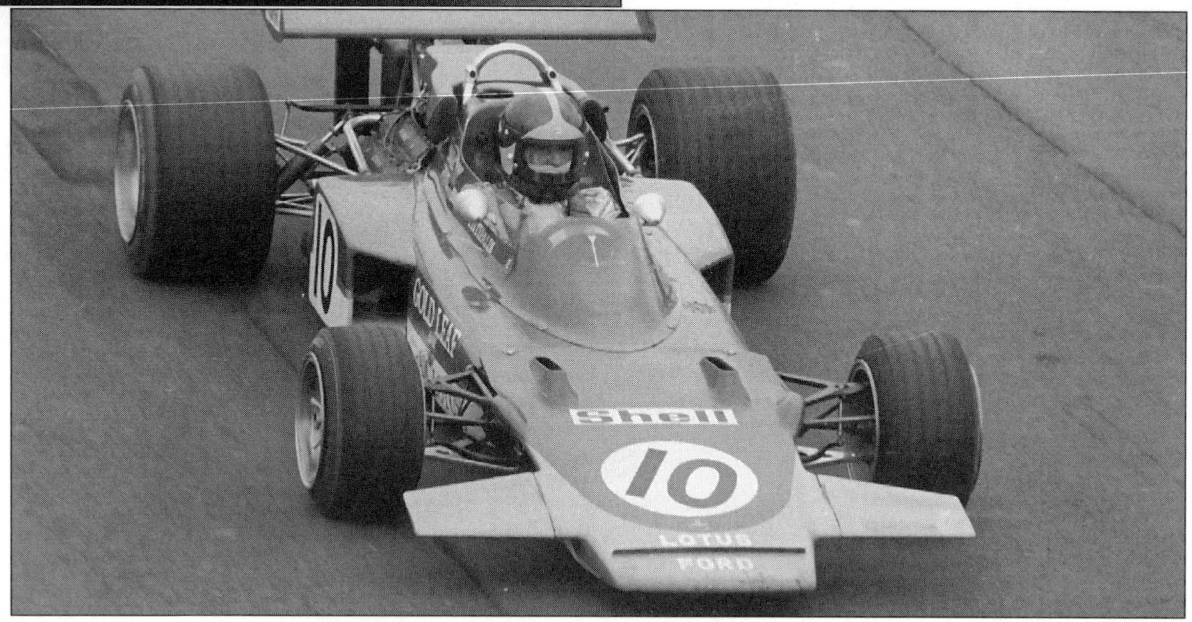

Emerson Fittipaldi driving Lotus 72/5, with a 3-liter Cosworth Ford DFV V-8. Fittipaldi had trouble with the transistor box and finished seventh place overall.

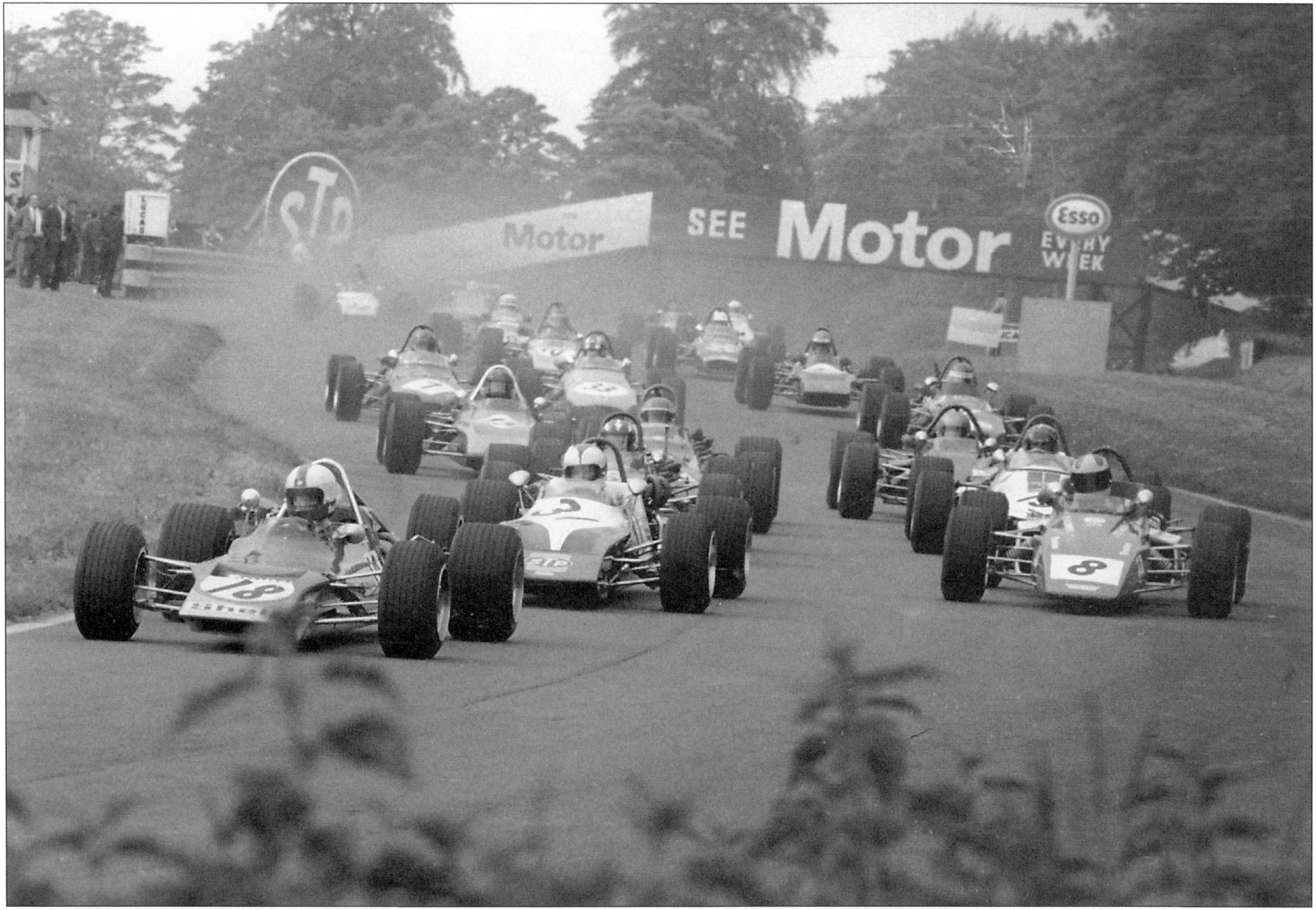

David Walker, driving a Lotus 69 Formula 3, leads the field at Old Hall corner during the 1971 British Empire Trophy for Formula 3 cars at Oulton Park.

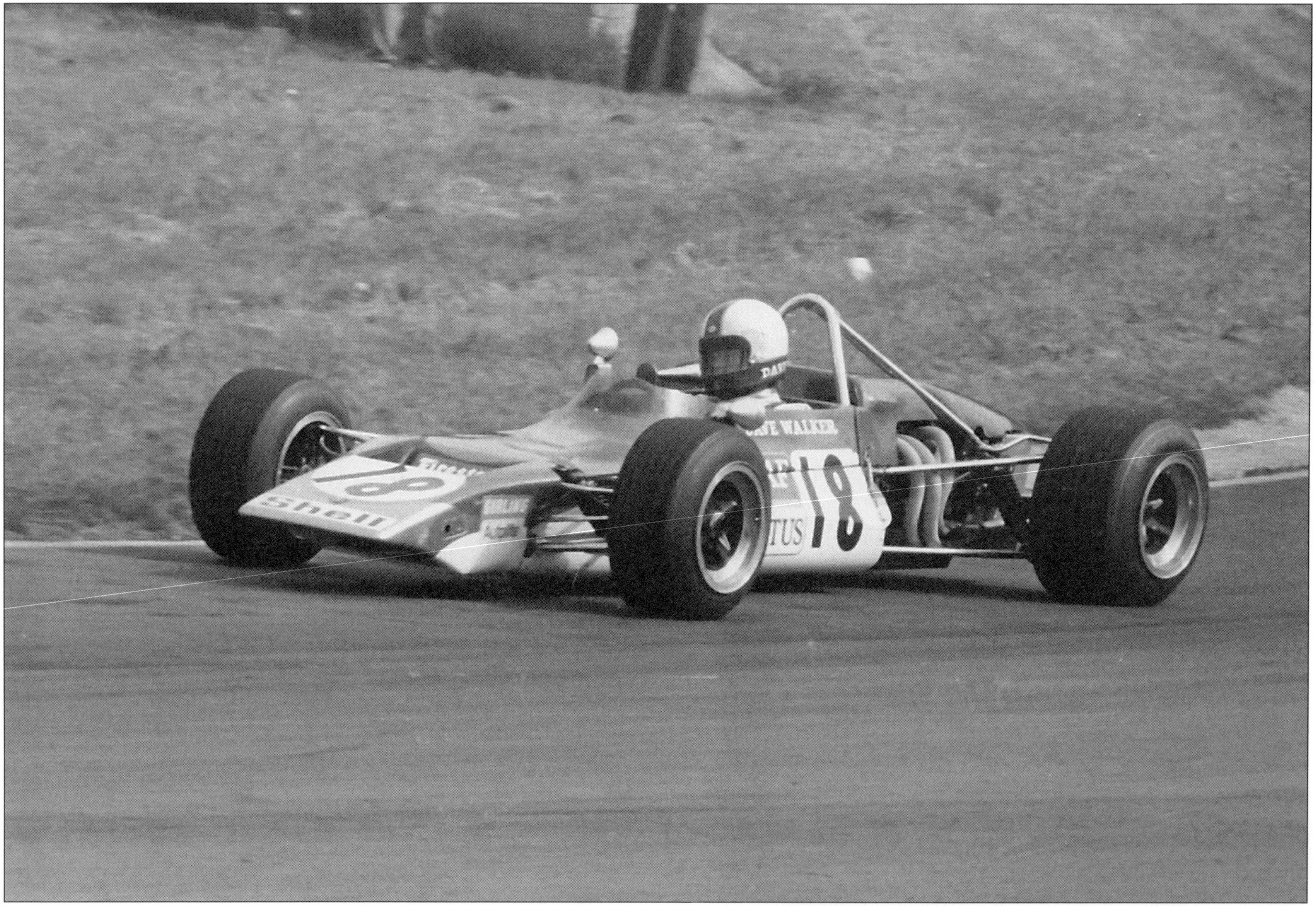

David Walker won the 1971 British Empire Trophy Race at Oulton Park in a 1.6-liter Gold Leaf Team Lotus 69.

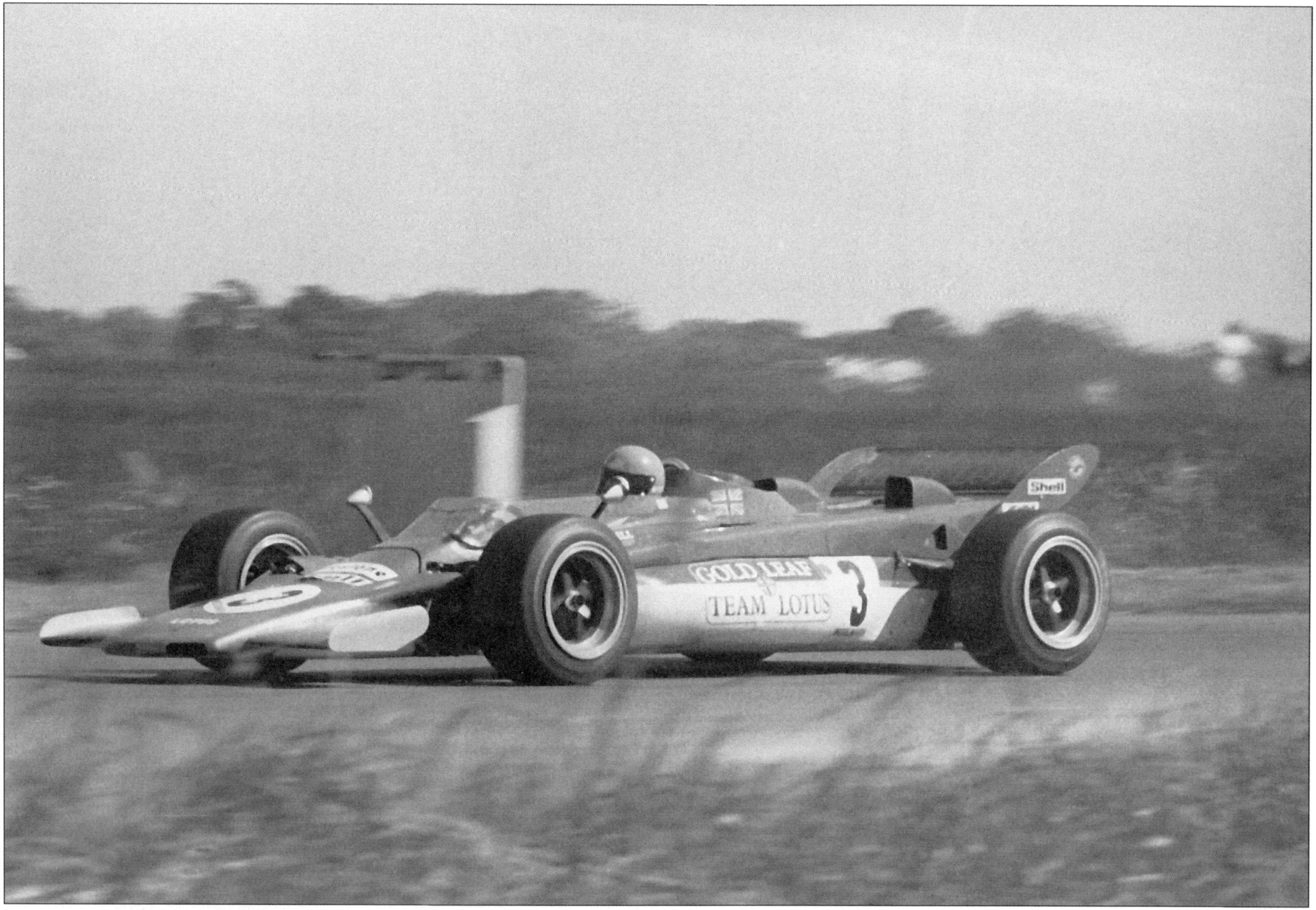

Reine Wisell driving Lotus 56B/1, with a Pratt & Whitney Turbine, in the 1971 British Grand Prix at Silverstone. The car finished but had throttle linkage problems throughout the race.

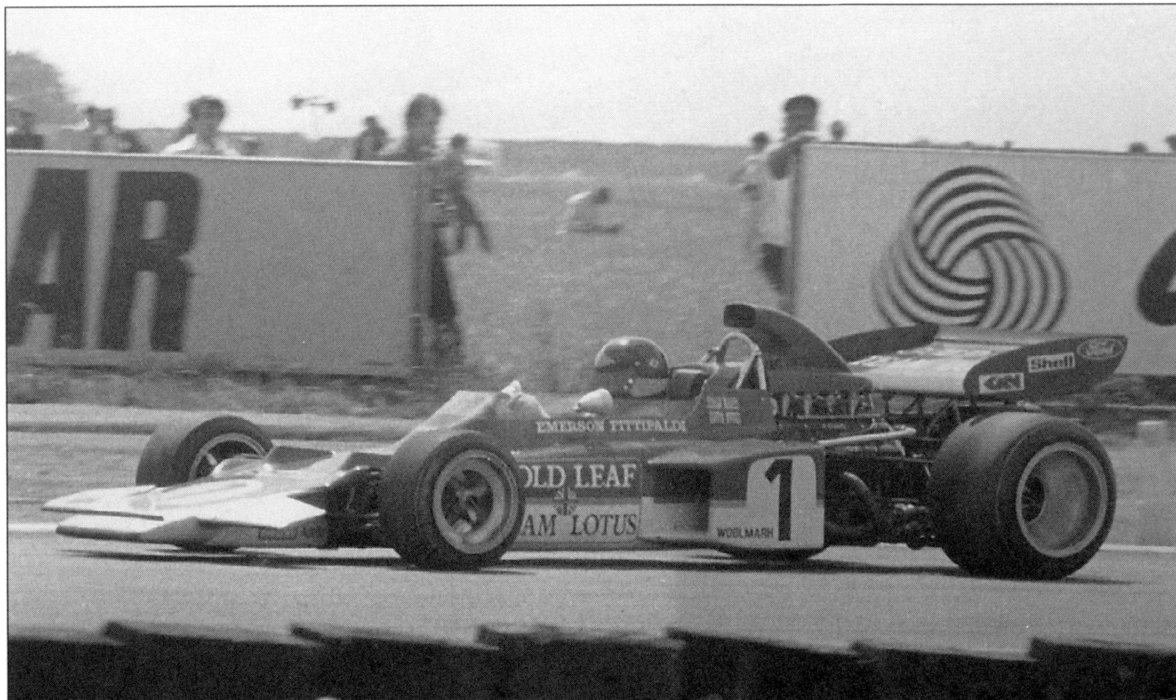

1971 British Grand Prix at Silverstone. Emerson Fittipaldi driving Lotus 72D/5, with a 3-liter Ford Cosworth DFV V-8. Plagued by problems during the race, Fittipaldi managed a lucky third place.

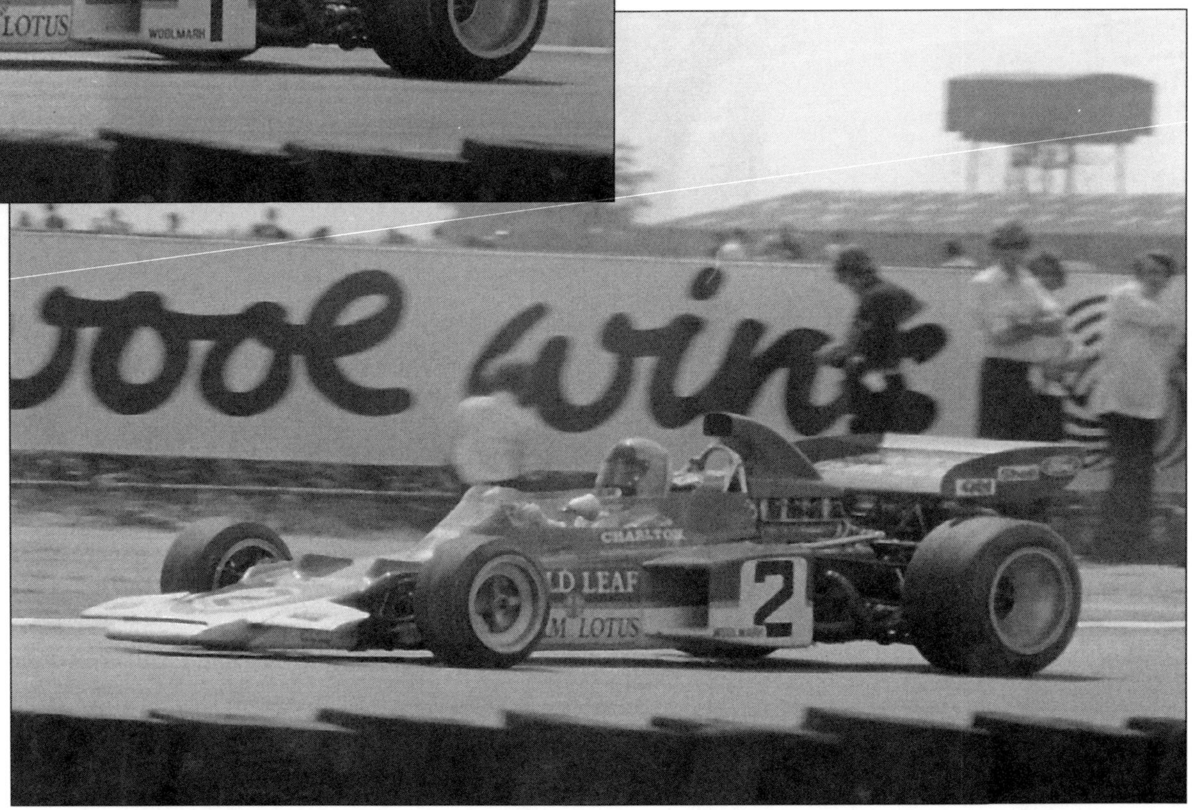

Dave Charlton, in Lotus 72D/3, completed one lap before the engine gave out.

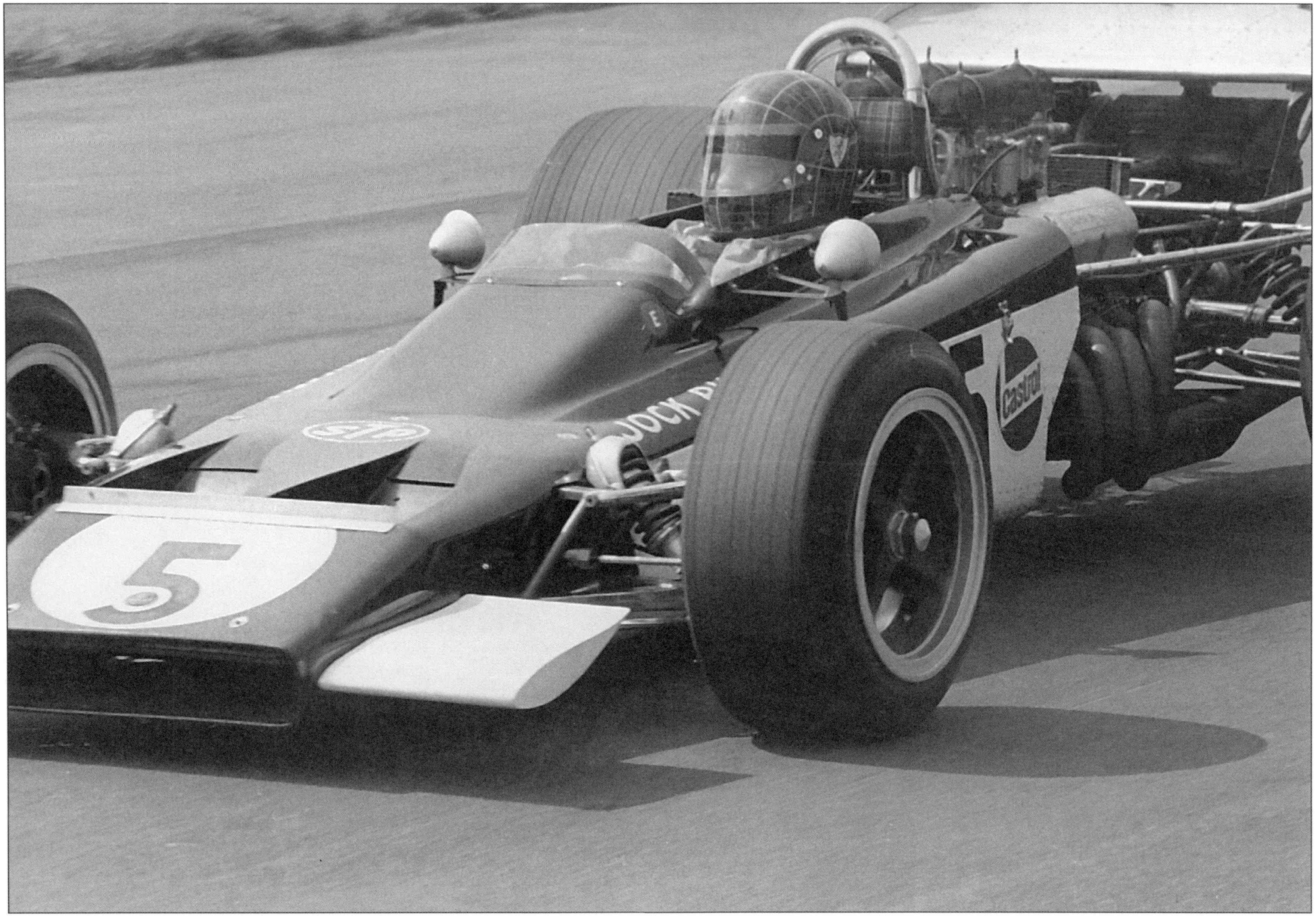

Jock Russell driving a 5.0 Lotus 70 in the 1971 Rothmans International Gold Cup Race at Oulton Park. Russell's car broke a camshaft on the first lap.

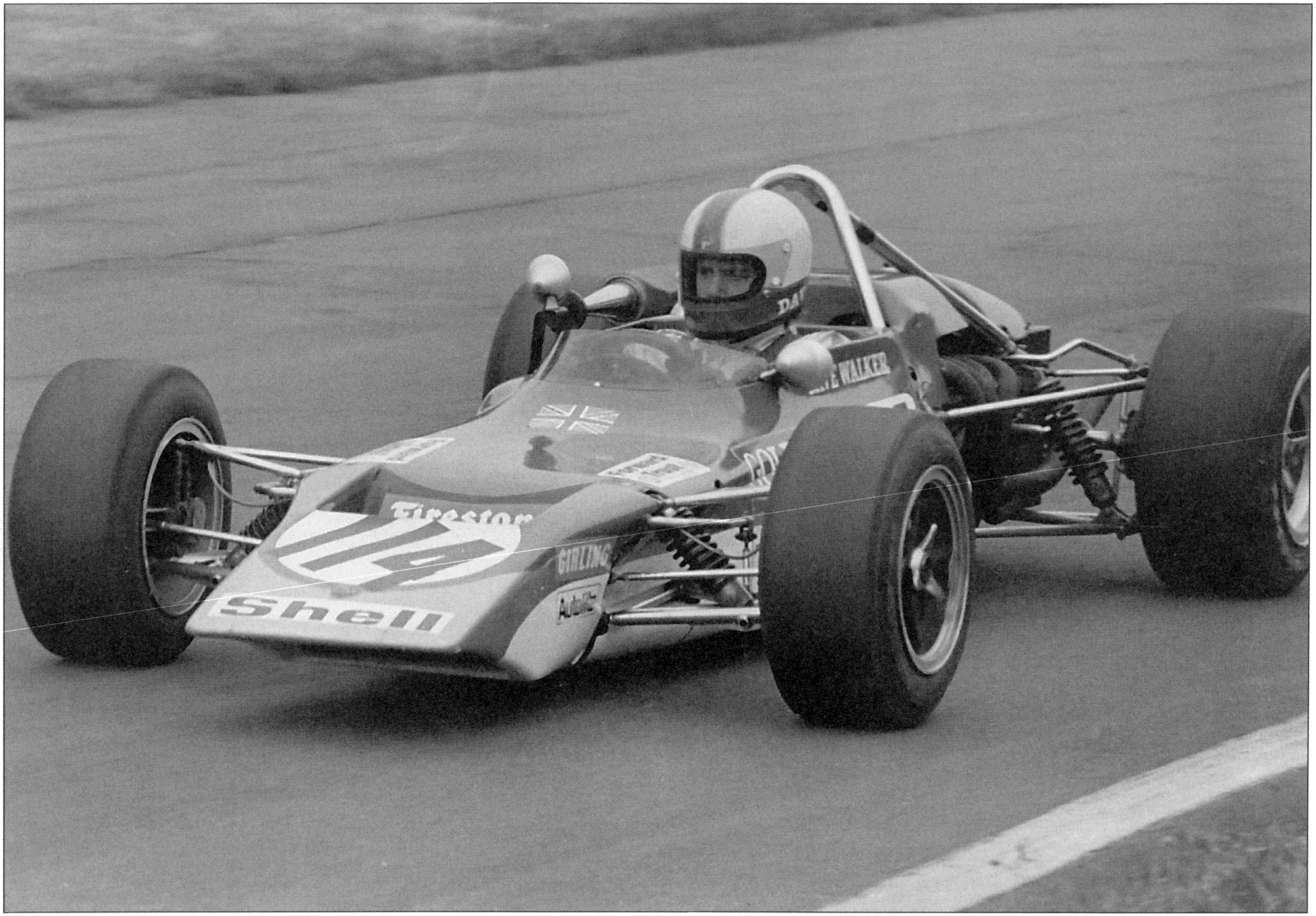

David Walker won the support race at the 1971 Gold Cup Race, Oulton Park, driving a 1.6-liter Lotus 69 Novamotor.

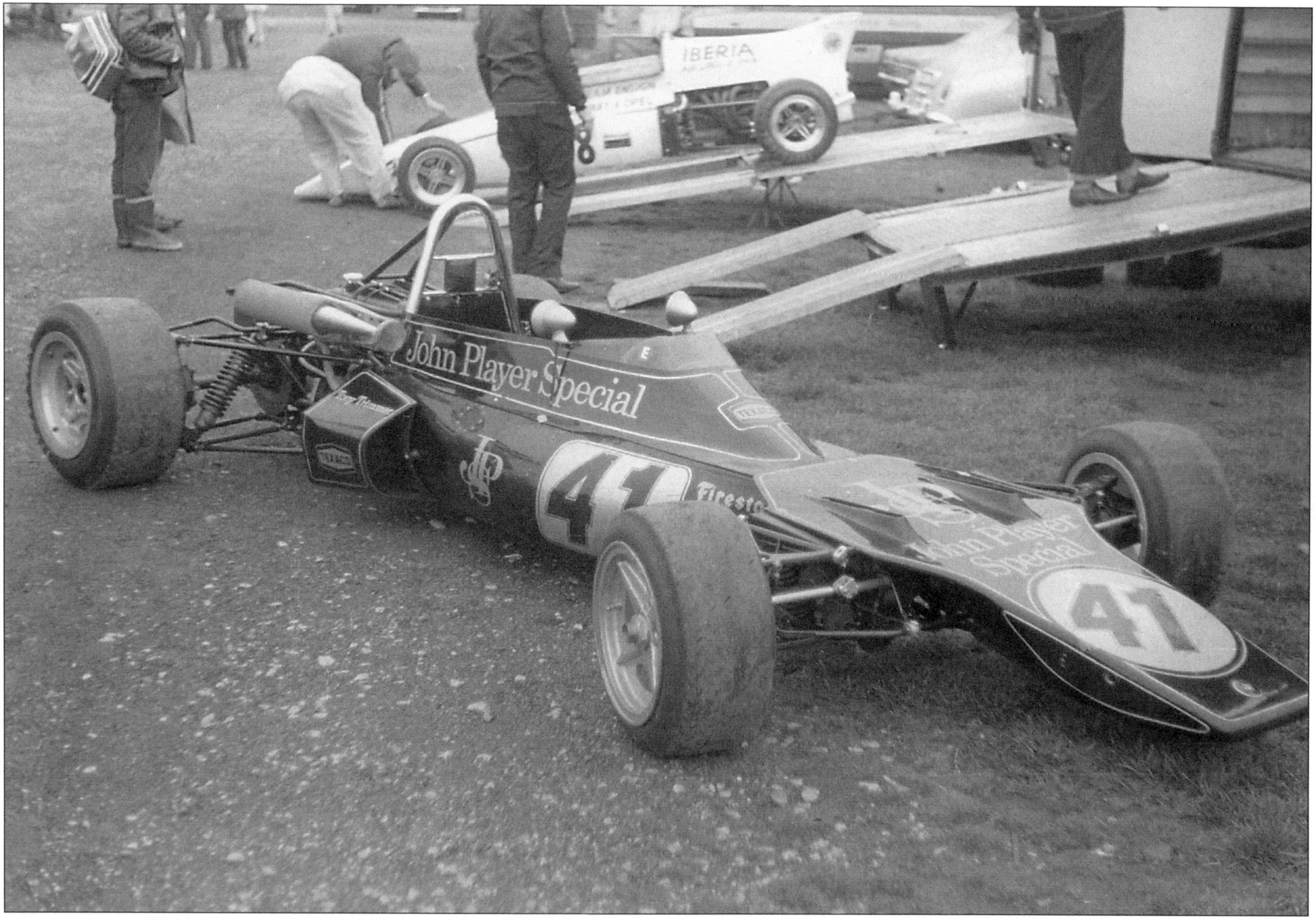

Tony Trimmer's John Player Special F3 Ford Novamotor in the paddock of Oulton Park in 1972. Note the word "Lotus" is missing, one of the first cars produced by Lotus to be named John Player Special.

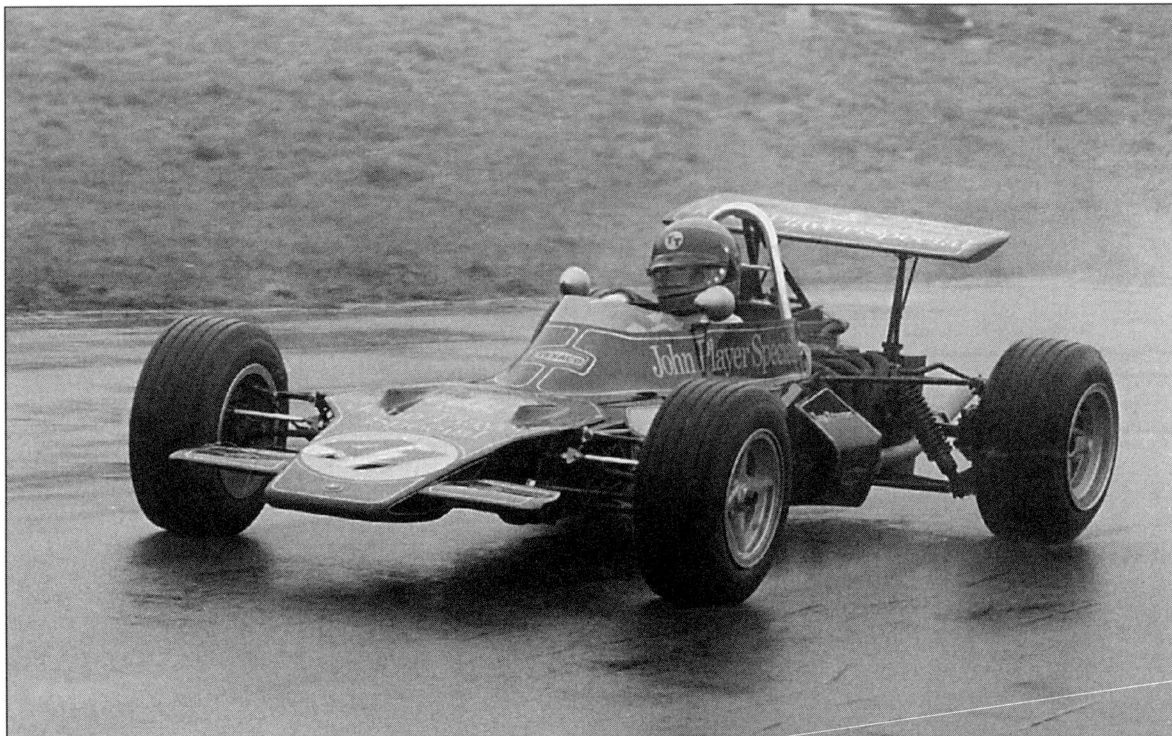

1972 International Gold Cup at Oulton Park. Tony Trimmer's John Player Special F3 finished seventh in the support race.

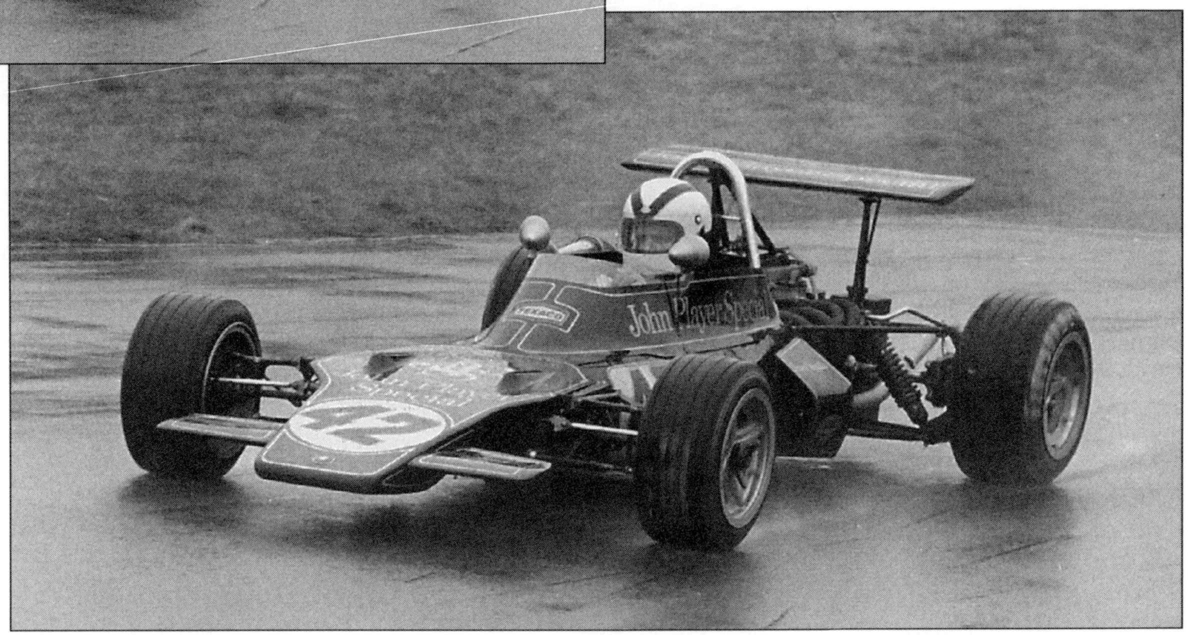

Bernard Vennilio's John Player Special F3 Ford Novamotor finished thirteenth and last during the support race.

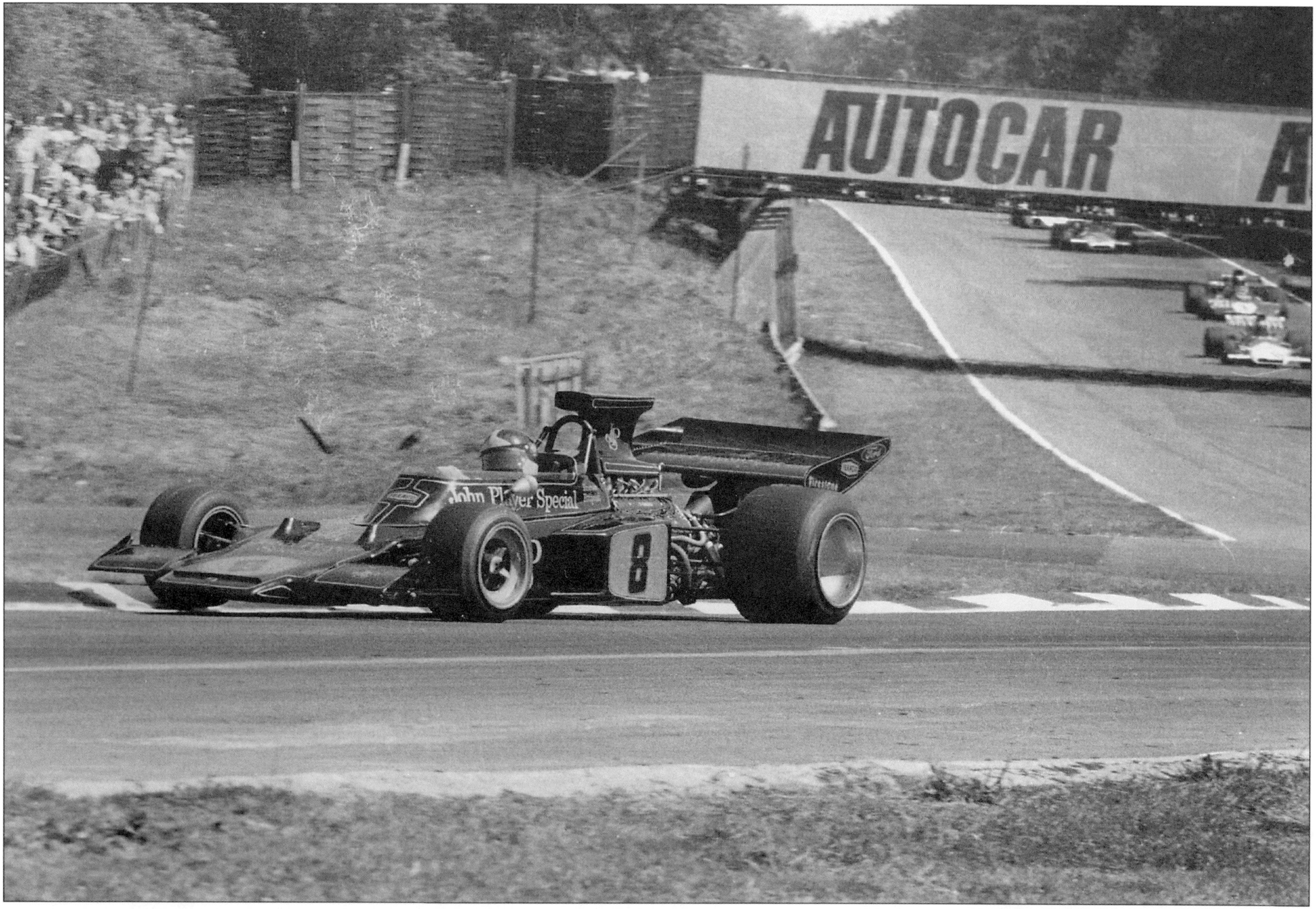

Emerson Fittipaldi winning the 1972 British Grand Prix at Brands Hatch in great style. Fittipaldi was driving John Player Special 72D/7, with a 3-liter Ford Cosworth DFV V-8.

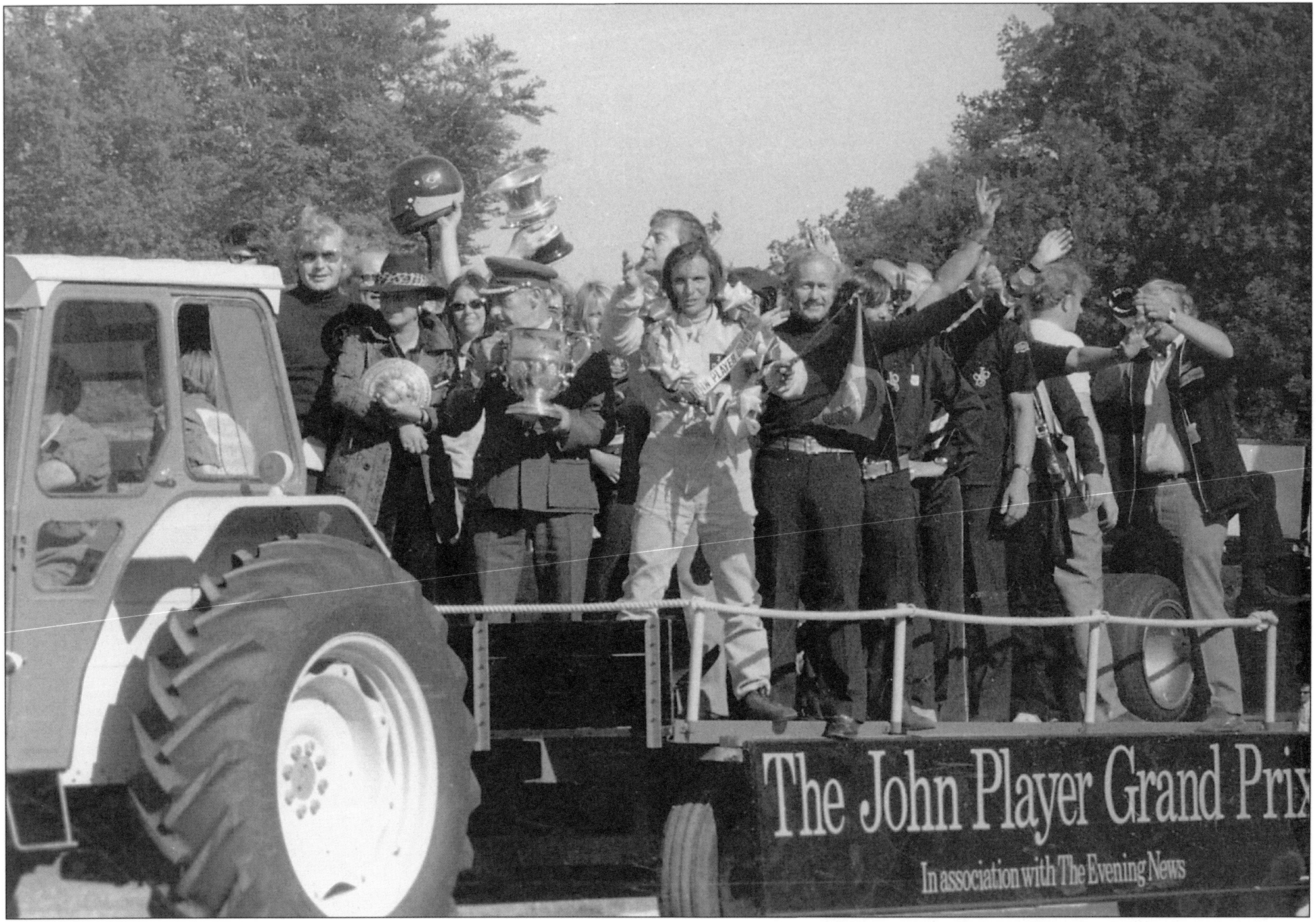

Emerson Fittipaldi and Colin Chapman on the victory float following the 1972 British Grand Prix at Brands Hatch.

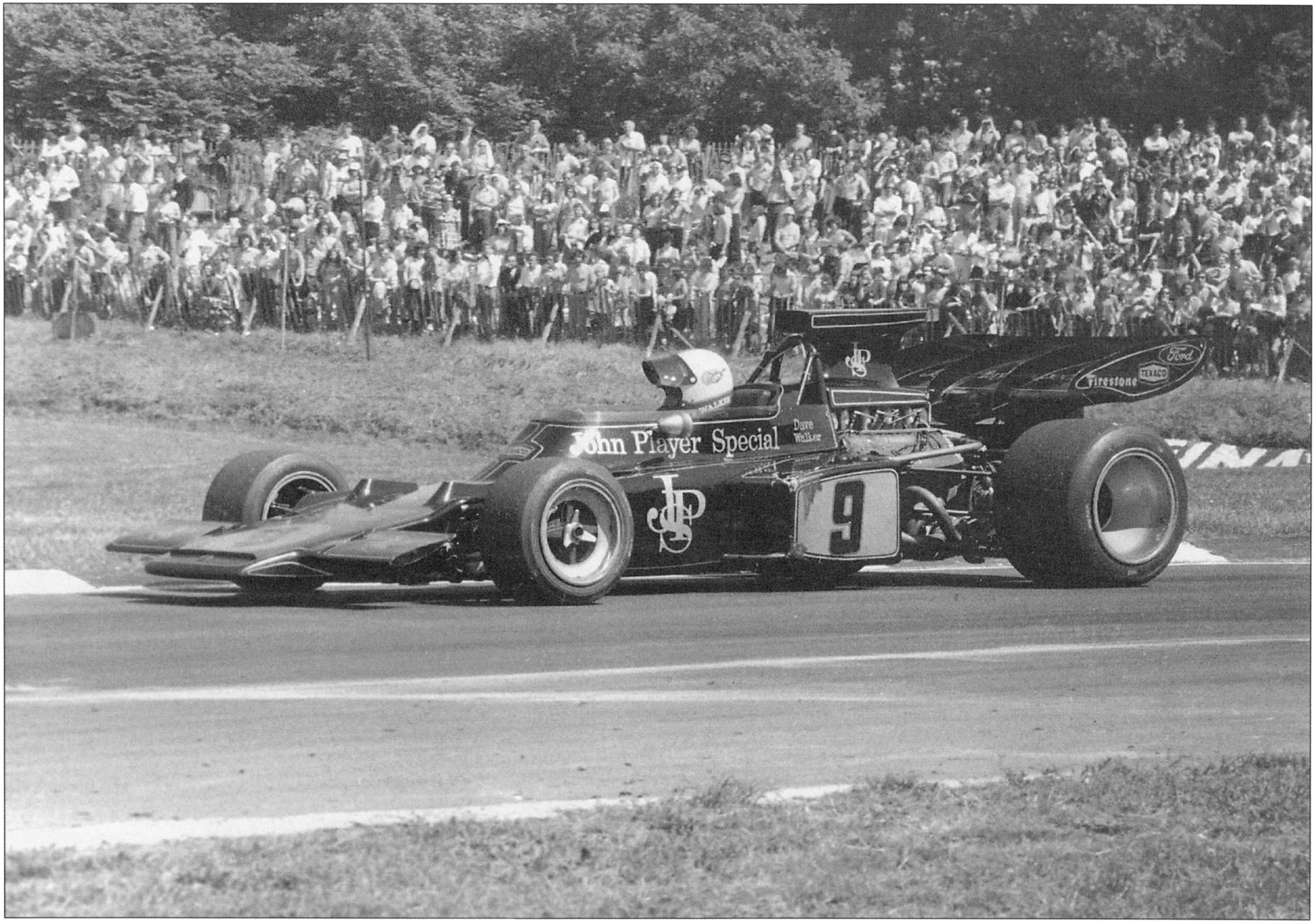

Dave Walker driving John Player Special 72D/6, with a 3-liter Ford Cosworth DFV V-8 in the 1972 British Grand Prix at Brands Hatch. Walker retired during the race when a shock absorber mounting broke.

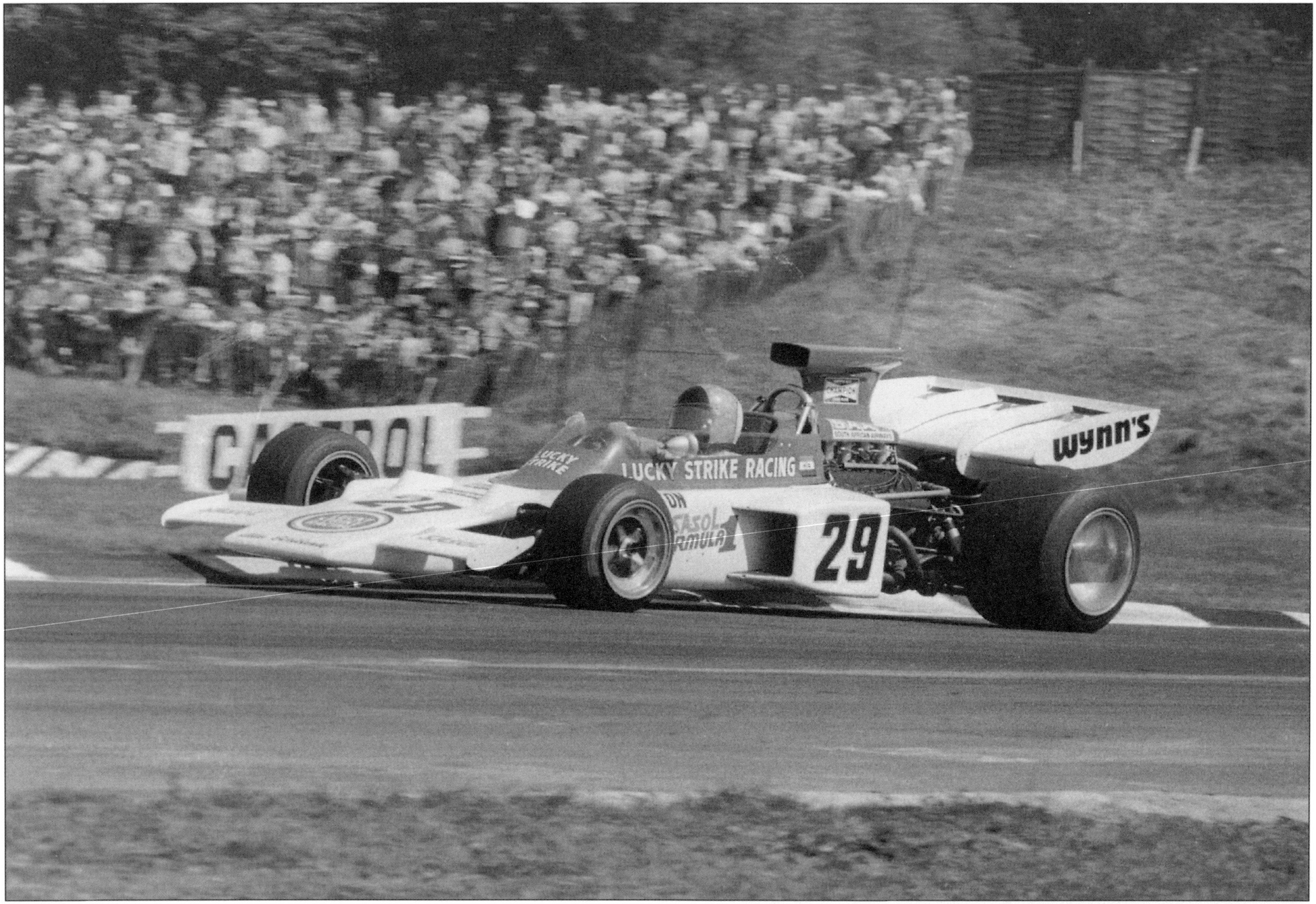

Dave Charlton's 3-liter Ford Cosworth DFV V-8 powered Lotus 72D/3 retired after 22 laps with a gear selection problem during the 1972 British Grand Prix at Brands Hatch.

1974 Rothmans Gold Cup Race's support race at Oulton Park. John Roberts driving a 2.5-liter Lotus 16.

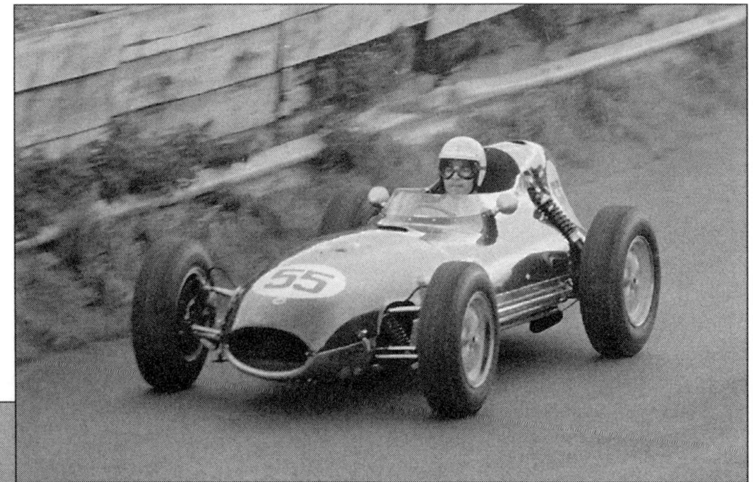

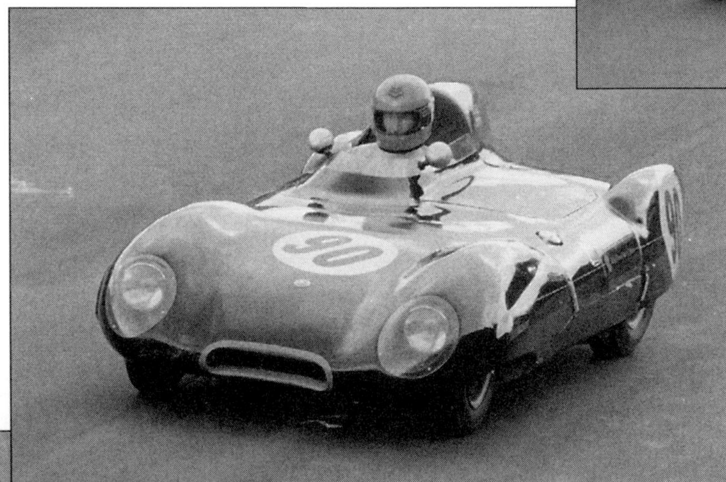

Roger Friend in a 1098cc Lotus 11 LeMans.

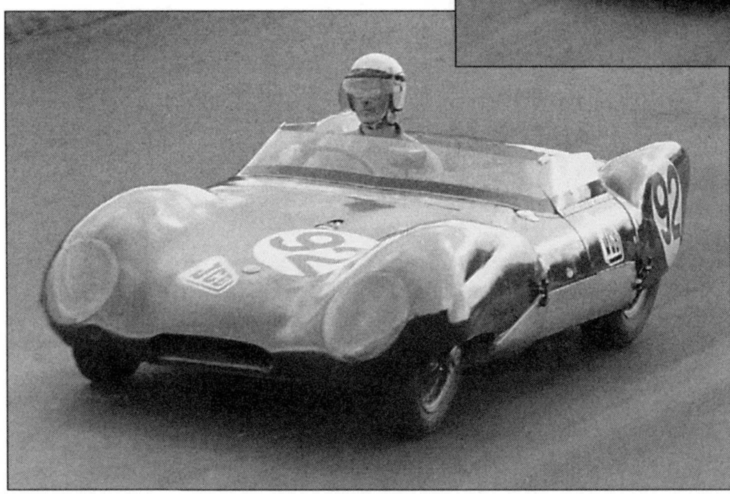

Terry Harrison also driving a 1098cc Lotus 11 LeMans.

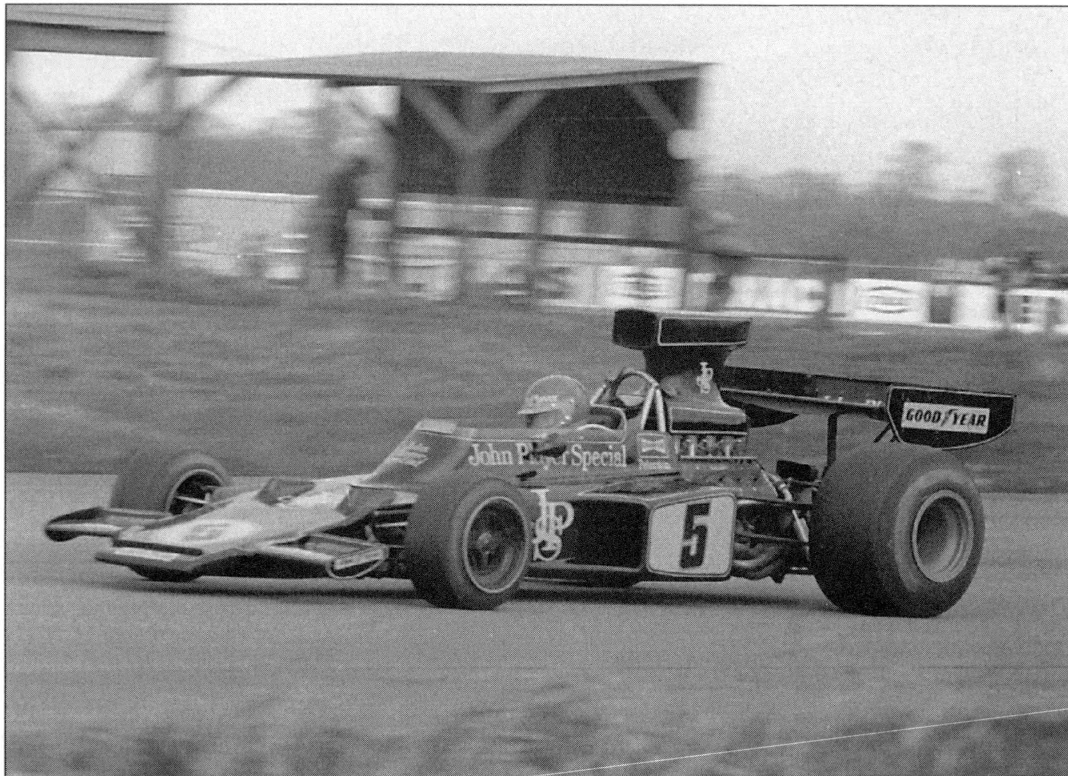

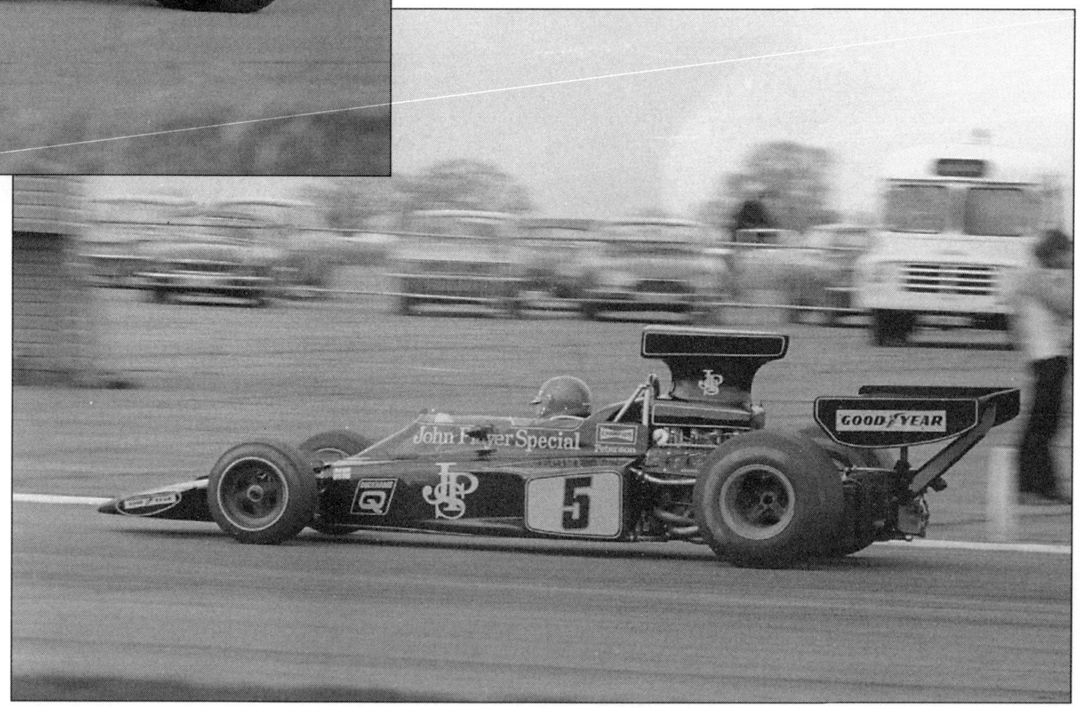

Ronnie Peterson driving Lotus 72E/9, powered by a 3-liter Ford Cosworth DFV V-8 during warm-up at the 1975 BRDC International Trophy at Silverstone. Peterson did not start the race due to engine failure in the warm-up.

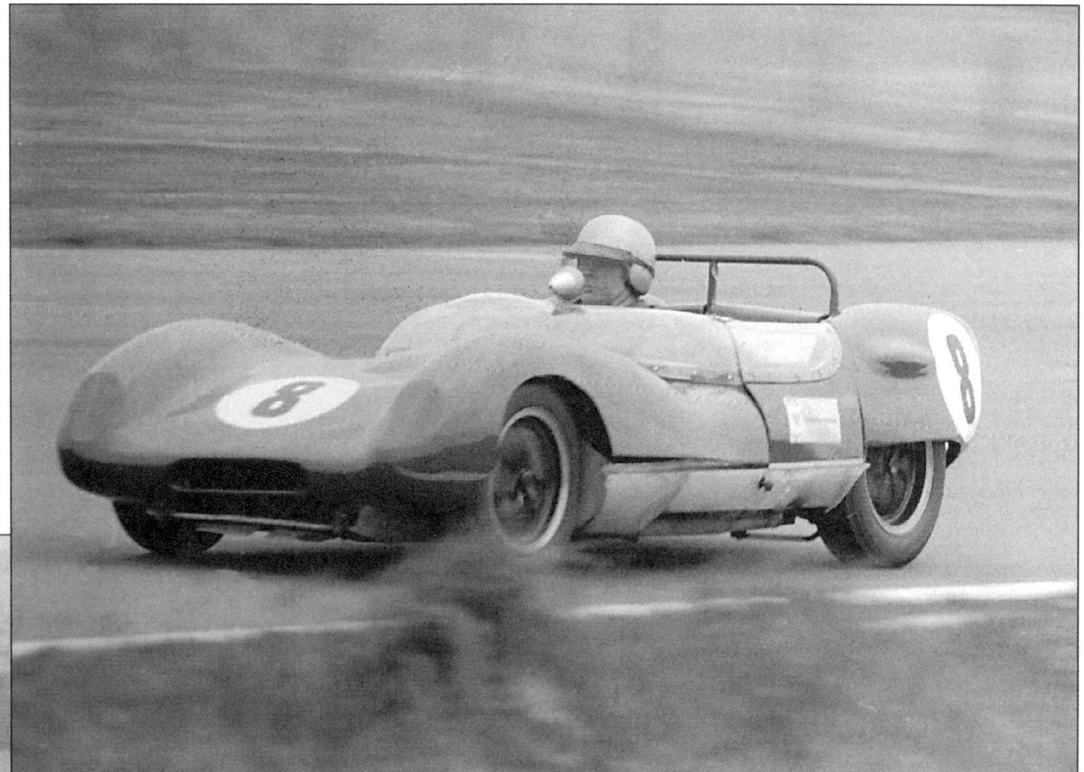

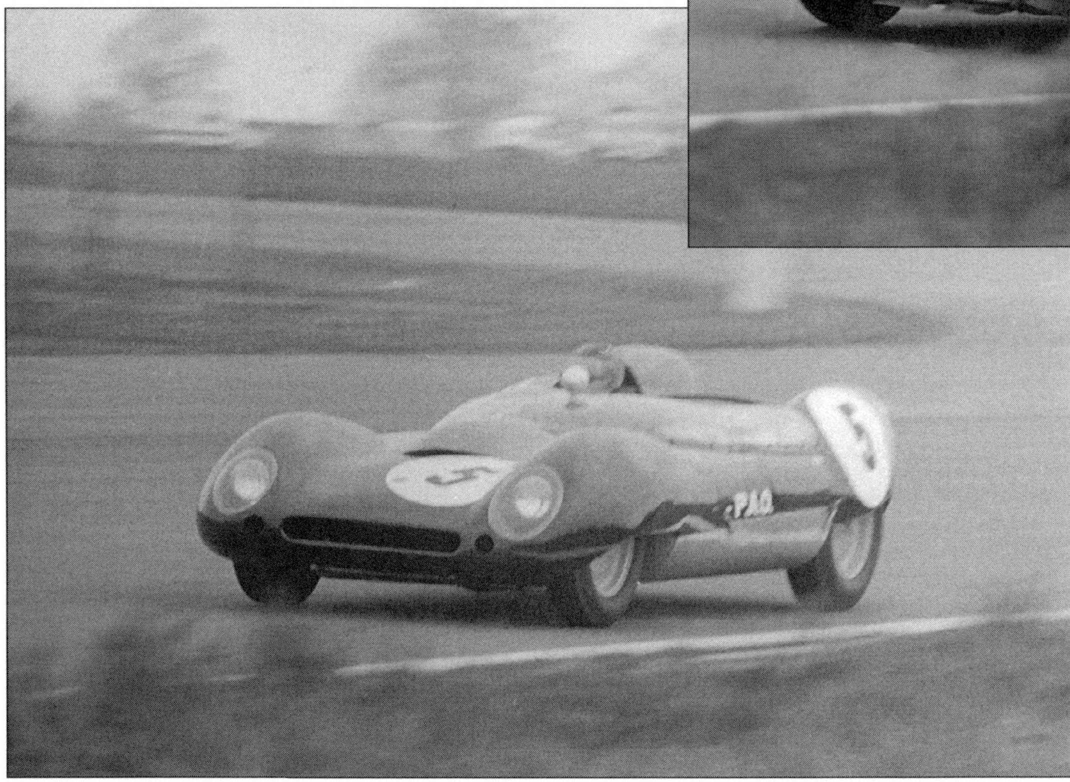

As a tribute, at the Graham Hill Trophy Race of 1976, two of the early Lotus cars that Graham Hill drove during his racing career, were driven around the Silverstone track. Upper right a Lotus 17, lower left a Lotus 15.

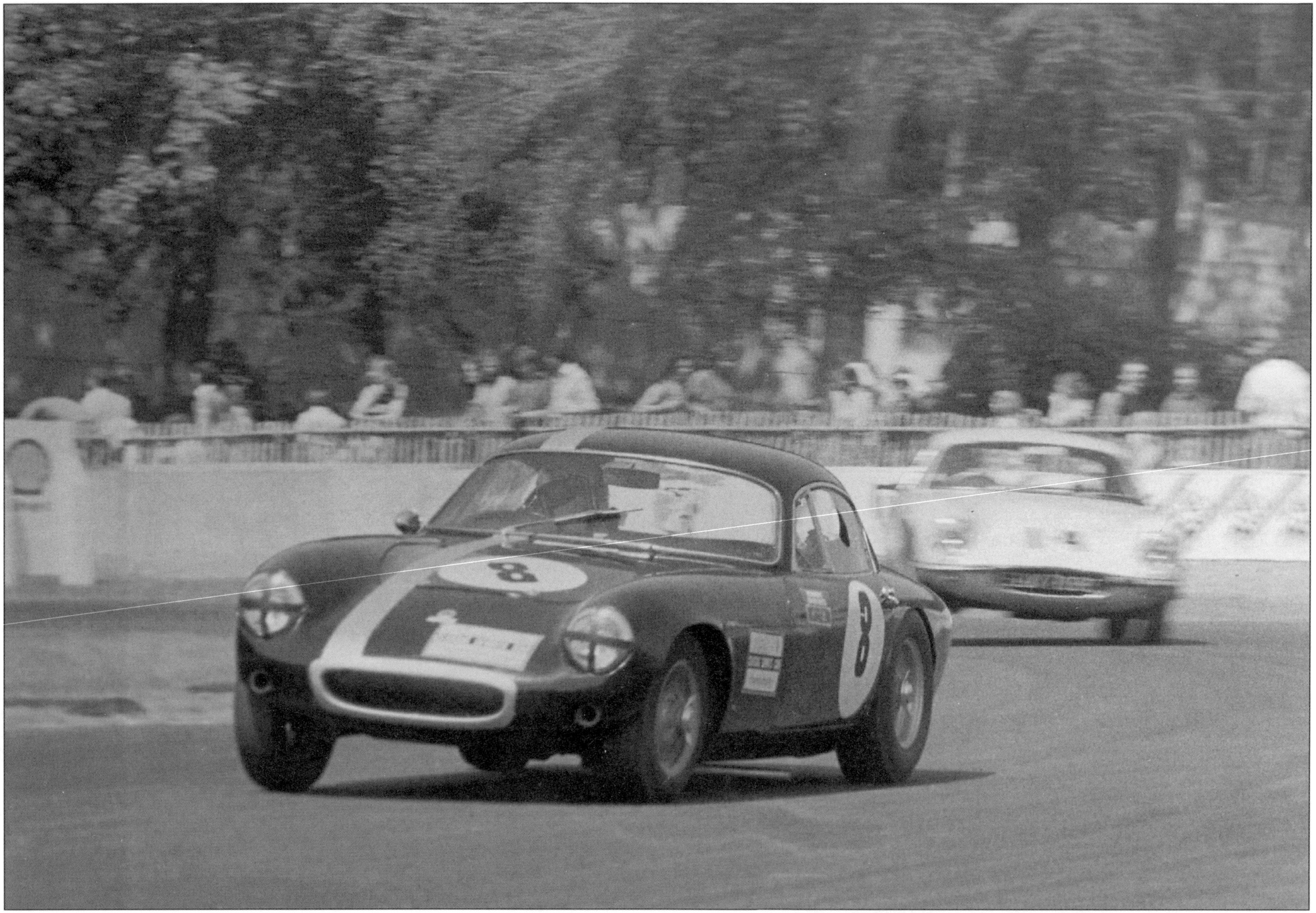

Alan Hall driving a 1220cc Lotus Elite Mk. 14 at the May 28, 1977 re-opening of Donington Park which had been closed since 1939.

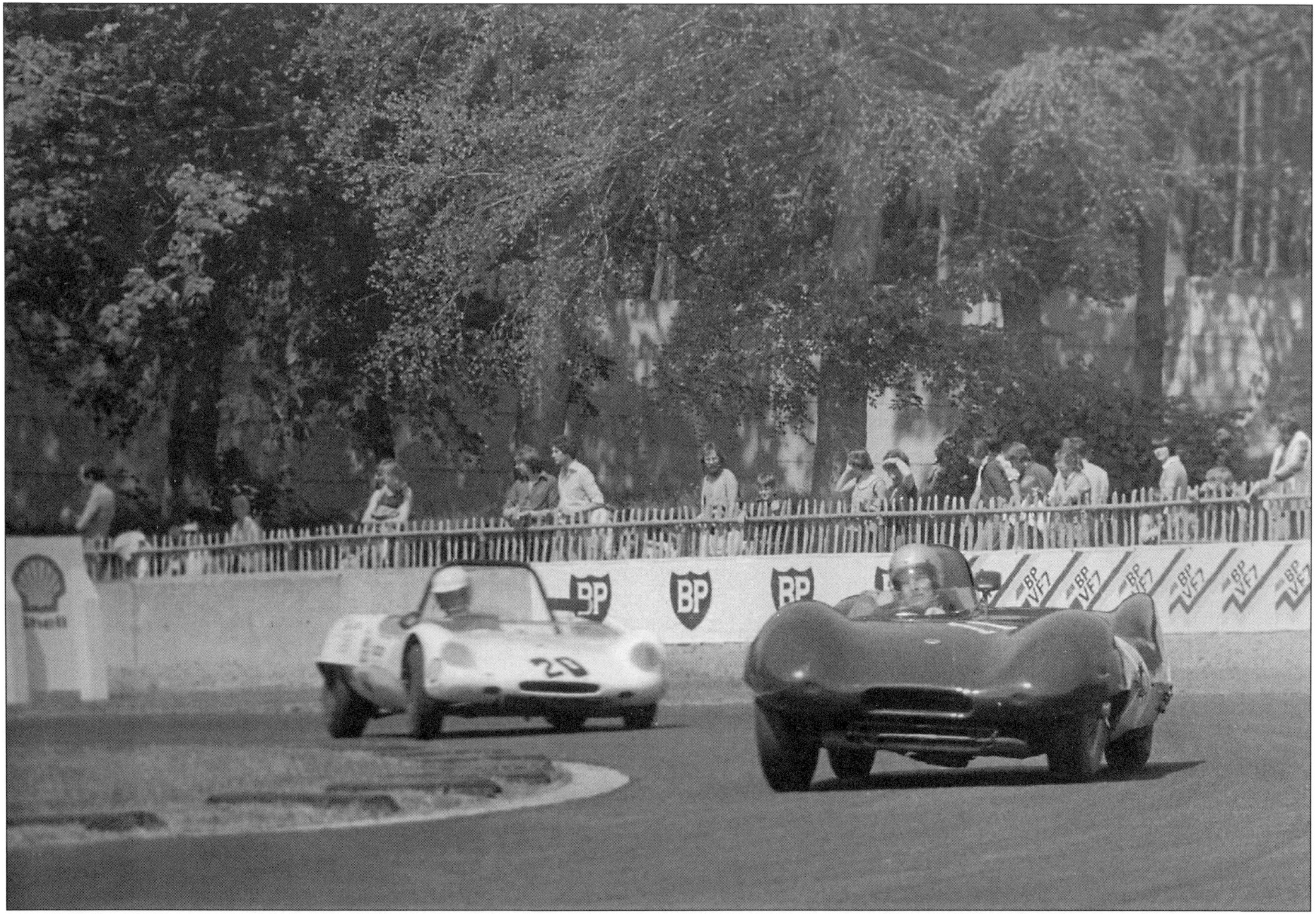

Michael Cambell-Bowling driving a 1220cc. Lotus Mk. 11 LeMans at the re-opening of Donington Park.

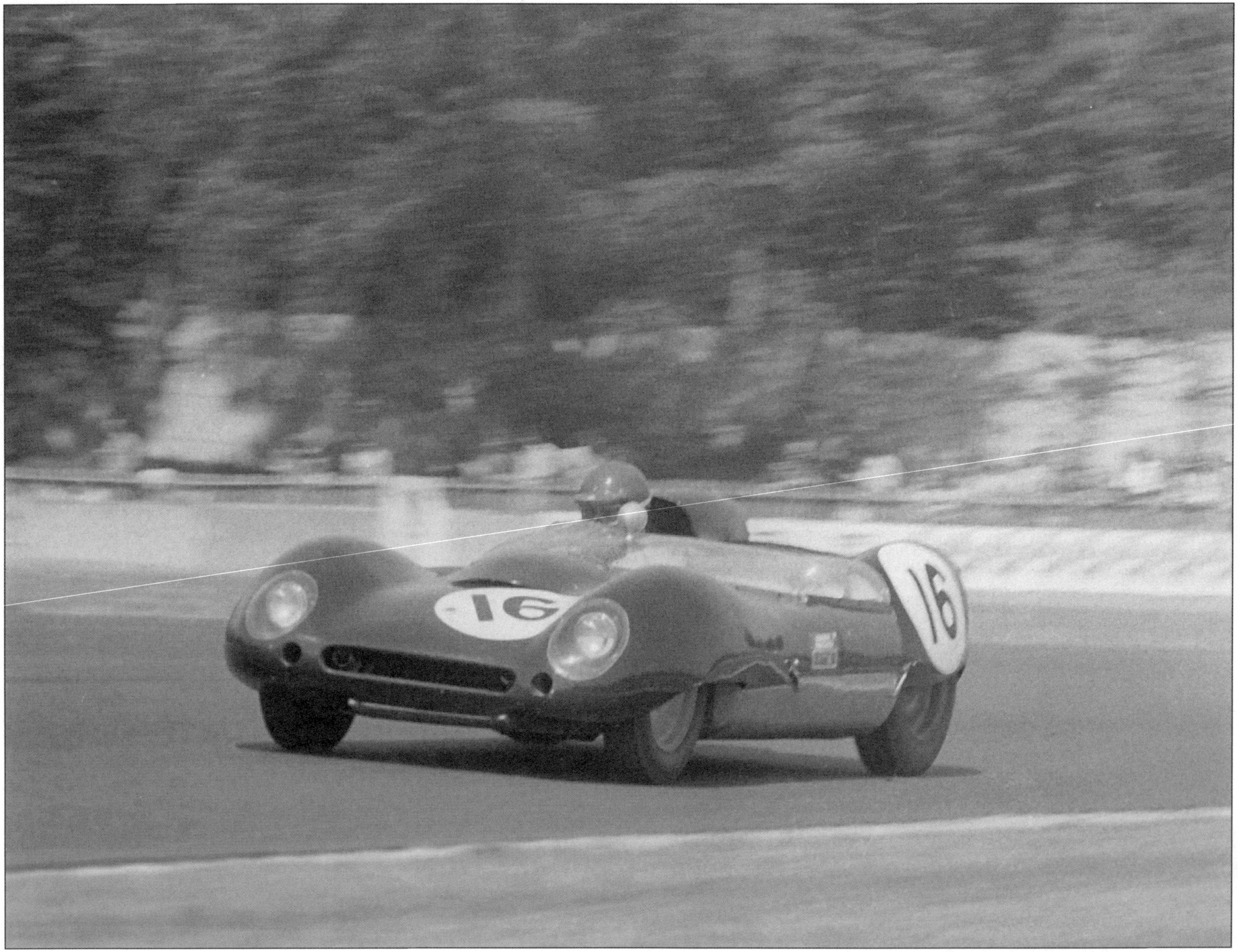

John Harper in a 2.0 Lotus 15 at the 1977 re-opening of Donington Park.

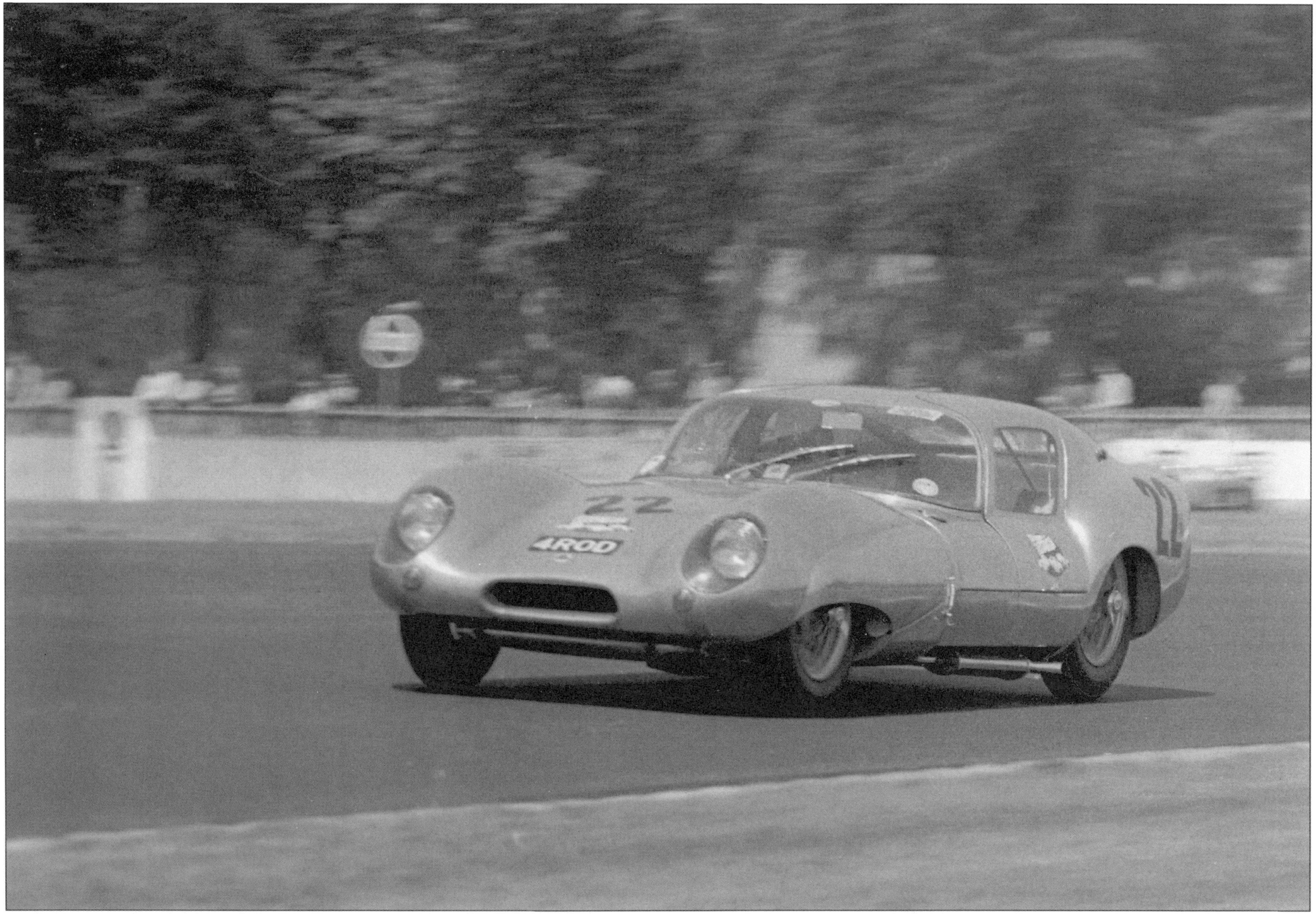

Chris Drake driving a 1098cc Lotus 11 at the 1977 re-opening of Donington Park.

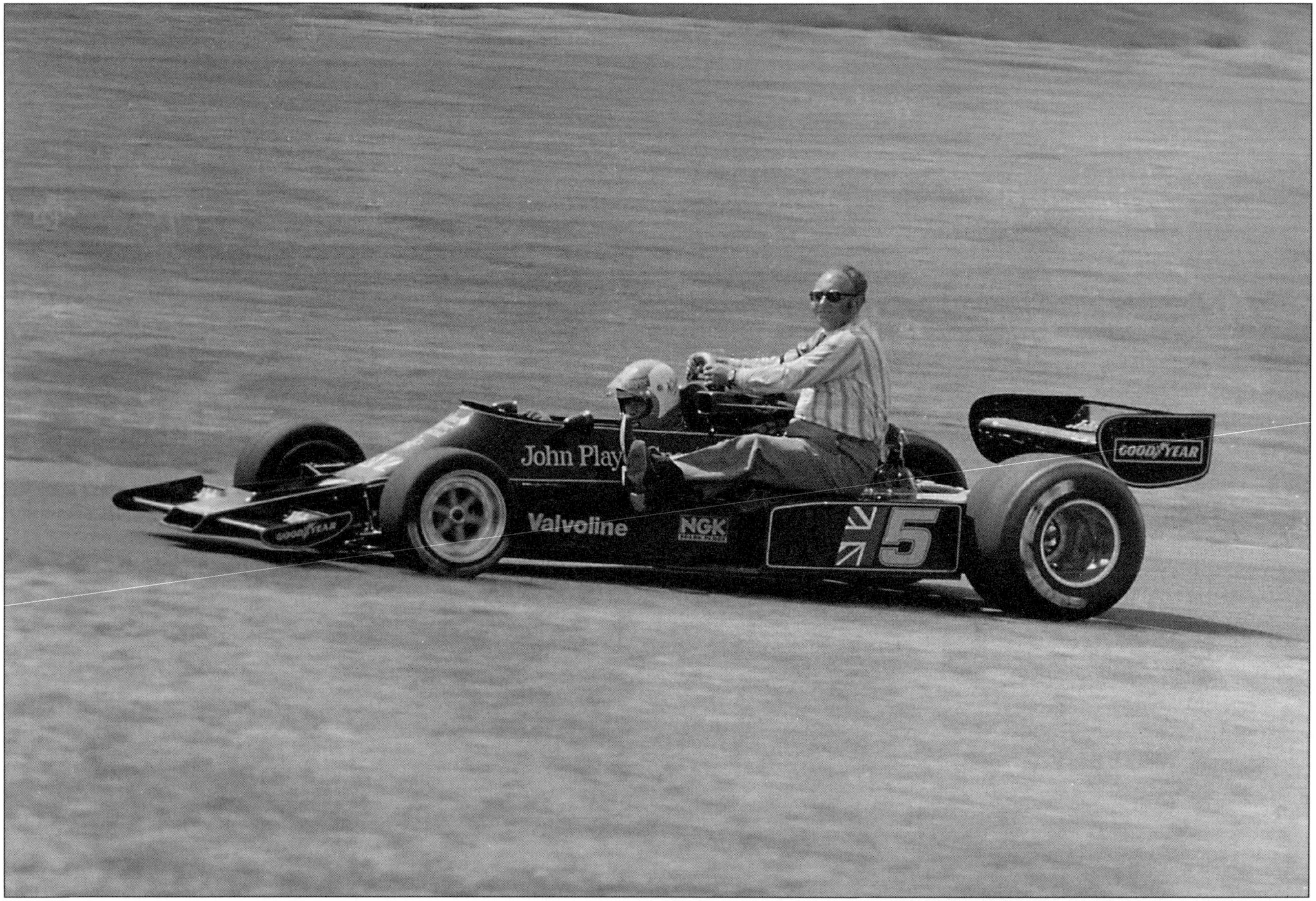

Gunnar Nilsson, in a John Player Special Lotus 78, drives circuit owner Tom Wheatcroft round Donington Park to officially open the newly rebuilt circuit on May 28, 1977.

1977 British Grand Prix at Silverstone. Mario Andretti driving John Player Special 78/3, with a Ford Cosworth DFV V-8 engine. Andretti retired in lap 62 when the engine seized.

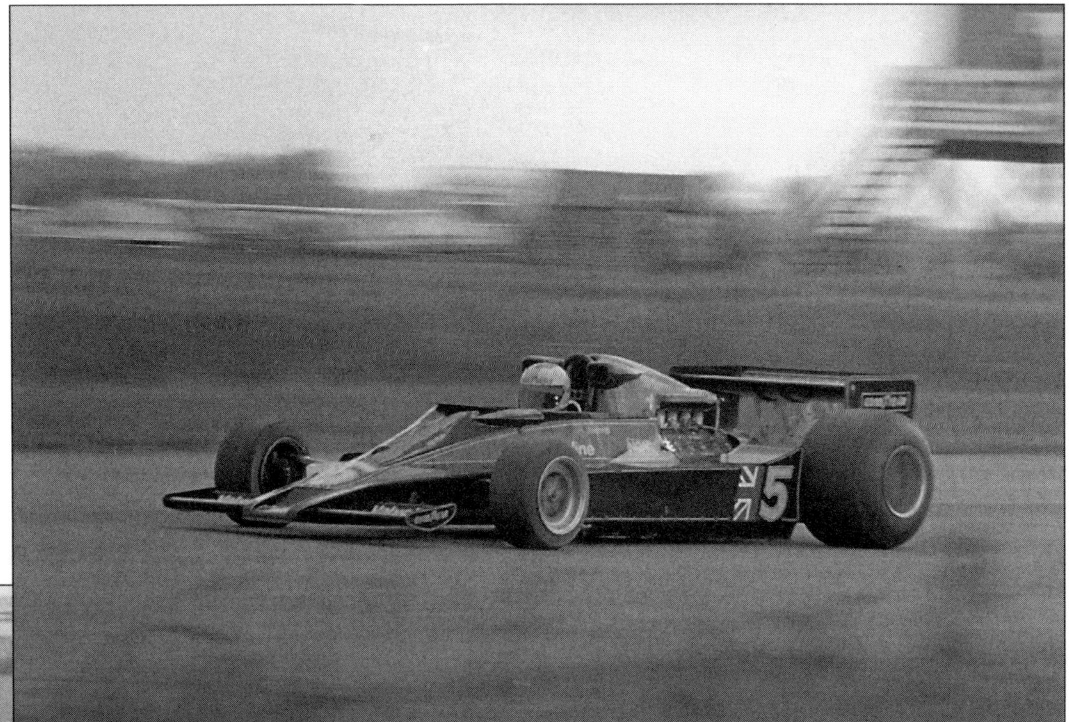

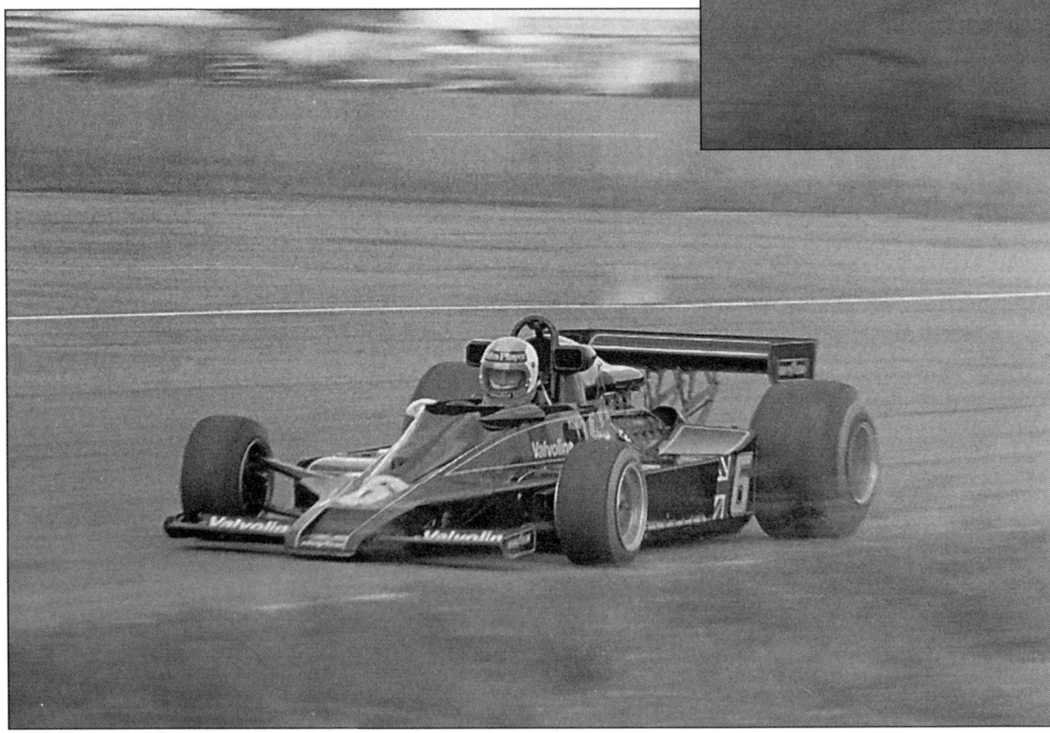

Gunnar Nilsson in John Player Special 78/2 put on a great display to finish in third place overall.

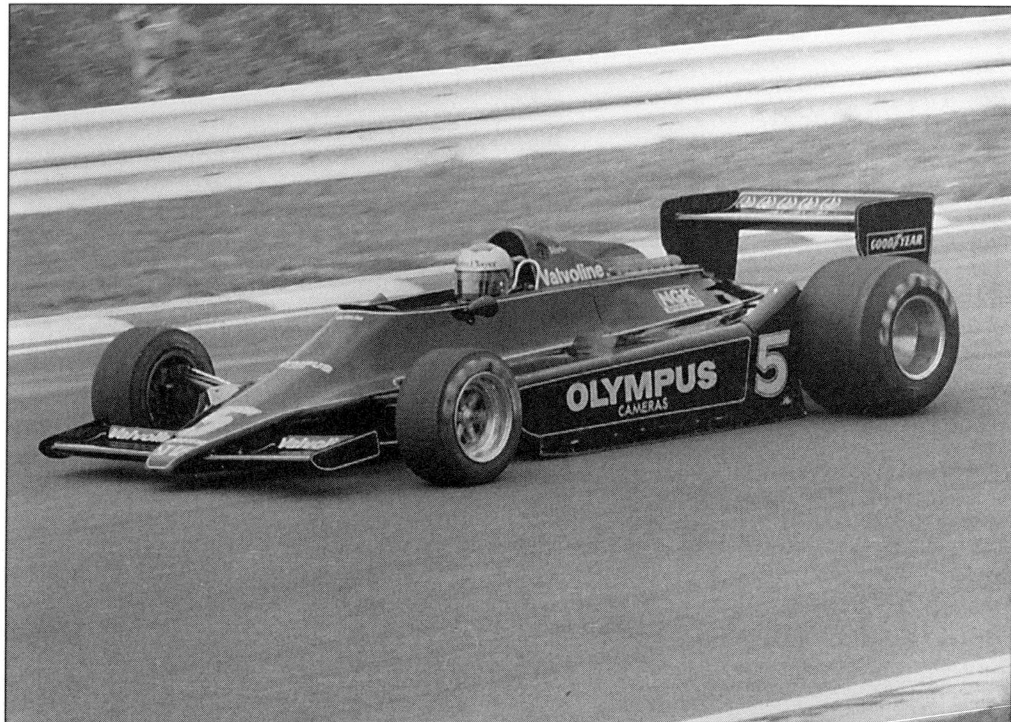

1978 British Grand Prix at Brands Hatch. Mario Andretti driving Lotus 79/3, with 3-liter Ford Cosworth DFV V-8. Andretti led the race for more than twenty laps until he succumbed to a blown engine.

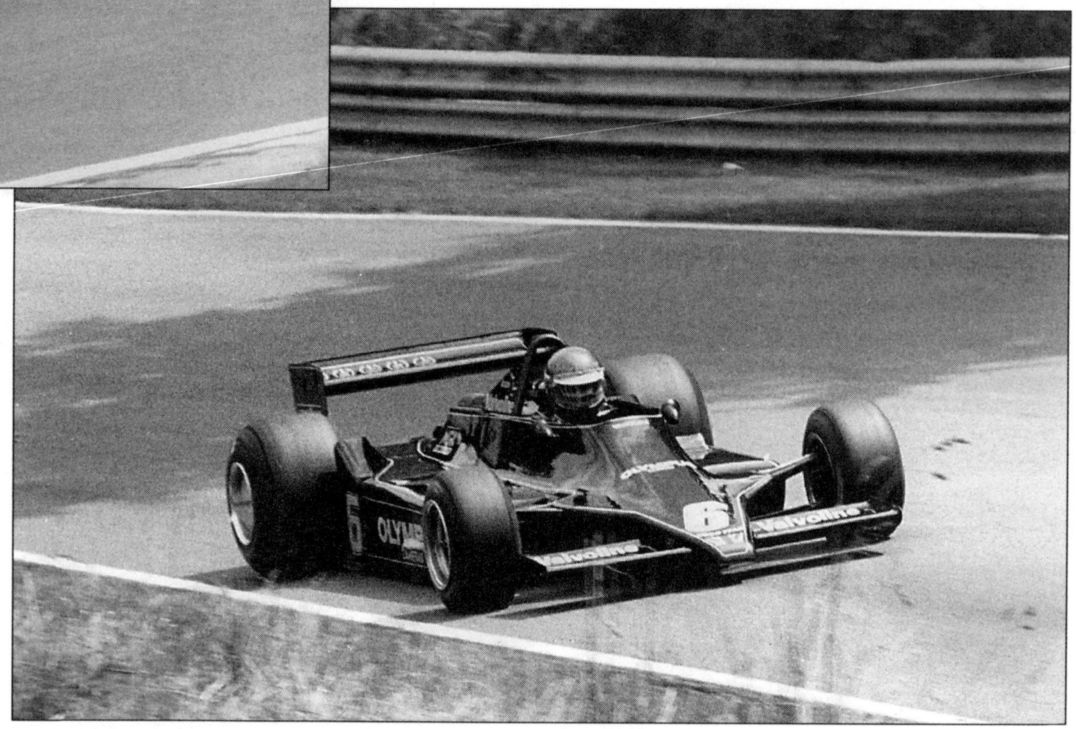

Ronnie Peterson, in Lotus 79/2, was uncatchable during practice, but during the race his fuel pump failed on the sixth lap.

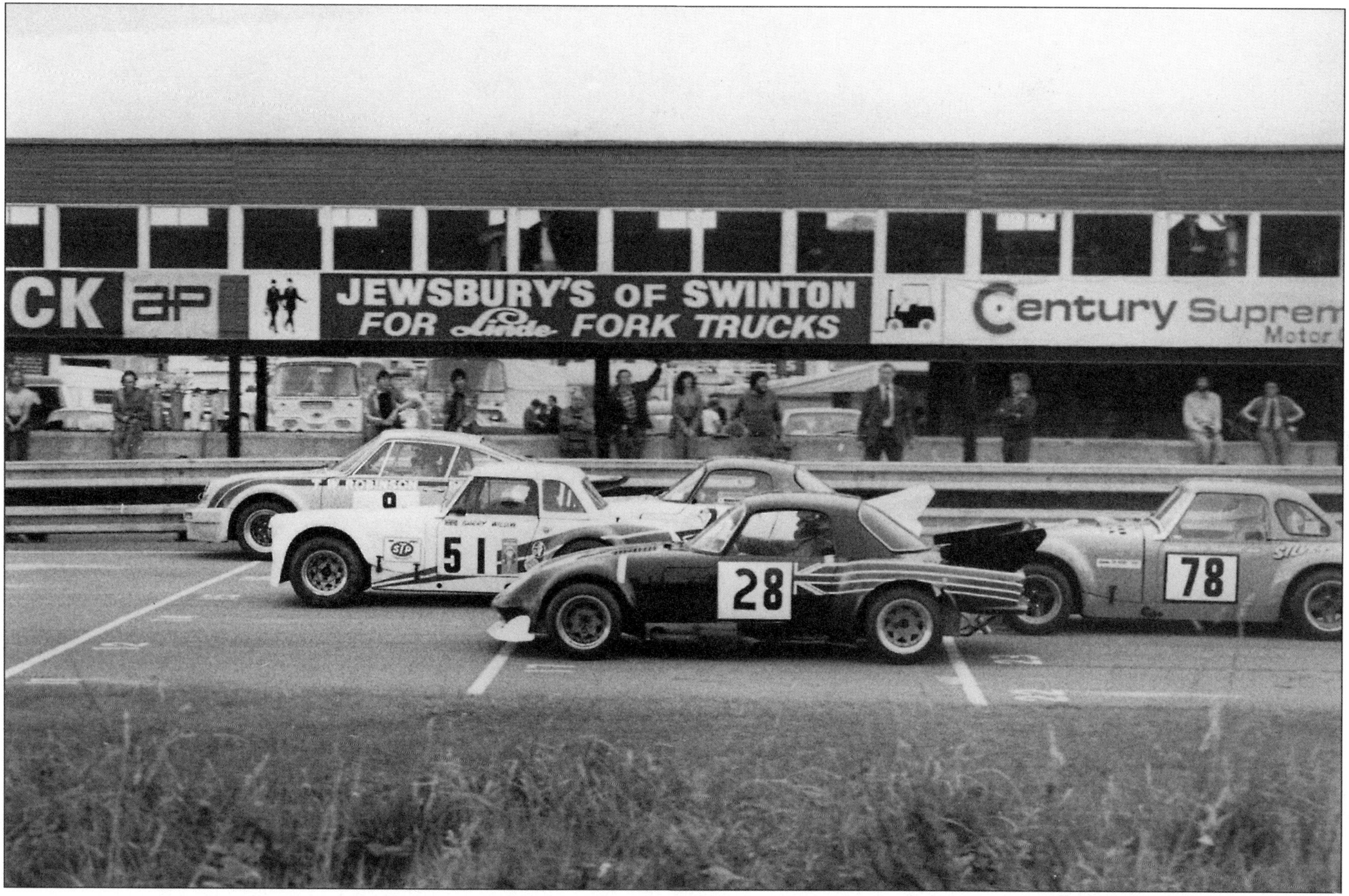

A much modified Lotus 36 waiting to start in the 1979 Mod Sports Car Race at Oulton Park.

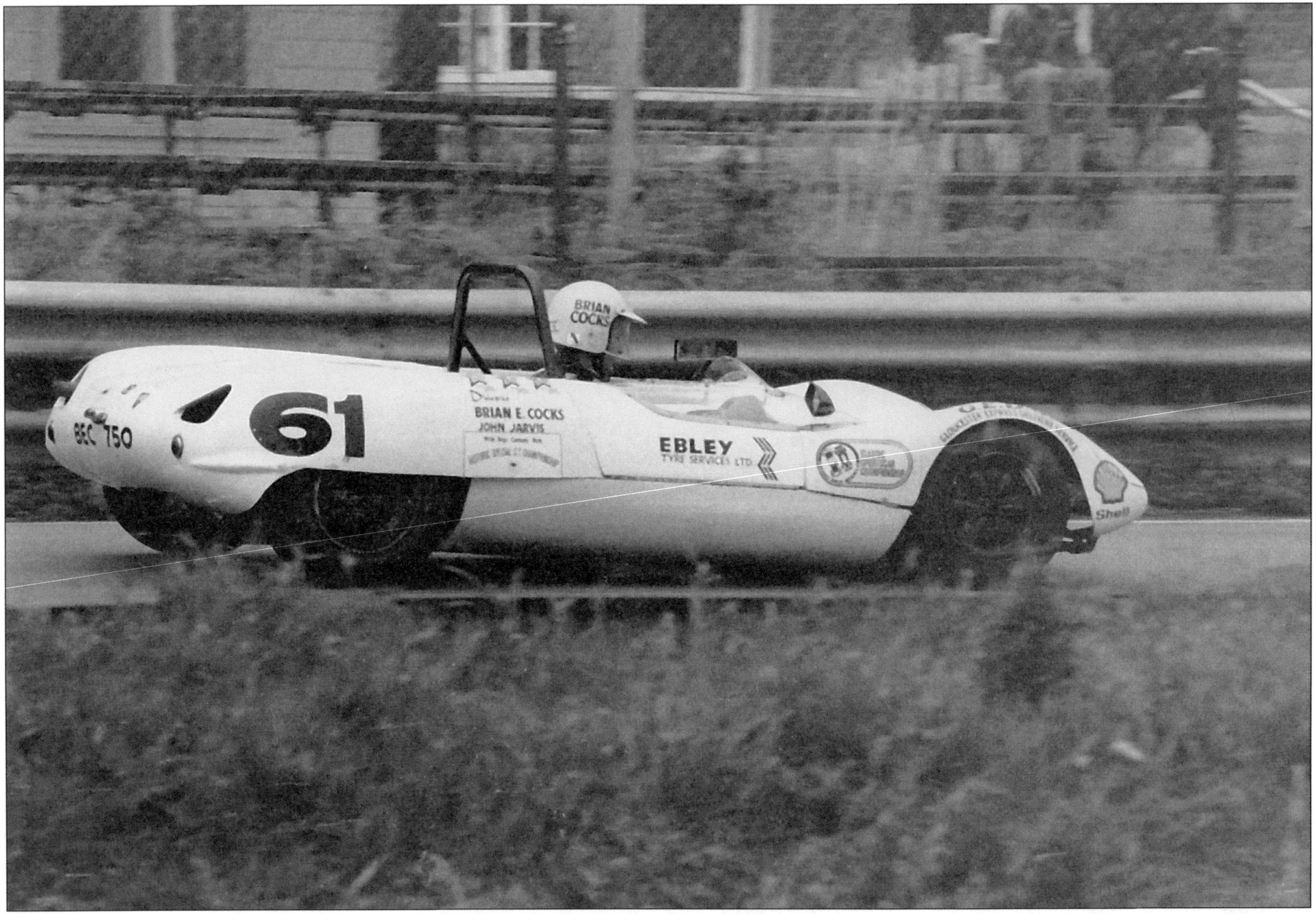

Brian Cocks' Lotus 23 approaching Lodge Corner at Oulton Park in 1979.

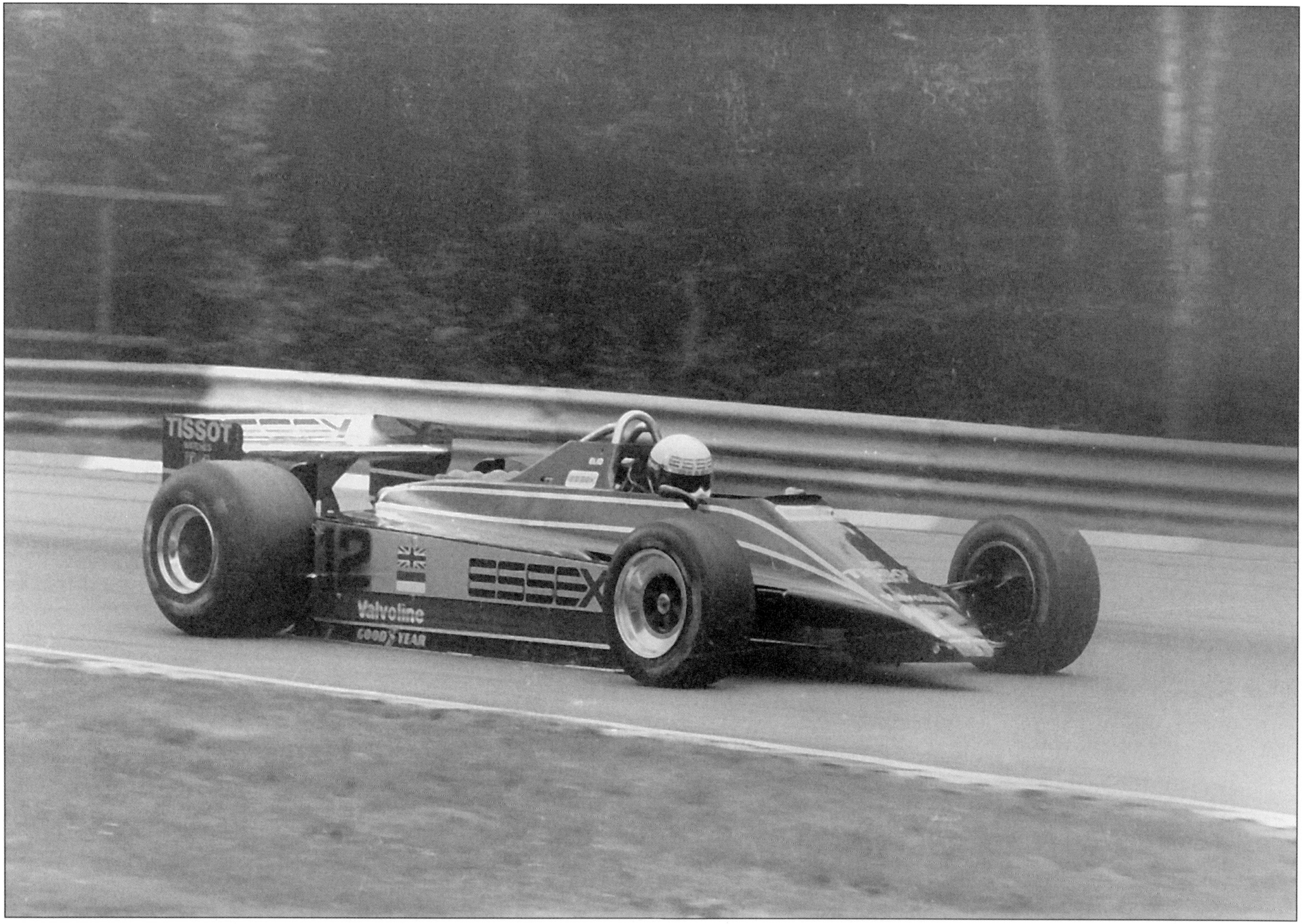

Elio de Angelis driving Essex Lotus 81/1, powered by a 3-liter Ford Cosworth DFV V-8, retired early in the 1980 British Grand Prix at Brands Hatch with a broken rear cross member.

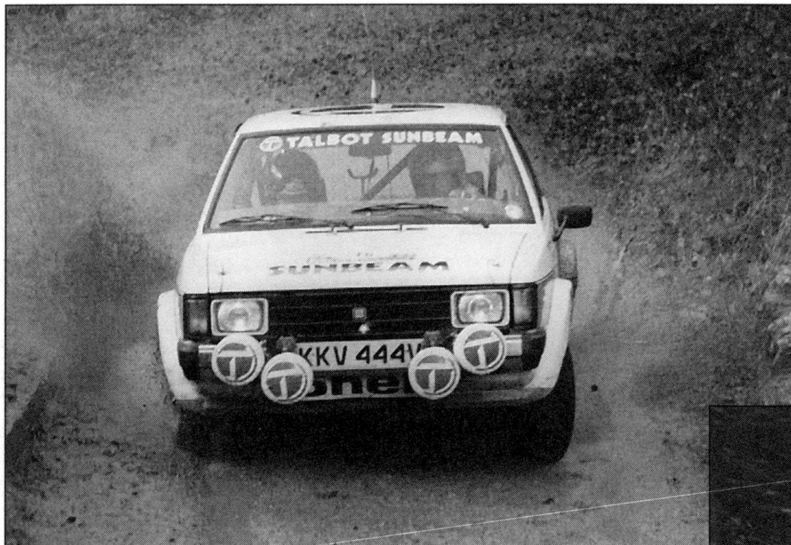

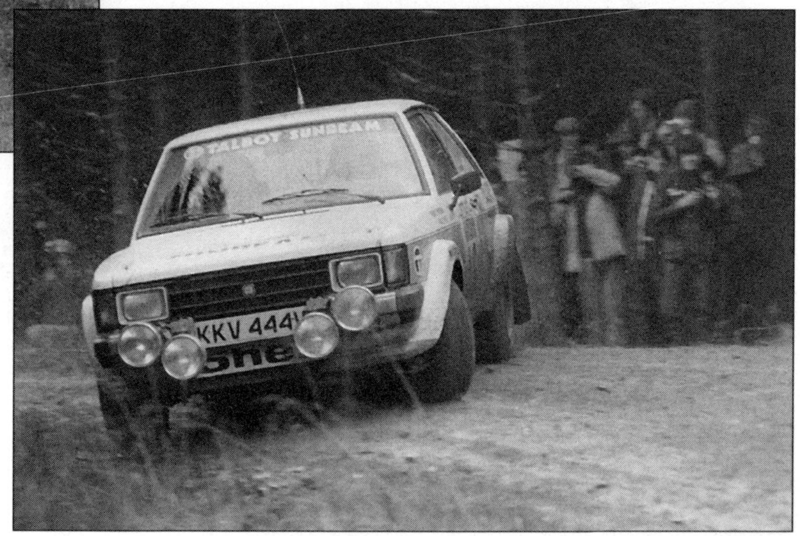

Two shots of Henry Toivonen and Paul White driving a Talbot Sunbeam Lotus through Greystokes Forest in the Lake District on their way to win the 1980 Lombard RAC Rally of Great Britain.

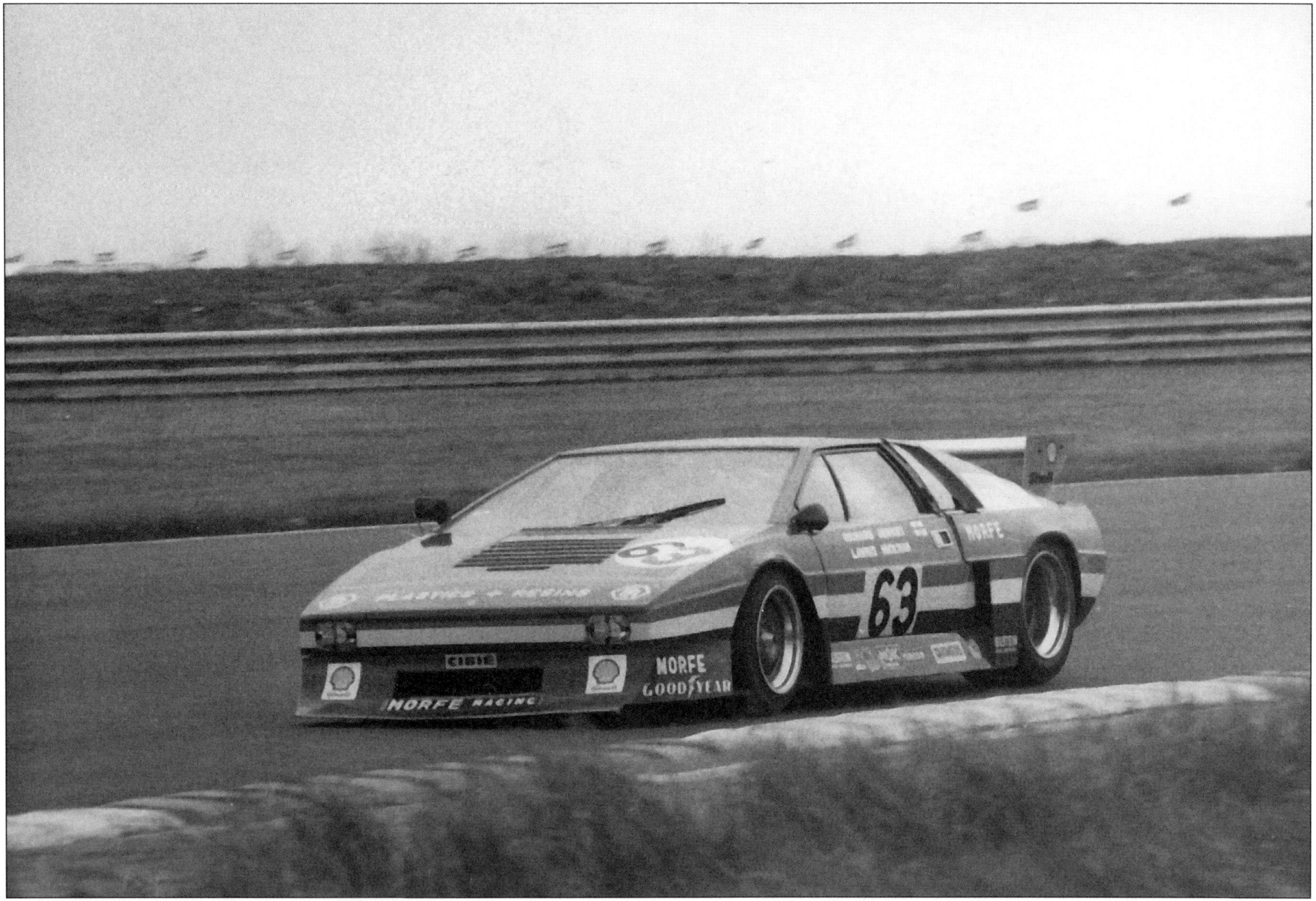

1981 Silverstone World Endurance Sports Car Race. Richard Jenvey and Lawrie Hickinan in a 2-liter Lotus Esprit. The car did not start the race after the engine exploded during practice.

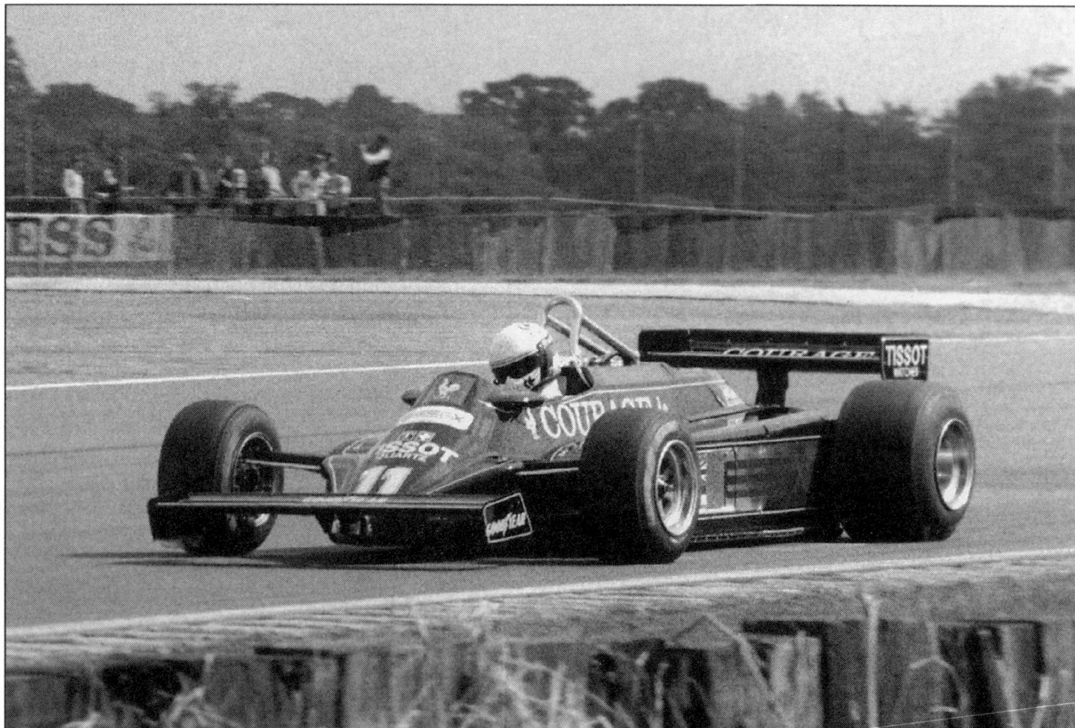

1981 British Grand Prix at Silverstone. Elio de Angelis driving 3-liter John Player Special Lotus 87/3 was black flagged during the race for overtaking another car under two yellow flags. De Angelis got out of his car and took no further part in the race.

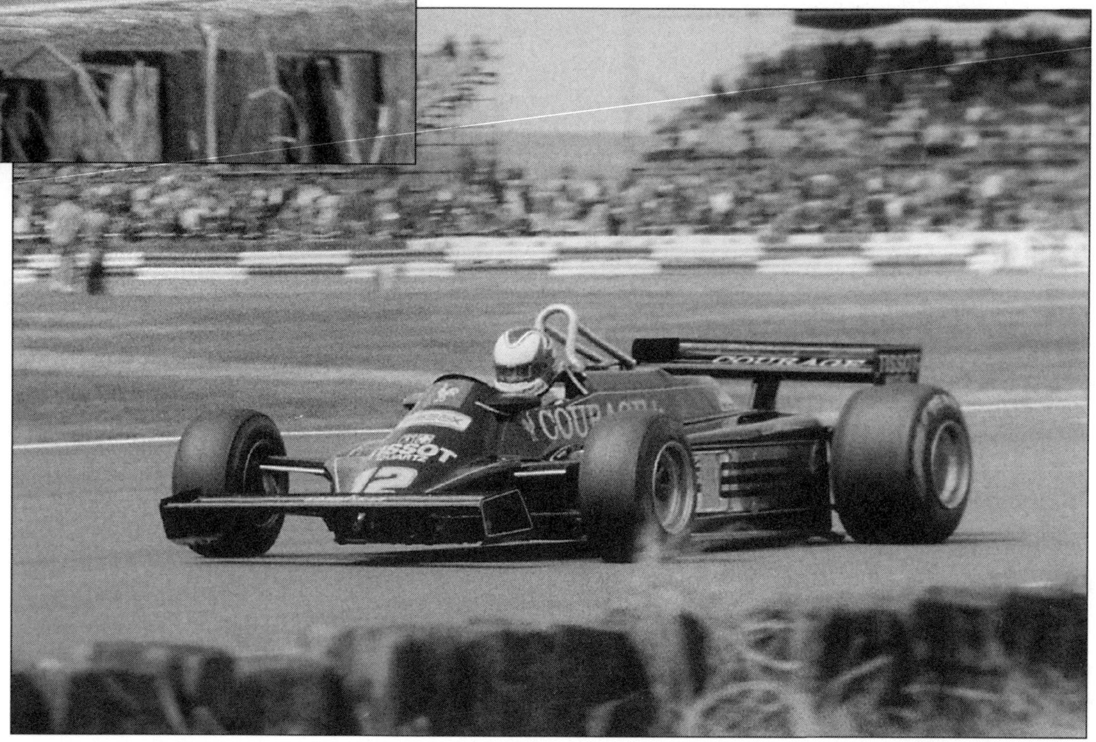

Nigel Mansell in Lotus 87/2. Mansell should have been racing the new Type 88B, but the car was banned after Thursday's practice. Mansell was unable to qualify the type 87 into the race.

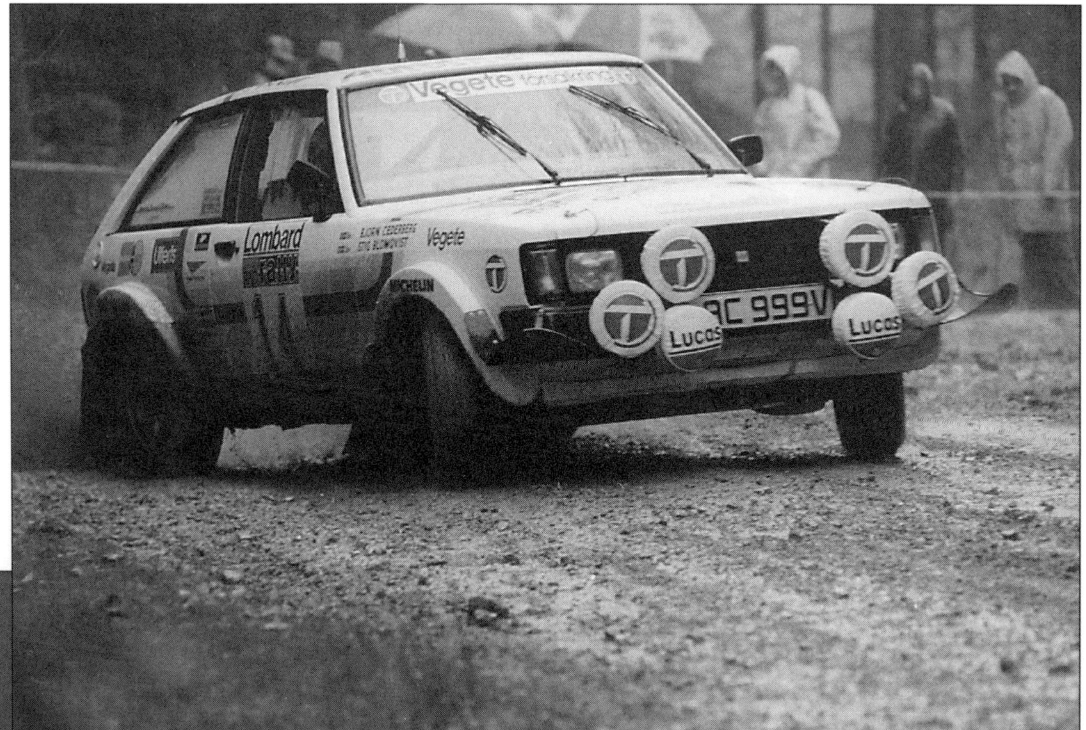

1981 Lombard RAC Rally. Stig Blomquist and Bjorn Cederberg's Talbot Sunbeam Lotus finished in third place. This ensured that Talbot Sunbeam Lotus Team took the World Makes Championship.

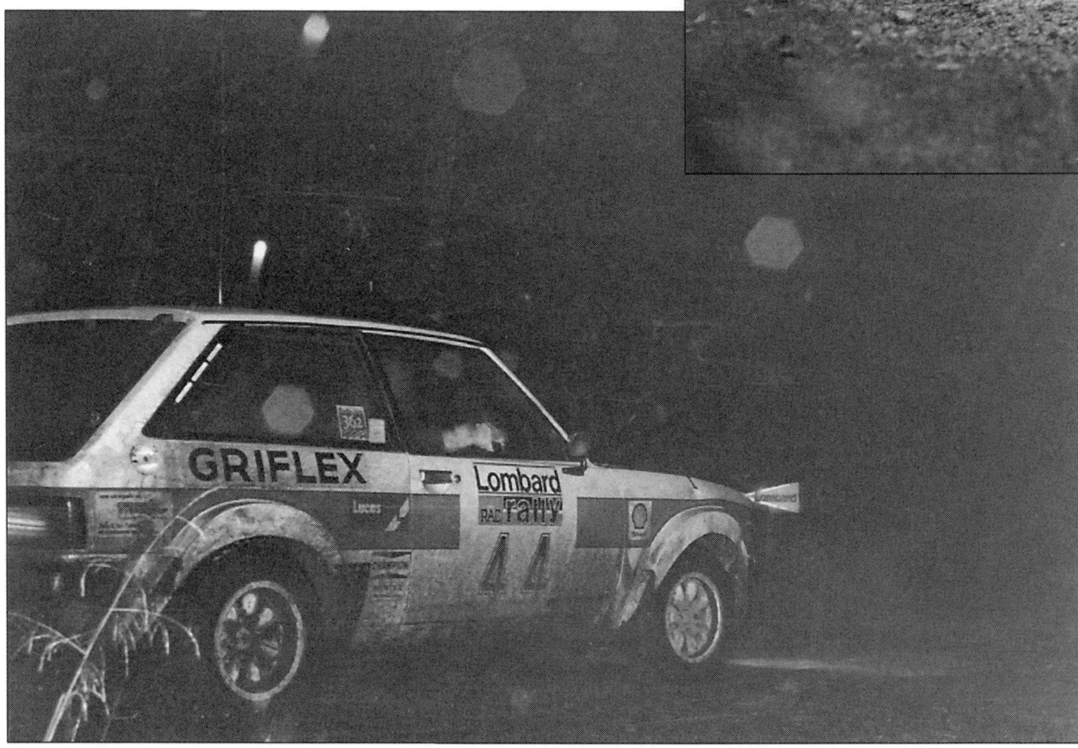

Night time and very wet in Kershope Forrest with Chris Lord and Ernest Waldron's Talbot Sunbeam Lotus. They finished thirteenth overall.

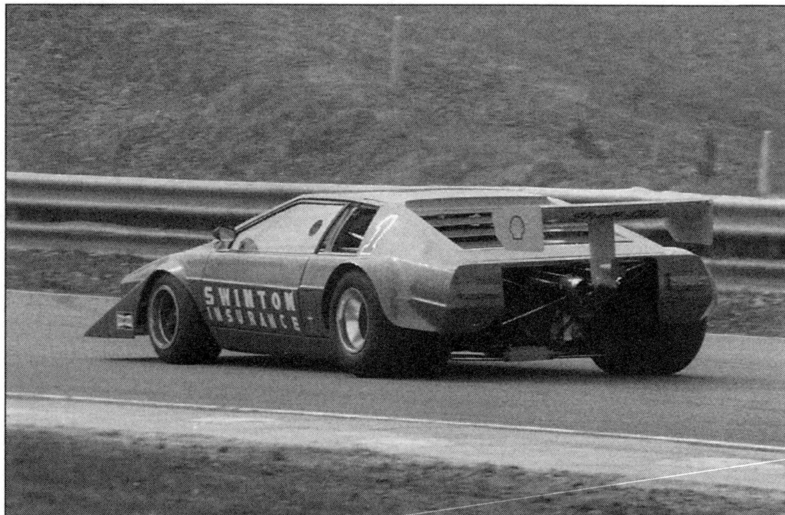

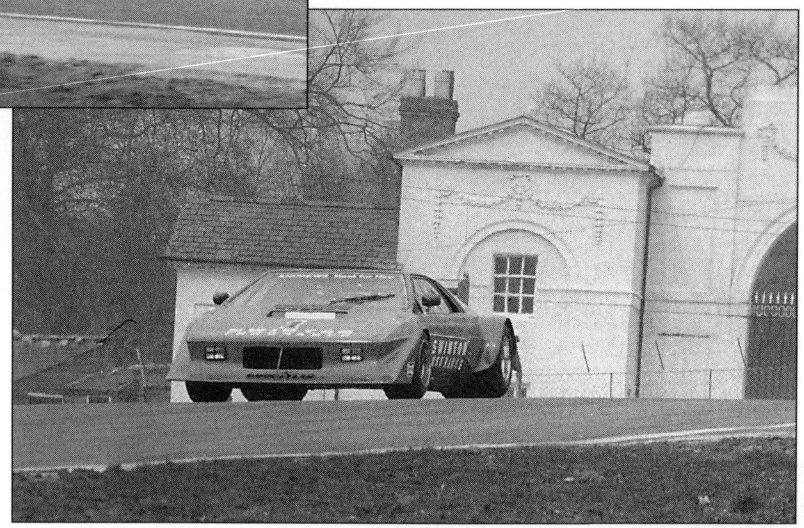

Two views of George "Welly" Potter's 7200cc Lotus Esprit in the GT Challenge at Oulton Park in 1982. Potter finished in second place.

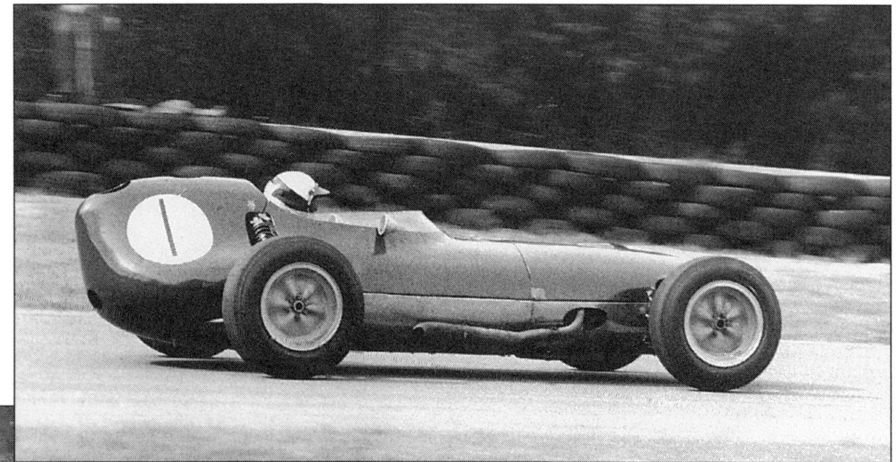

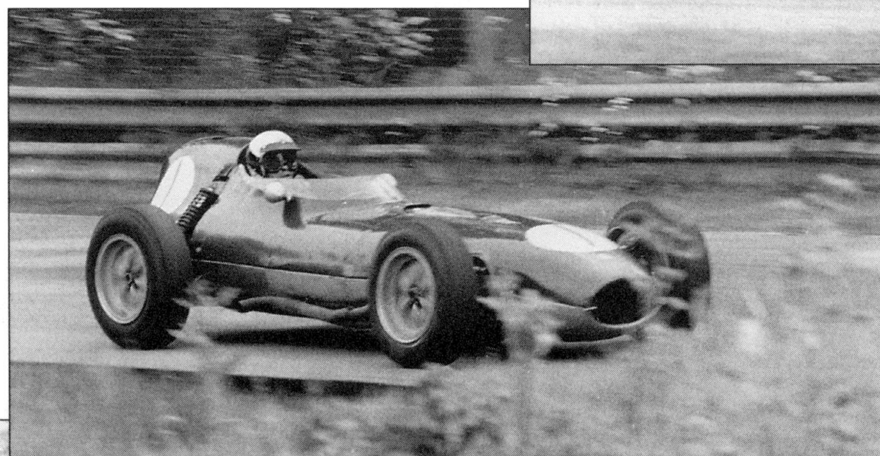

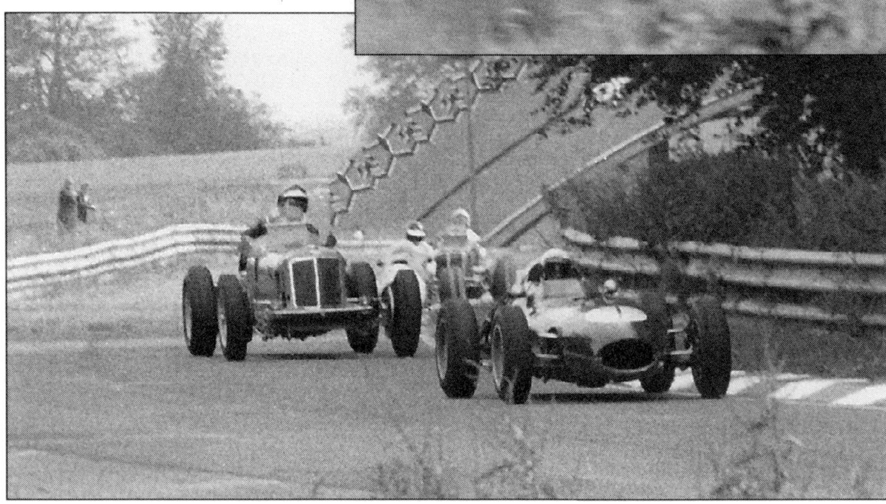

Three views of Bruce Halford driving a 2.5-liter Lotus 16 in the Allcomers Race at the 1982 Richard Seaman Trophy Races, Oulton Park. Halford went on to win.

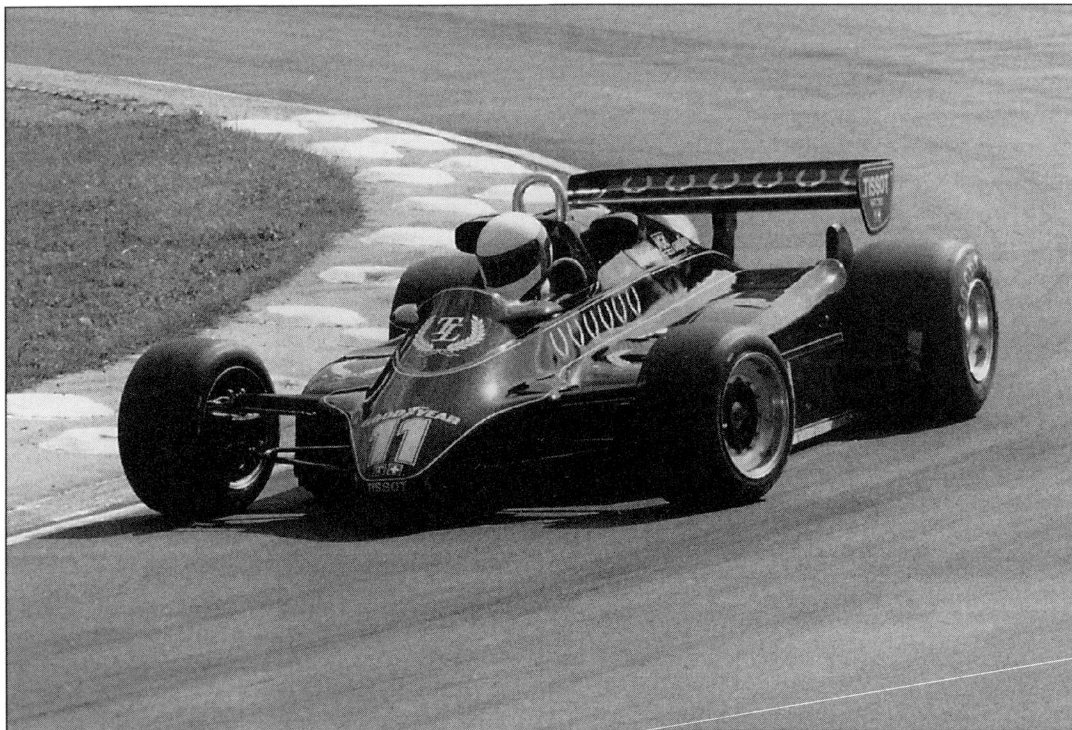

1982 British Grand Prix at Brands Hatch. Elio de Angelis' John Player Special Lotus 91/8 was in third place until the last lap, but an engine misfire intervened — dropping him to fourth place overall.

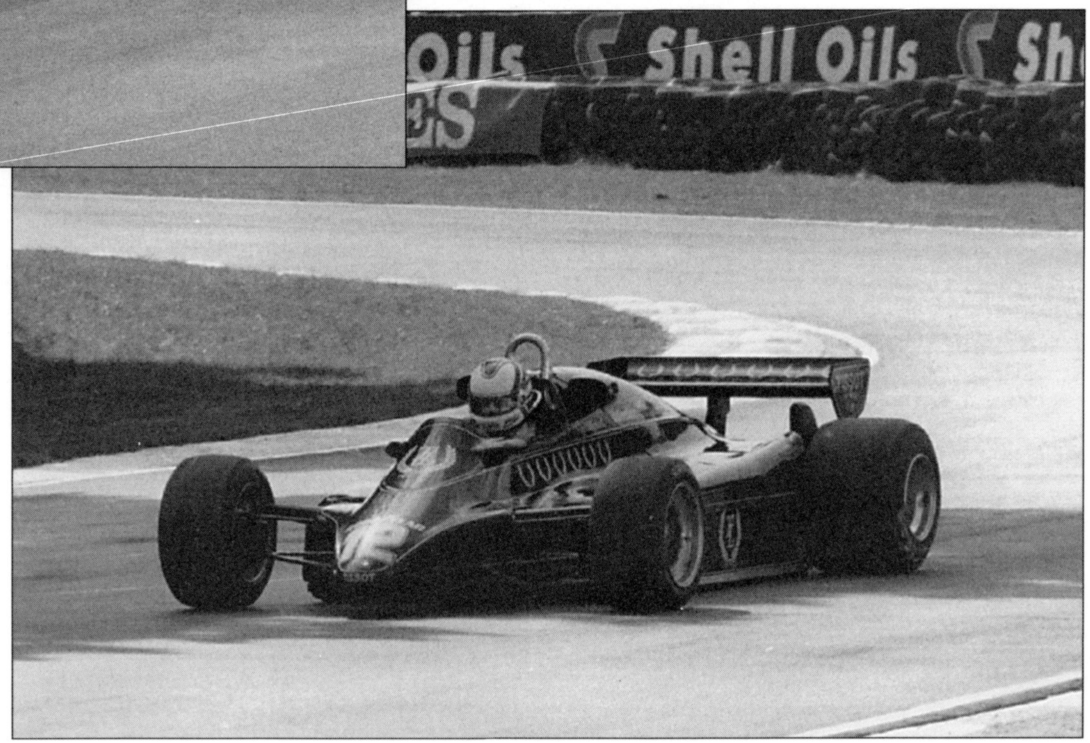

Nigel Mansell driving John Player Special Lotus 91/7. An injured arm forced him to retire during the race.

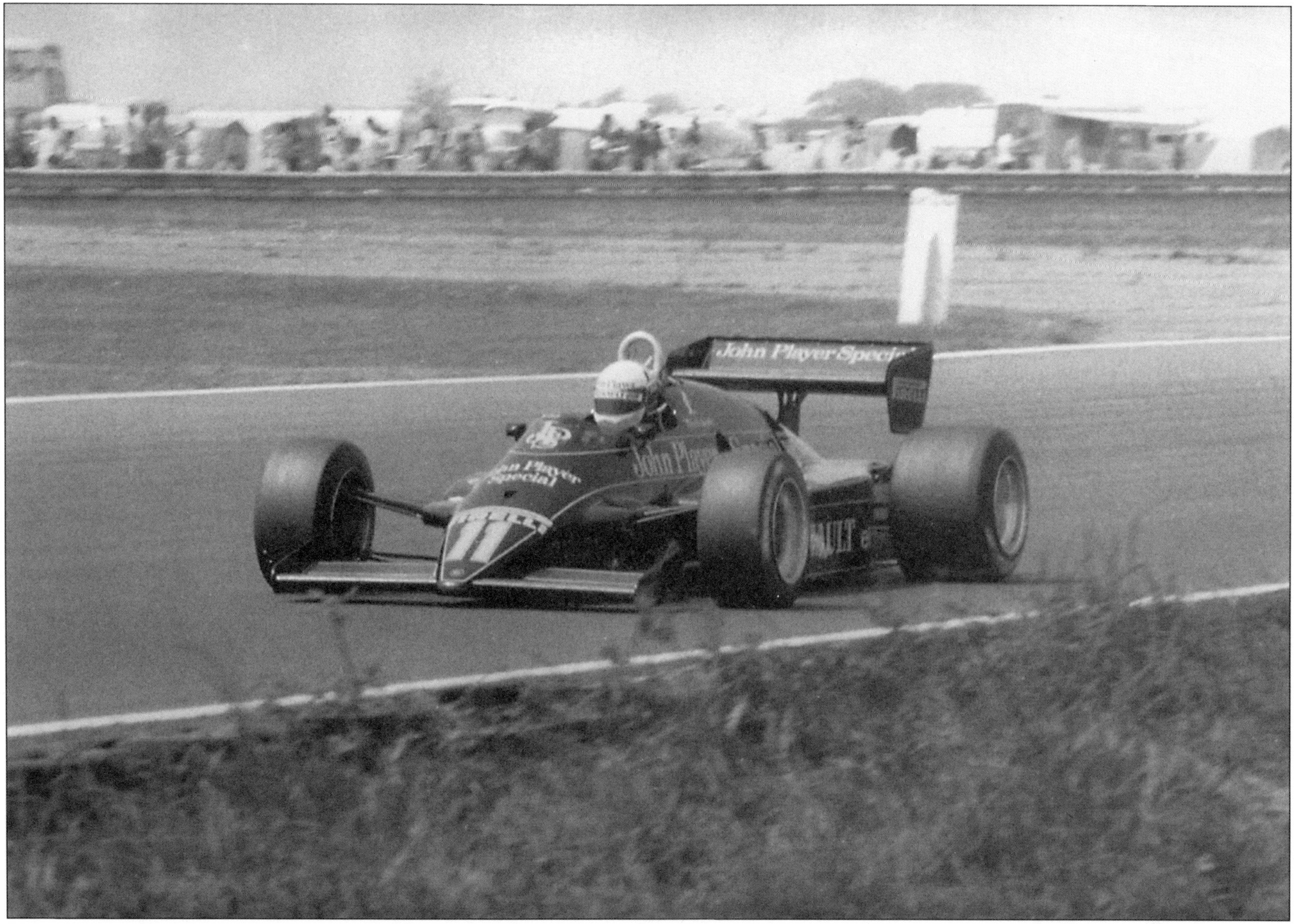

Elio de Angelis' 1.5-liter Lotus 94T/1 during the 1983 British Grand Prix at Silverstone. He retired in lap two with a broken turbocharger.

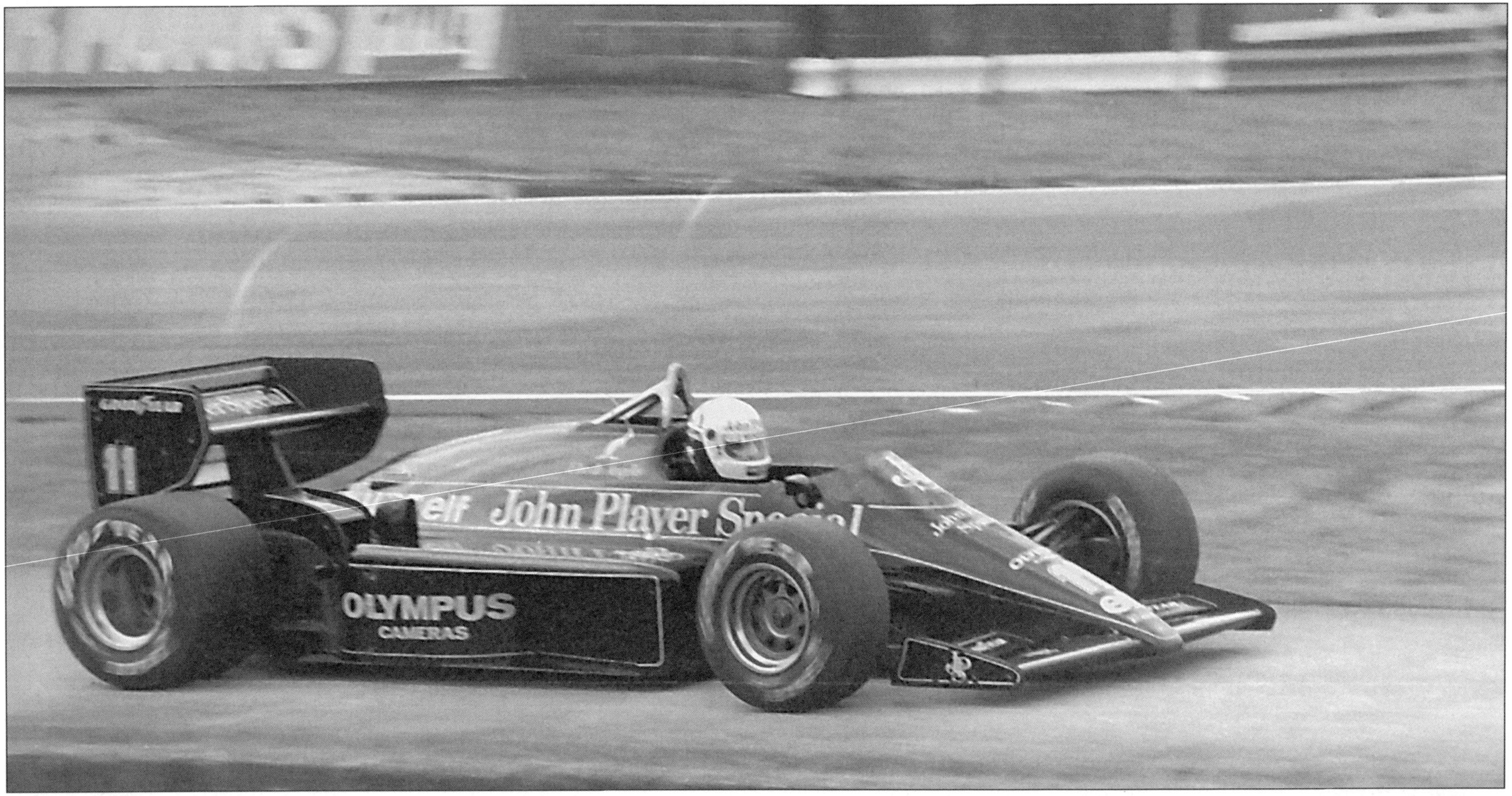

The 1.5-liter Lotus 97T/3 Renault V-6 Turbo of Elio de Angelis at the 1985 British Grand Prix, Silverstone. Having problems with his engine, he finished but was not classified.

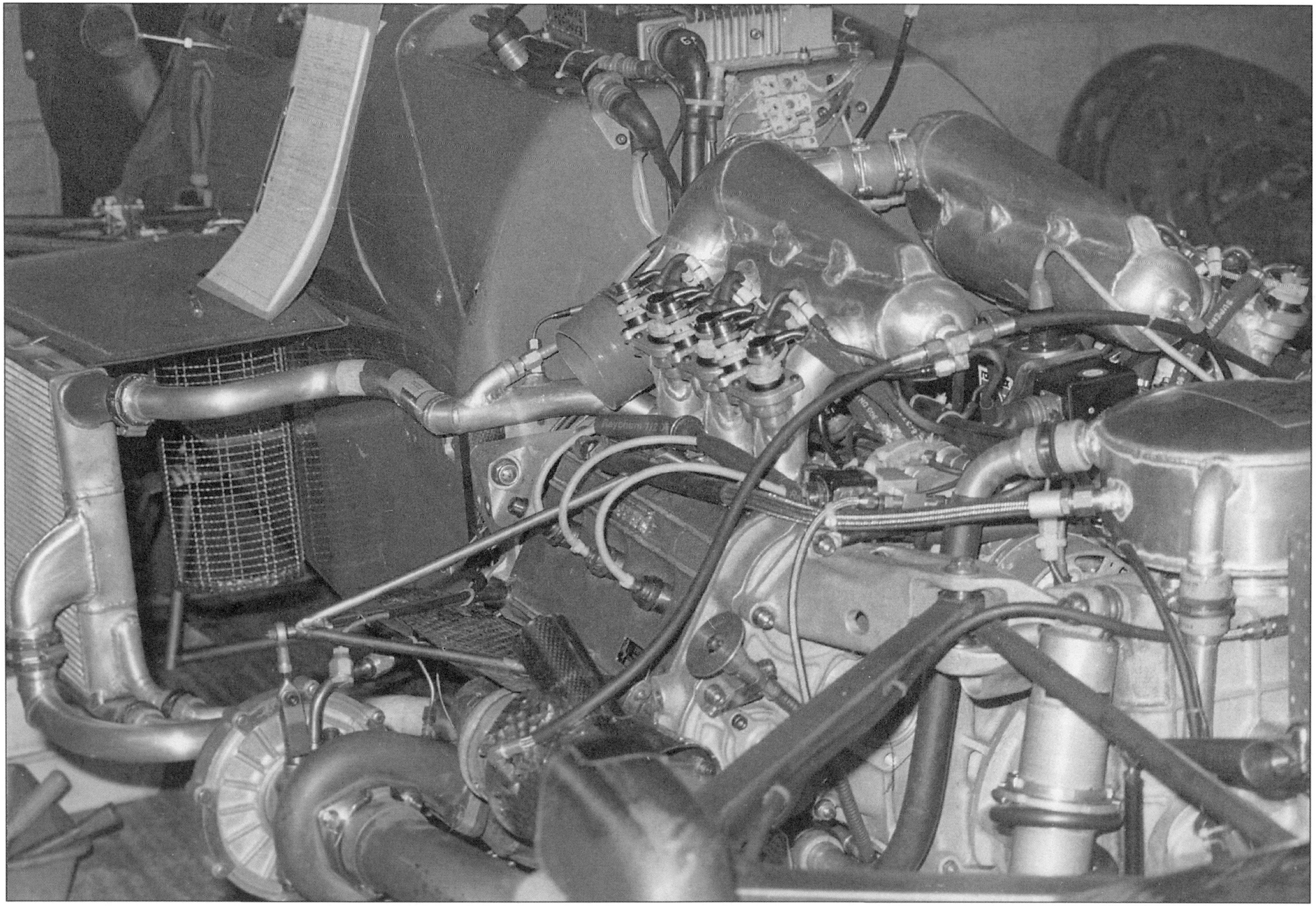

A close-up of the Renault V-6 Turbo engine used by Lotus cars in 1985.

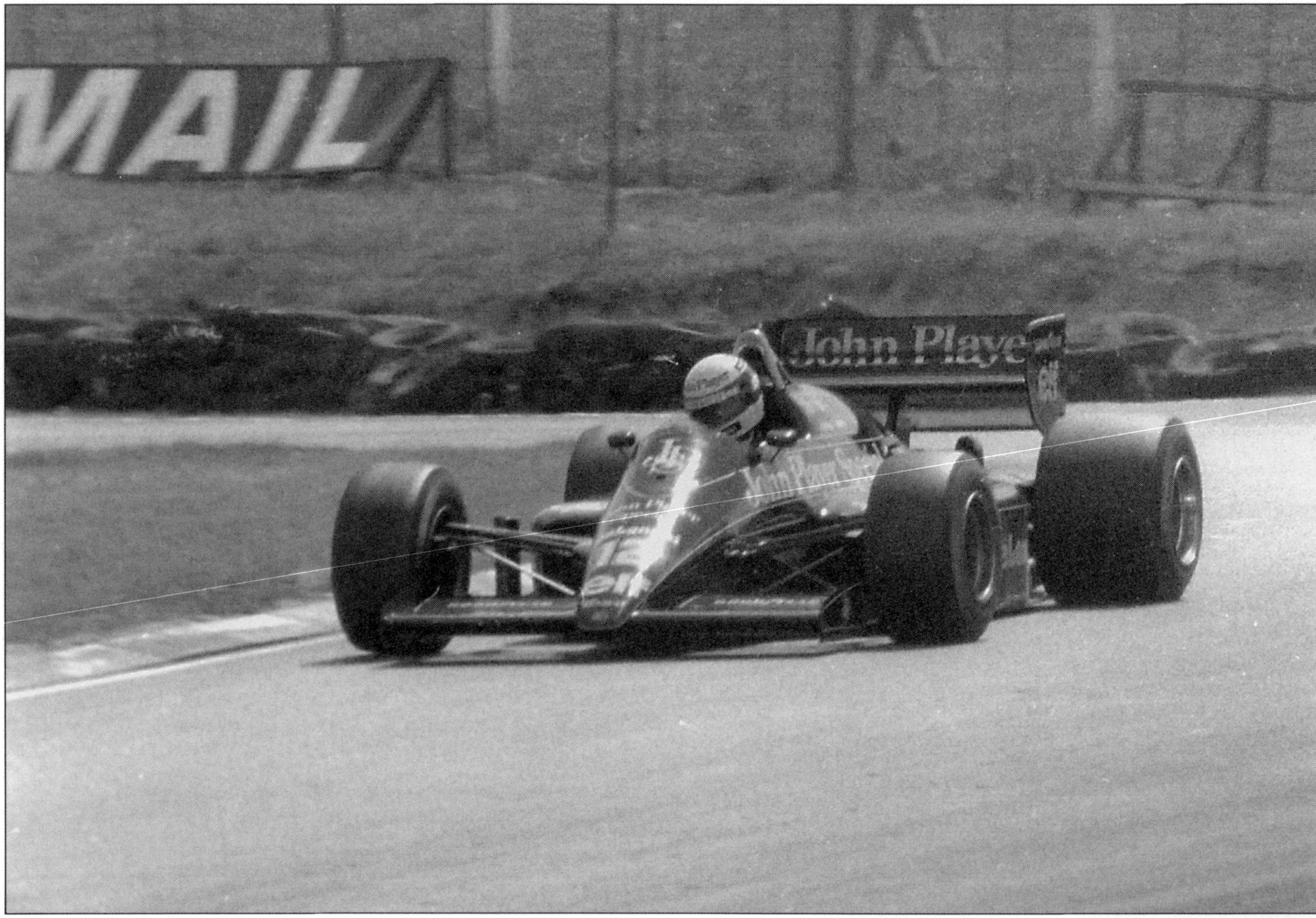

Aryton Senna's Lotus 98T/1, with the 1.5-liter Renault V-6 Turbo, at the 1986 British Grand Prix, Brands Hatch. Senna retired in lap 27 with transmission problems.

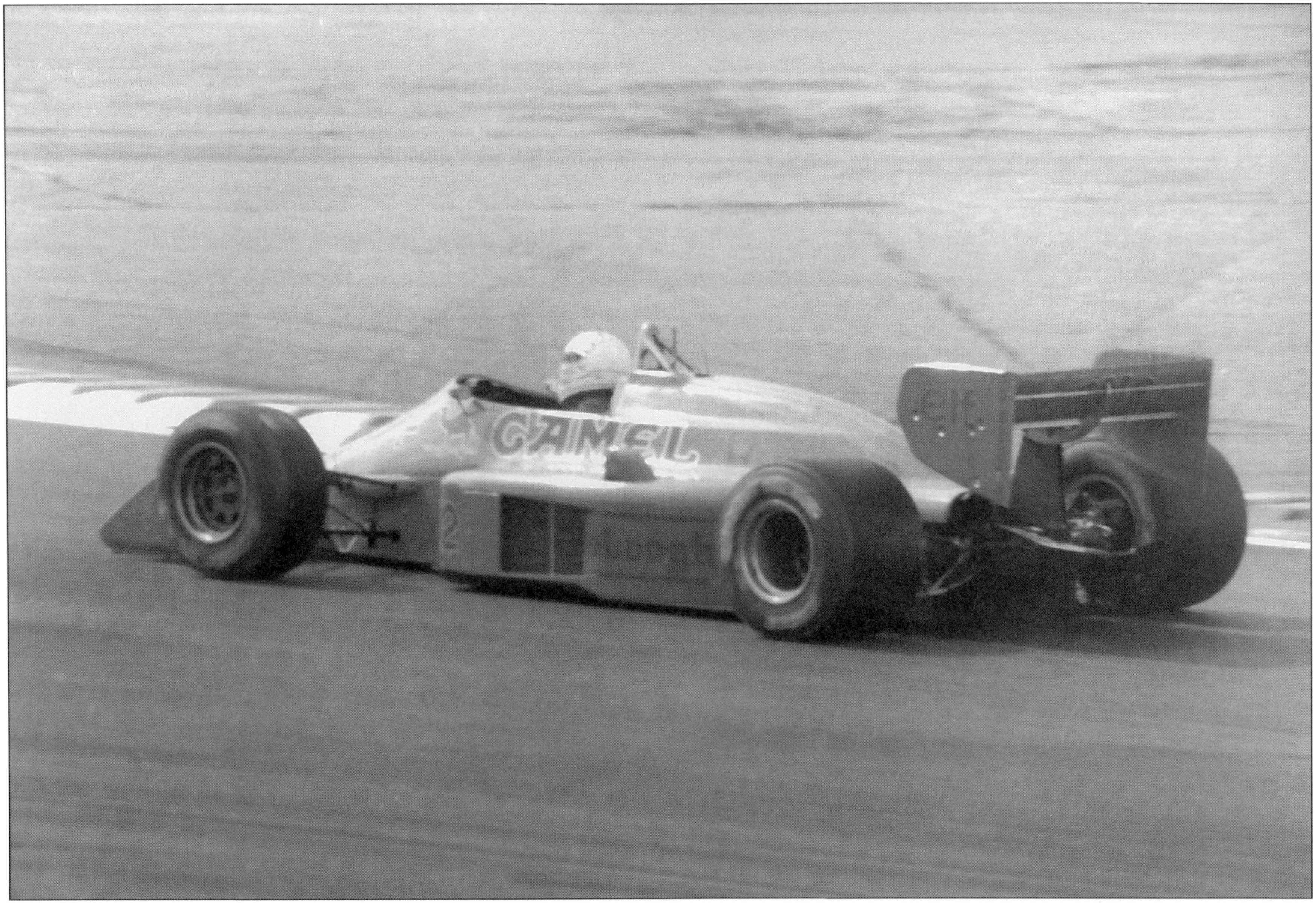

Satoru Nakajima driving Lotus 99T/5, with a 1.5-liter Honda V-6 turbo. Nakajima finished the Silverstone 1987 British Grand Prix in fourth place.

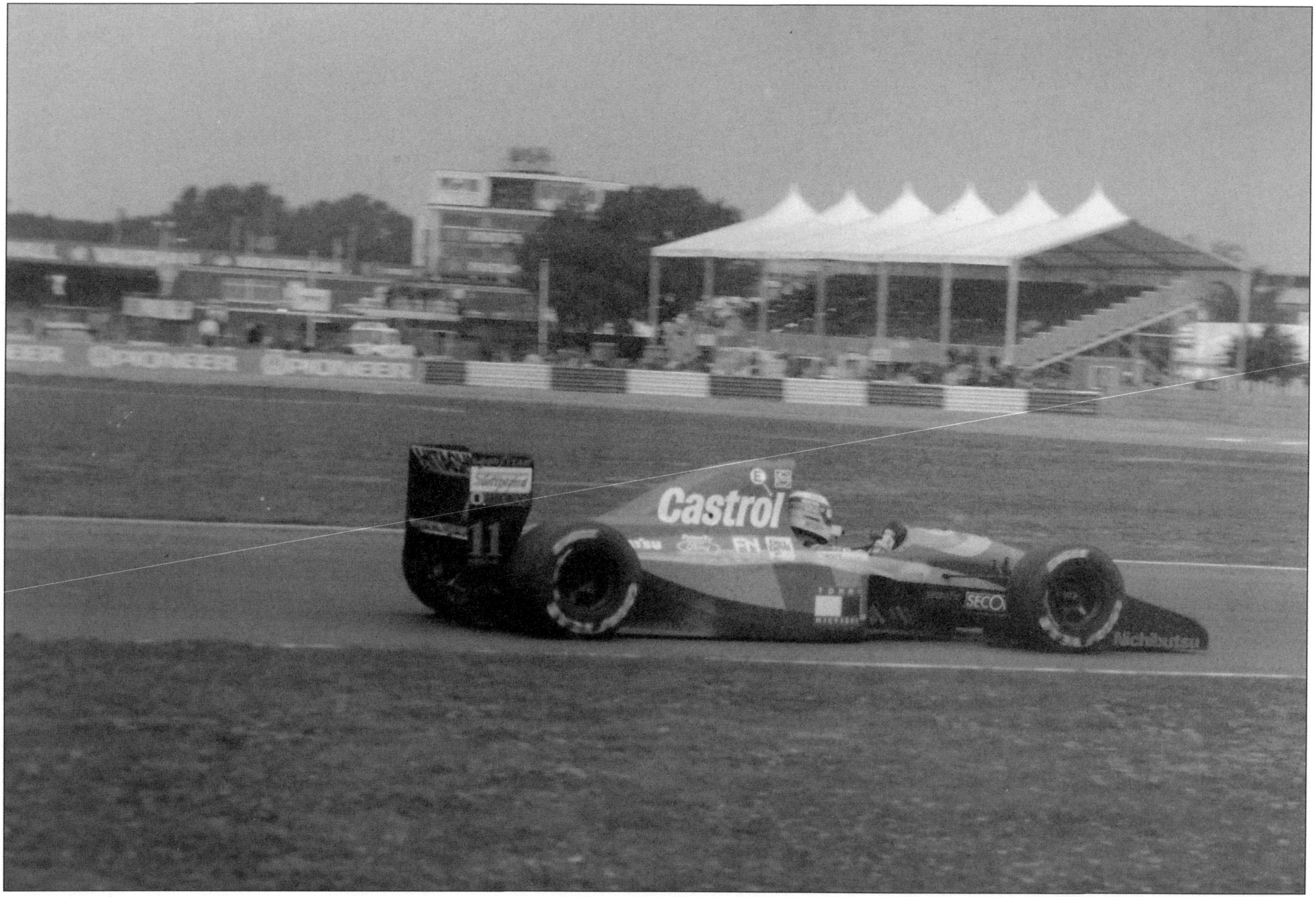

Mika Hakkinen's Lotus 107/2, powered by a 3.5-liter Ford HB V-8, finished the 1992 British Grand Prix at Silverstone, in sixth place.

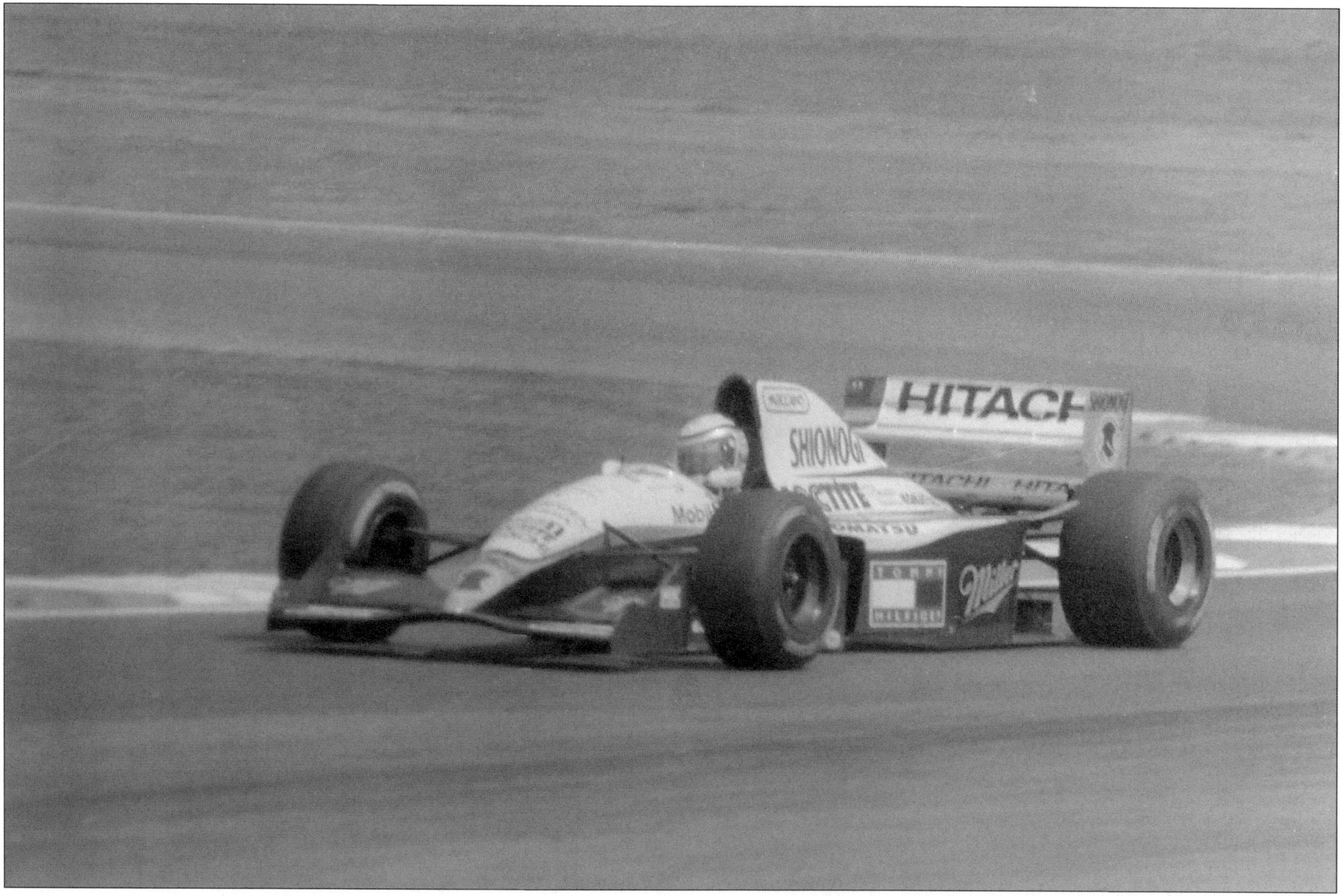

Allessandro Zanardi driving Lotus 109C/2, with a 3.5-liter Mugen Honda, during the 1994 British Grand Prix at Silverstone. Starting from the pit-lane due to an engine problem during the warm-up lap, he pulled off in lap 5 with a blown engine. This was the last season of Grand Prix racing for the Lotus Team.

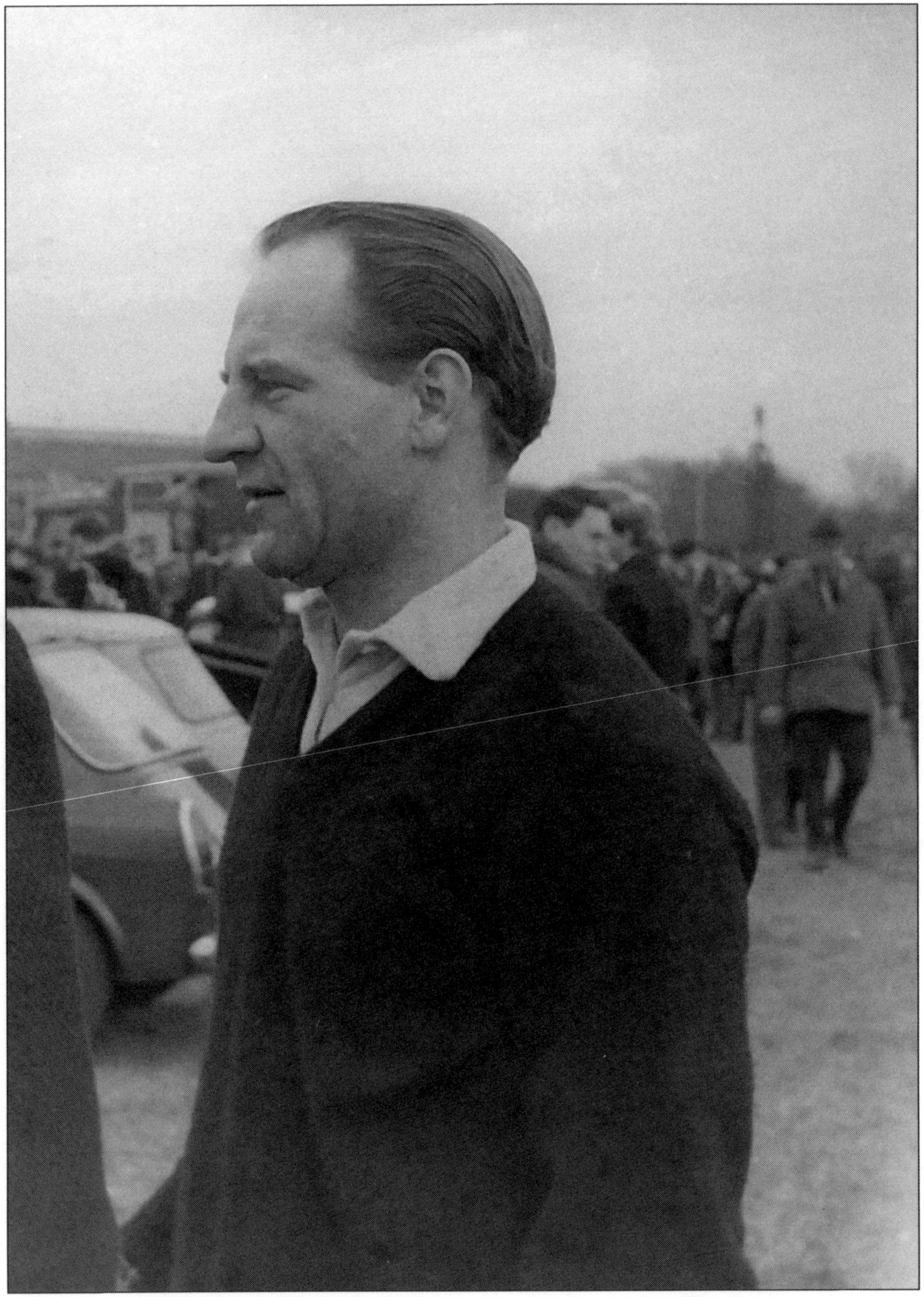

Innes Ireland.

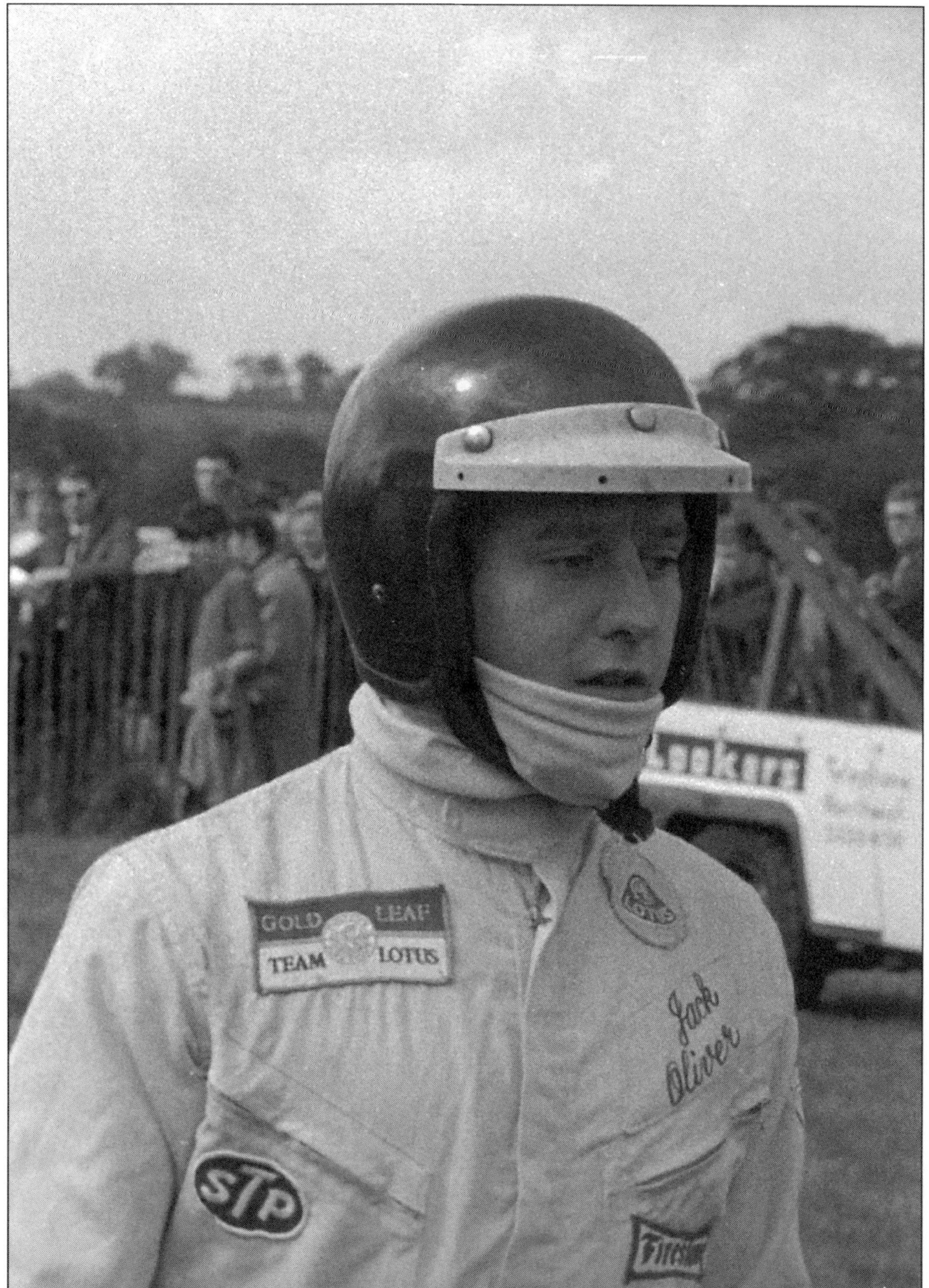

Jackie Oliver.

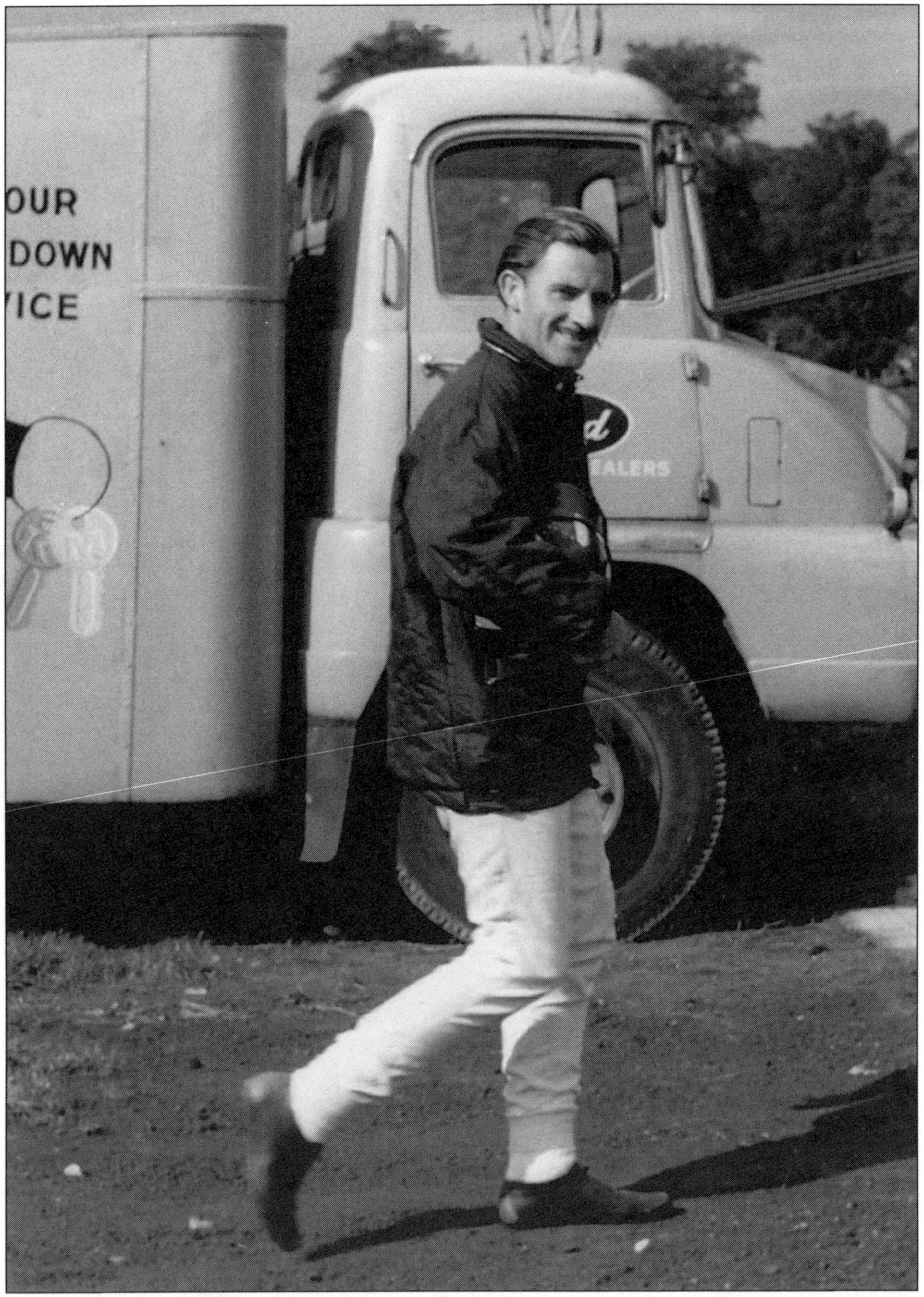

Graham Hill.

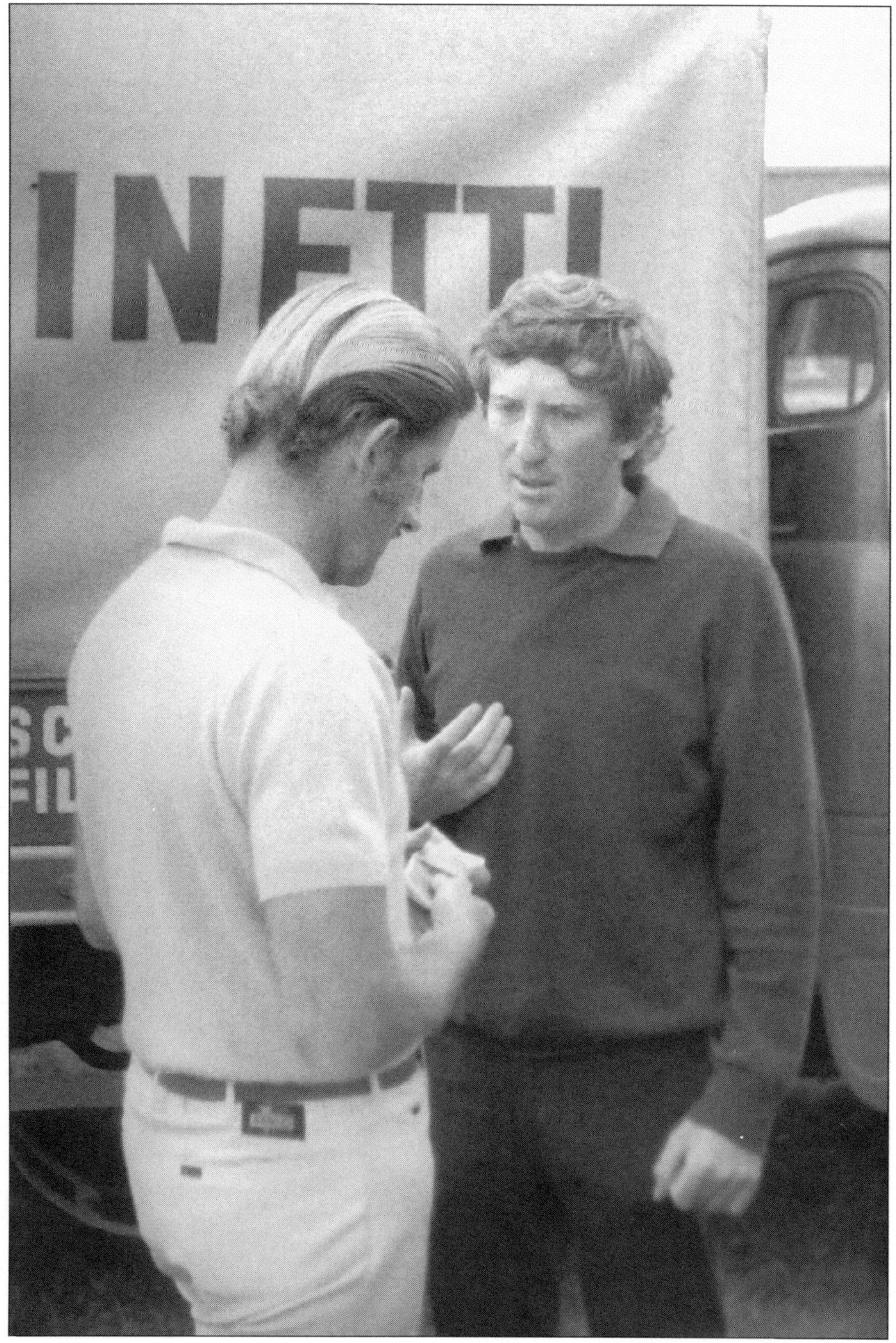

Jochen Rindt.

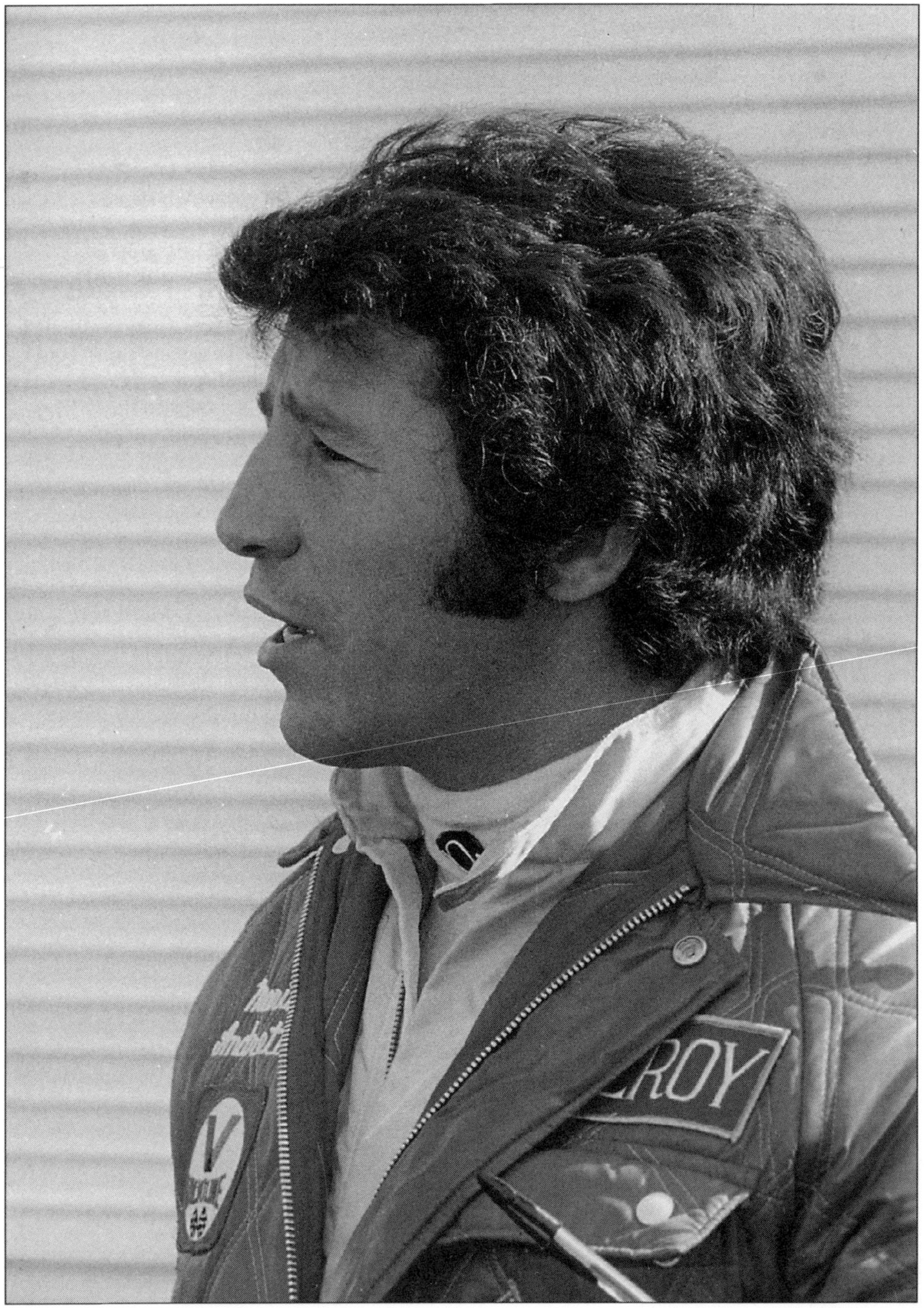

Mario Andretti.

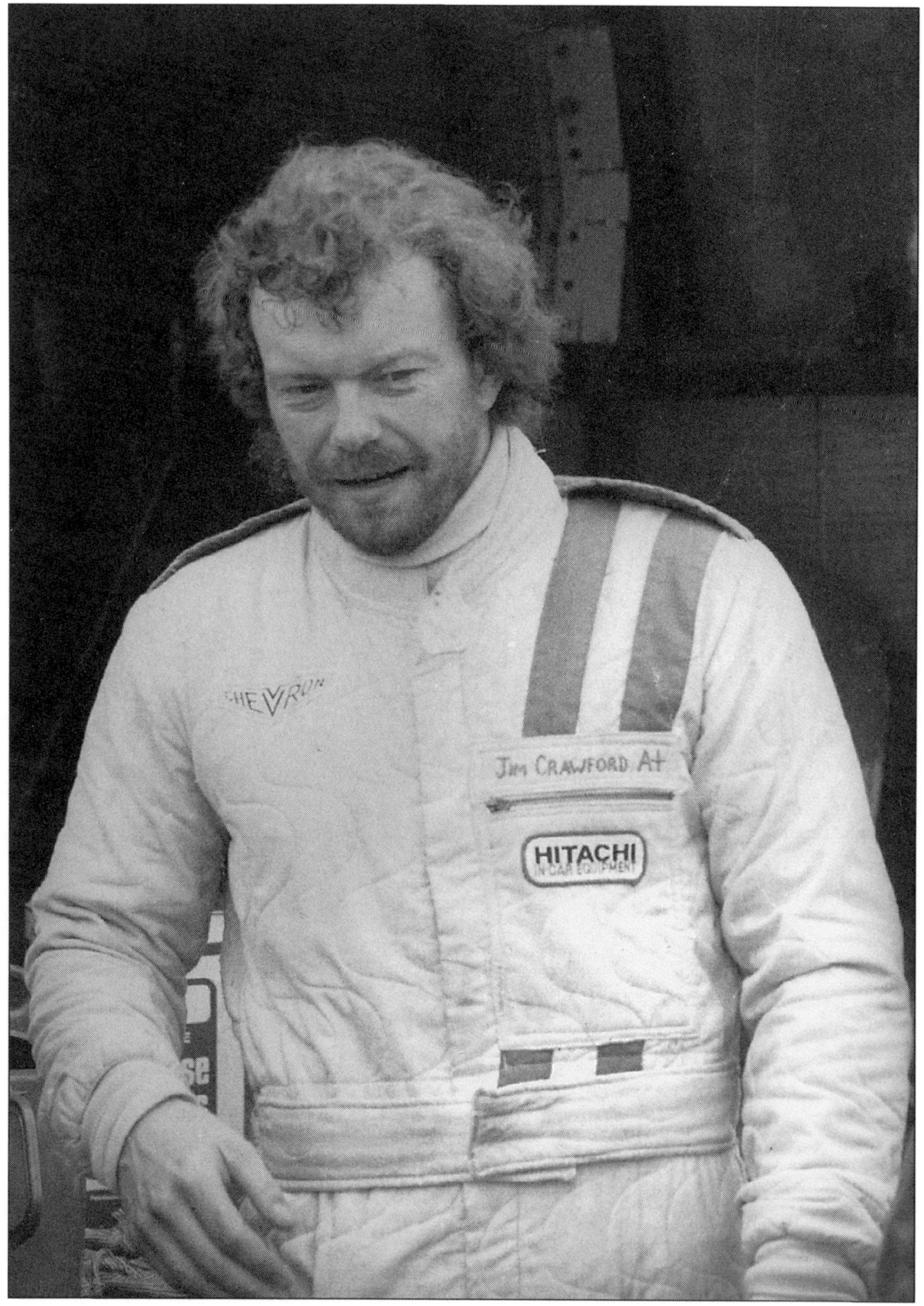

Jim Crawford.

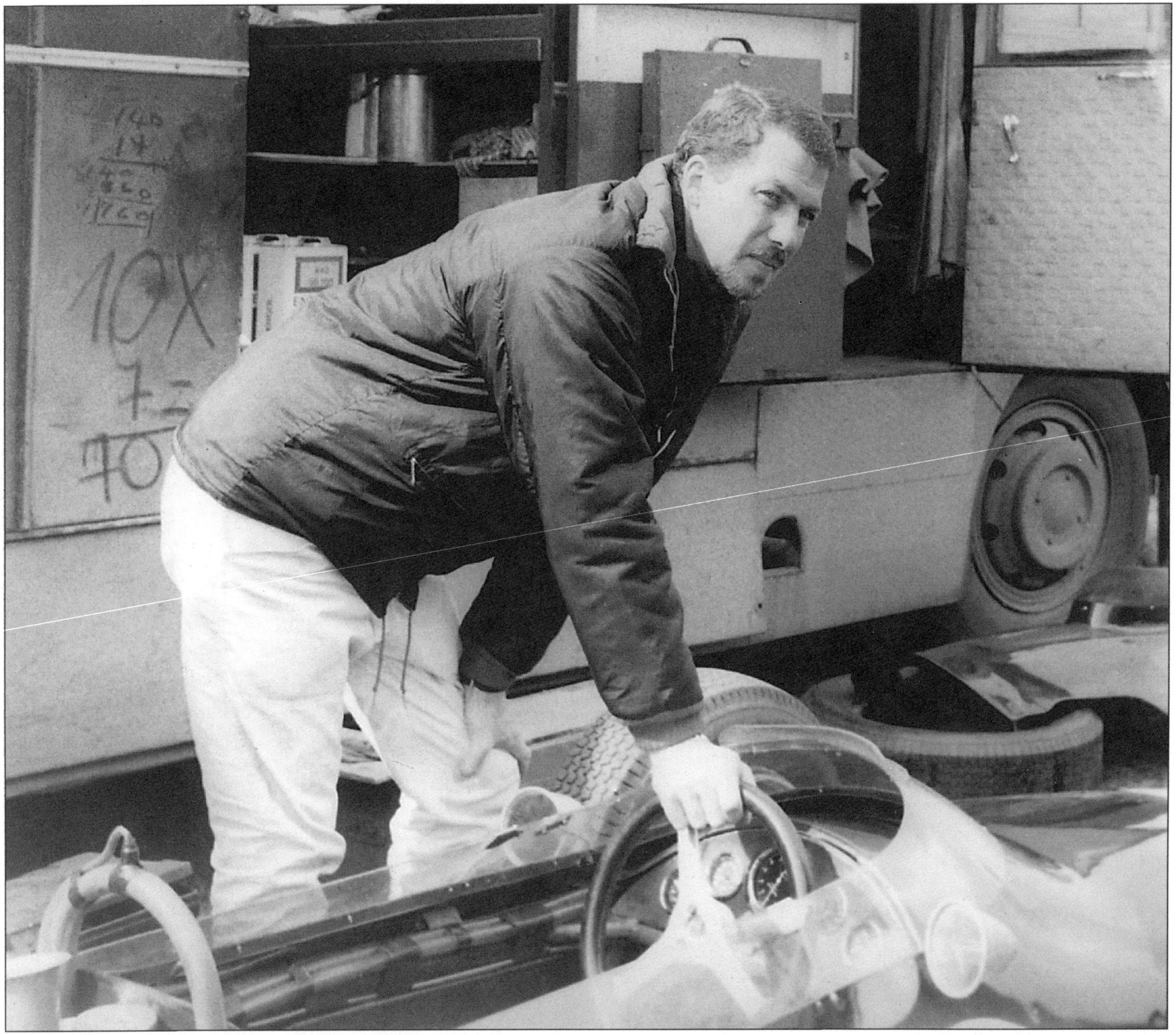

Jo Bonnier.

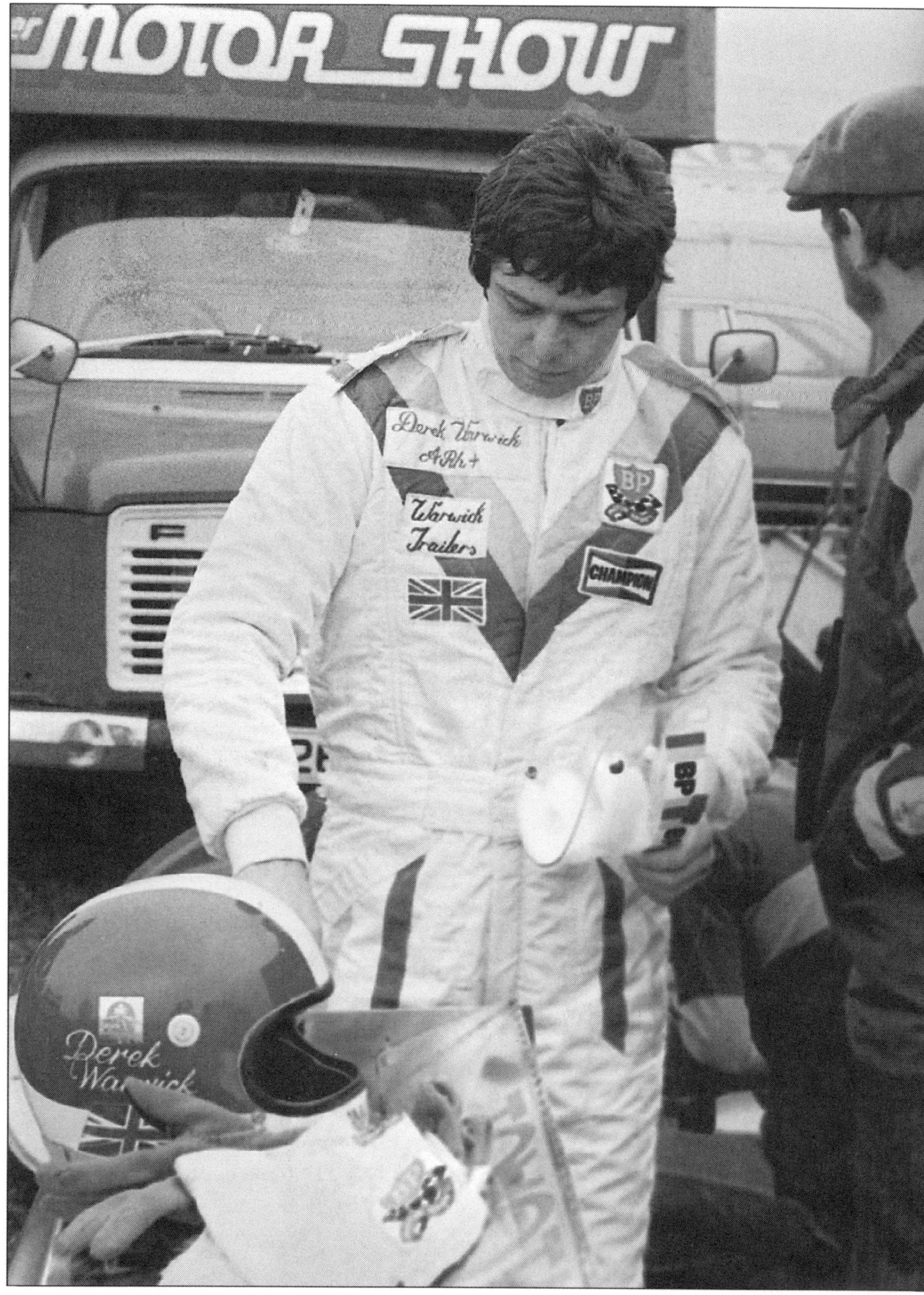

Derek Warwick.

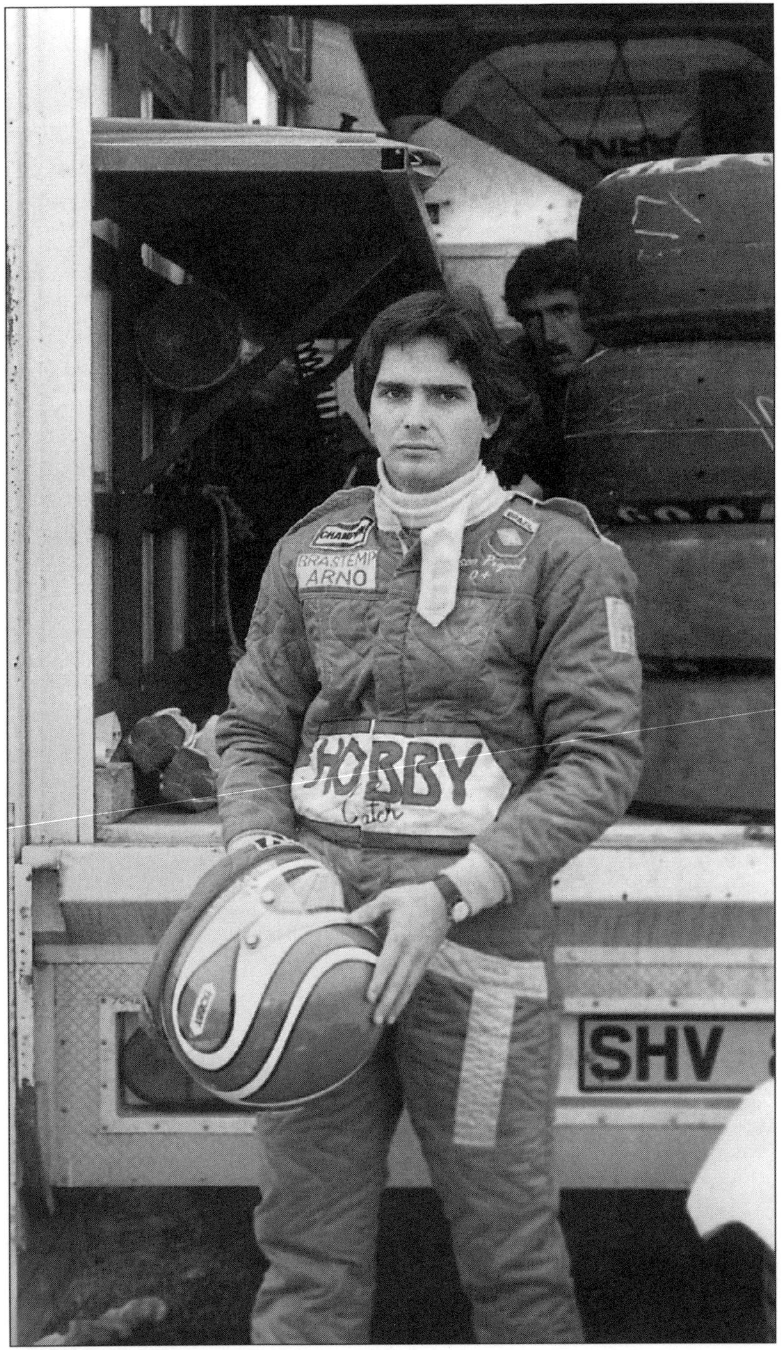

Nelson Piquet.

The Iconografix Photo Archive Series includes:

AMERICAN CULTURE	
AMERICAN SERVICE STATIONS 1935-1943	ISBN 1-882256-27-1
COCA-COLA: A HISTORY IN PHOTOGRAPHS 1930-1969	ISBN 1-882256-46-8
COCA-COLA: ITS VEHICLES IN PHOTOGRAPHS 1930-1969	ISBN 1-882256-47-6
PHILLIPS 66 1945-1954	ISBN 1-882256-42-5
AUTOMOTIVE	
FERRARI PININFARINA 1952-1996	ISBN 1-882256-65-4
GT40	ISBN 1-882256-64-6
IMPERIAL 1955-1963	ISBN 1-882256-22-0
IMPERIAL 1964-1968	ISBN 1-882256-23-9
LE MANS 1950: THE BRIGGS CUNNINGHAM CAMPAIGN	ISBN 1-882256-21-2
LINCOLN MOTOR CARS 1920-1942	ISBN 1-882256-57-3
LINCOLN MOTOR CARS 1946-1960	ISBN 1-882256-58-1
MG 1945-1964	ISBN 1-882256-52-2
MG 1965-1980	ISBN 1-882256-53-0
PACKARD MOTOR CARS 1935-1942	ISBN 1-882256-44-1
PACKARD MOTOR CARS 1946-1958	ISBN 1-882256-45-X
SEBRING 12-HOUR RACE 1970	ISBN 1-882256-20-4
STUDEBAKER 1933-1942	ISBN 1-882256-24-7
STUDEBAKER 1946-1958	ISBN 1-882256-25-5
VANDERBILT CUP RACE 1936 & 1937	ISBN 1-882256-66-2
TRACTORS AND CONSTRUCTION EQUIPMENT	
CASE TRACTORS 1912-1959	ISBN 1-882256-32-8
CATERPILLAR MILITARY TRACTORS VOLUME 1	ISBN 1-882256-16-6
CATERPILLAR MILITARY TRACTORS VOLUME 2	ISBN 1-882256-17-4
CATERPILLAR SIXTY	ISBN 1-882256-05-0
CLETRAC AND OLIVER CRAWLERS	ISBN 1-882256-43-3
ERIE SHOVEL	ISBN 1-882256-69-7
FARMALL CUB	ISBN 1-882256-71-9
FARMALL F–SERIES	ISBN 1-882256-02-6
FARMALL MODEL H	ISBN 1-882256-03-4
FARMALL MODEL M	ISBN 1-882256-15-8
FARMALL REGULAR	ISBN 1-882256-14-X
FARMALL SUPER SERIES	ISBN 1-882256-49-2
FORDSON 1917-1928	ISBN 1-882256-33-6
HART-PARR	ISBN 1-882256-08-5
HOLT TRACTORS	ISBN 1-882256-10-7
INTERNATIONAL TRACTRACTOR	ISBN 1-882256-48-4
INTERNATIONAL TD CRAWLERS 1933-1962	ISBN 1-882256-72-7
JOHN DEERE MODEL A	ISBN 1-882256-12-3
JOHN DEERE MODEL B	ISBN 1-882256-01-8
JOHN DEERE MODEL D	ISBN 1-882256-00-X
JOHN DEERE 30 SERIES	ISBN 1-882256-13-1
MINNEAPOLIS-MOLINE U-SERIES	ISBN 1-882256-07-7
OLIVER TRACTORS	ISBN 1-882256-09-3
RUSSELL GRADERS	ISBN 1-882256-11-5
TWIN CITY TRACTOR	ISBN 1-882256-06-9
RAILWAYS	
CHICAGO, ST. PAUL, MINNEAPOLIS & OMAHA RAILWAY 1880-1940	ISBN 1-882256-67-0
CHICAGO&NORTH WESTERN RAILWAY 1975-1995	ISBN 1-882256-76-X
GREAT NORTHERN RAILWAY 1945-1970	ISBN 1-882256-56-5
MILWAUKEE ROAD 1850-1960	ISBN 1-882256-61-1
SOO LINE 1975-1992	ISBN 1-882256-68-9
WISCONSIN CENTRAL LIMITED 1987-1996	ISBN 1-882256-75-1
WISCONSIN CENTRAL RAILWAY 1871-1909	ISBN 1-882256-78-6
TRUCKS	
BEVERAGE TRUCKS 1910-1975	ISBN 1-882256-60-3
*BROCKWAY TRUCKS 1948-1961**	ISBN 1-882256-55-7
DODGE TRUCKS 1929-1947	ISBN 1-882256-36-0
DODGE TRUCKS 1948-1960	ISBN 1-882256-37-9
LOGGING TRUCKS 1915-1970	ISBN 1-882256-59-X
*MACK® MODEL AB**	ISBN 1-882256-18-2
*MACK AP SUPER-DUTY TRUCKS 1926-1938**	ISBN 1-882256-54-9
*MACK MODEL B 1953-1966 VOLUME 1**	ISBN 1-882256-19-0
*MACK MODEL B 1953-1966 VOLUME 2**	ISBN 1-882256-34-4
*MACK EB-EC-ED-EE-EF-EG-DE 1936-1951**	ISBN 1-882256-29-8
*MACK EH-EJ-EM-EQ-ER-ES 1936-1950**	ISBN 1-882256-39-5
*MACK FC-FCSW-NW 1936-1947**	ISBN 1-882256-28-X
*MACK FG-FH-FJ-FK-FN-FP-FT-FW 1937-1950**	ISBN 1-882256-35-2
*MACK LF-LH-LJ-LM-LT 1940-1956 **	ISBN 1-882256-38-7
*MACK MODEL B FIRE TRUCKS 1954-1966**	ISBN 1-882256-62-X
*MACK MODEL CF FIRE TRUCKS 1967-1981**	ISBN 1-882256-63-8
STUDEBAKER TRUCKS 1927-1940	ISBN 1-882256-40-9
STUDEBAKER TRUCKS 1941-1964	ISBN 1-882256-41-7
WHITE TRUCKS 1900-1937	ISBN 1-882256-80-8

The Iconografix Photo Gallery Series includes:

CATERPILLAR PHOTO GALLERY	ISBN 1-882256-70-0

The Iconografix Photo Album Series includes:

CADILLAC 1948-1964	ISBN 1-882256-83-2
CORVETTE PROTOTYPES & SHOW CARS	ISBN 1-882256-77-8
DODGE PICKUPS 1939-1978	ISBN 1-882256-82-4
LOLA RACE CARS 1962-1990	ISBN 1-882256-73-5
LOTUS RACE CARS 1961-1994	ISBN 1-882256-84-0
McLAREN RACE CARS 1965-1996	ISBN 1-882256-74-3
PORSCHE 356 1948-1965	ISBN 1-882256-85-9

All Iconografix books are available from direct mail specialty book dealers and bookstores worldwide, or can be ordered from the publisher. For book trade and distribution information or to add your name to our mailing list contact

Iconografix
PO Box 446
Hudson, Wisconsin, 54016

Telephone: (715) 381-9755
(800) 289-3504 (USA)
Fax: (715) 381-9756

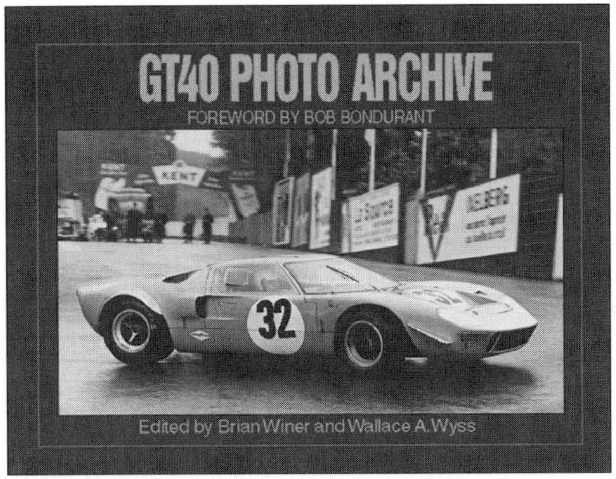

MORE GREAT BOOKS FROM ICONOGRAFIX

GT40 *Photo Archive* ISBN 1-882256-64-6

PORSCHE 356 1948-1965
Photo Album ISBN 1-882256-85-9

LOLA RACE CARS 1962-1990
Photo Album ISBN 1-882256-73-5

LE MANS 1950: THE BRIGGS CUNNINGHAM CAMPAIGN *Photo Archive*
ISBN 1-882256-21-2

McLAREN RACE CARS 1965-1996
Photo Album ISBN 1-882256-74-3

VANDERBILT CUP RACE 1936 & 1937
Photo Archive ISBN 1-882256-66-2

SEBRING 12-HOUR RACE 1970 ISBN
Photo Archive ISBN 1-882256-20-4

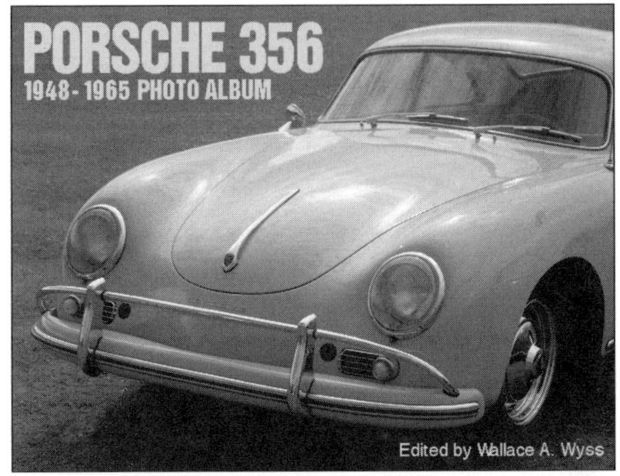

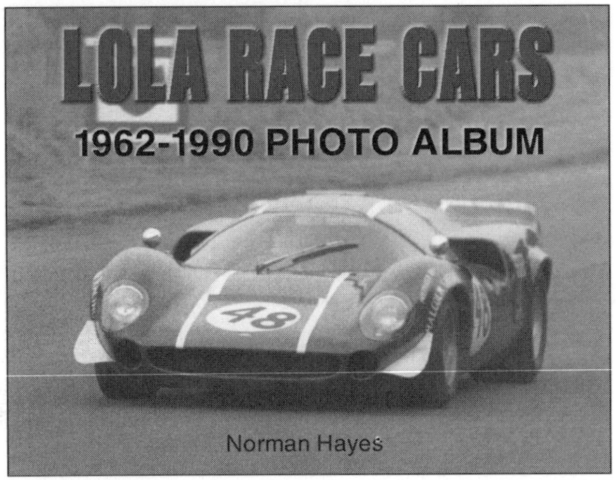

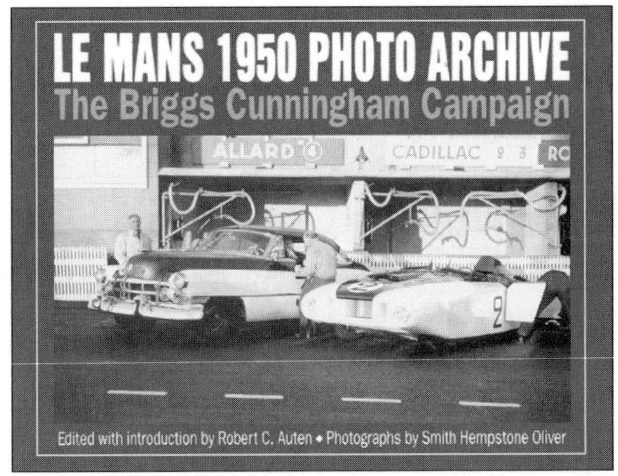

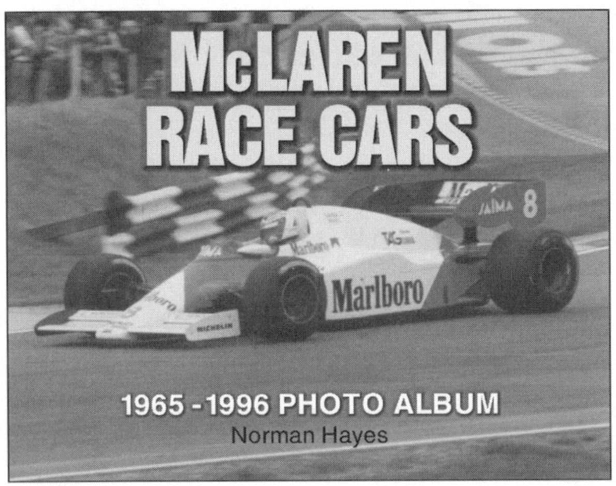

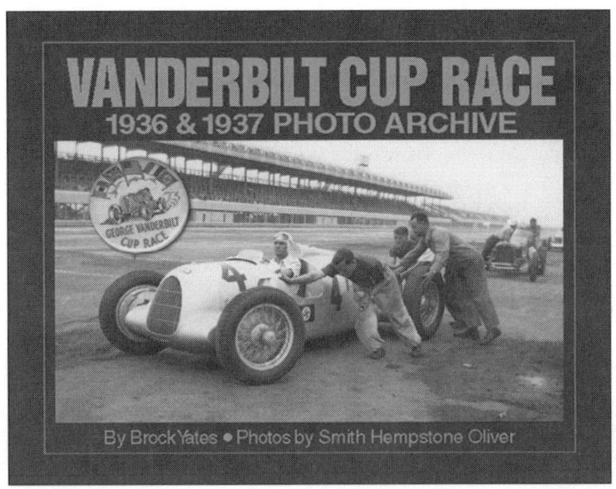

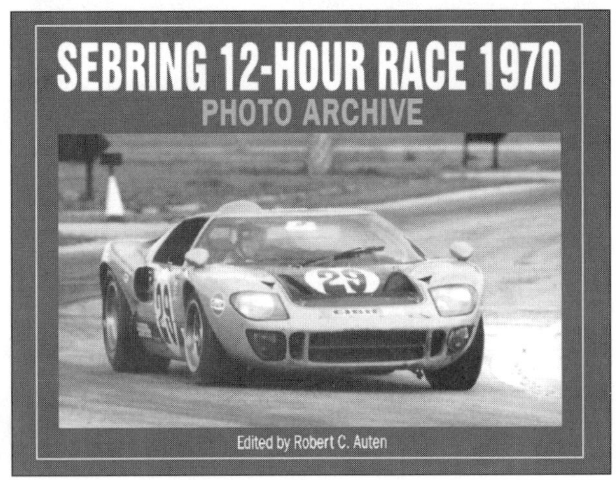